CCAR Journal
The Reform Jewish Quarterly

Symposium Issue on Judaism, Health, and Healing

Contents

CONTENTS

CONTENTS

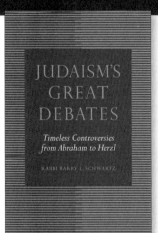

At the Gates — בִּשְׁעָרִים

Today's medical students stand a good chance of encountering both ritual and storytelling as part of their education to become physicians. Ritual may enter, among other places, when they first don their white coats, and when they begin and conclude their working relationship with a particular cadaver. Storytelling figures if their curriculum includes a component of "Narrative Medicine," a relatively new field that asserts the importance to a person's health of their whole life story—a story that includes ancestors and friends, work and love, interests and spiritual orientation.

Narrative Medicine often uses fictional models as it encompasses the awareness of health and disease into a storied structure. Likely to appear on the syllabus of any course dealing with medicine and literature is Leo Tolstoy's justly famous novella *The Death of Ivan Ilych*. For *CCAR Journal* readers who've not encountered this memorable story, I hope that my reference here will spur you to locate and read it; for others, perhaps time can be found for a rereading.

Ivan Ilych serves as a fitting introduction to this symposium issue on Judaism, Health, and Healing—an issue that seeks to wrap its arms around a multifaceted and important new field; a field whose impact is increasingly felt within congregational and communal Jewish life, as well as within academic circles. In terms of the field's development, my bringing in a work of fiction offers an indirect tribute to Rabbi William Cutter, founding director of the Kalsman Institute on Judaism and Health and professor emeritus at HUC, who has mined literary texts for educational and pastoral purposes throughout his career. Within this symposium issue, it is Michele Prince, Professor Cutter's worthy successor at Kalsman, and her co-guest editor, Nancy H. Wiener, founding director of the Blaustein Center for Pastoral Counseling, who gather and reflect upon multiple strands in the field's evolving story.

Turning again to Tolstoy's novella, let me highlight just a few parallels. Bioethicists often use it to educate clinicians about how patients experience serious illness. Ivan's doctors seem to give up on or pontificate to him, and his family behaves as if he has brought his illness upon himself. In the face of what is clearly his imminent death, his household continues to behave as if nothing much has changed. Both physicians and family lack compassion, empathy, and attentiveness. Only Ivan's servant Gerasim—"a fresh, clean peasant lad"—provides honest sympathy and generous attention to his needs. Only Gerasim recognizes and articulates the truth that "We shall all of us die."

As befits its title, *The Death of Ivan Ilych* both opens and closes with the death of the protagonist, beginning with the outside perspective of colleagues learning of his death and coming to reside inside Ivan's suffering mind/soul. In the middle, Tolstoy uses Ivan's death to shock us, with his protagonist, into awareness of what it means to be alive.

Like Tolstoy, Michele Prince and Nancy H. Wiener understand that healthy living includes spiritual, emotional, mental, social, and physical components, all intertwined. Furthermore, health and well-being, as well as their opposites and gradations, operate on the individual and communal levels. As Michele puts this in her report on the Research Roundtable, "the overarching goal . . . is to better understand the health of the Jewish people and to improve health and well-being in the Jewish community."

"Well-being" is a word that somehow means a great deal to me. It echoes inside whenever I read or use it, spreading out in harmonious circles. More than "happiness," this sometimes hyphenated, sometimes elided word seems to capture the state of a life being well-lived, even if the person living it may be sick, or conceivably dying.

Those of us who work hard to produce a publication worthy of readers' time and attention believe that the pieces contained in this and other issues can add to your well-being and enrich your life, though they cannot guarantee to extend it. Articles, book reviews, and *Maayanot* pieces do this mostly in rational ways; poetry does so through emotional and aesthetic channels. This issue includes the second publication under our new *Maayanot* rubric, a review of *Midrash and Medicine* that connects to the symposium, and a review essay on American Jewish identity as distilled in rabbis' sermons that nicely intersects. Also, we are delighted to include within this issue one or more poems by four poets, as well as selected "Words of Wisdom from Four Poets"—all of which emerged from a call for poems on the topic of this issue. The editorial board and I wish you learning and enjoyment, health and well-being, now and into the future.

Susan Laemmle, Editor

Introduction to this Issue from the Guest Editors

Michele Prince and Nancy H. Wiener

We are very pleased to present this special symposium issue of the *CCAR Journal*. The articles contained in this issue recognize that implicit within Judaism is a vision of well-being that is grounded in a passionate engagement with life. The articles acknowledge that community is the backdrop in which we grapple with modern dilemmas while honoring our sacred texts and rituals. They offer theological, historical, and rabbinic reflections on the intersection of Judaism, health, and healing, alongside a picture of contemporary congregational life. The articles represent the diverse ways contemporary, liberal Jews respond to the intersections between Jewish teachings and values, our understandings of illness and well-being—and what means we can employ to heal our body and soul when necessary.

Our call for papers generated a great deal of interest and the proposals we received for articles demonstrated the many ways that Judaism, health, and healing have meaning for us today. In fact, in the past six months, many of the authors themselves have dealt with a wide range of personal and family health issues that have enlivened their understandings and highlighted the ongoing relevance of this topic.

MICHELE PRINCE, MSW, LCSW, MAJCS (MAJCS, LA02) is the director of the Kalsman Institute on Judaism and Health of HUC-JIR. She is a licensed clinical social worker, specializing in oncology, and is co-founder of the Jewish Bereavement Project.

NANCY H. WIENER (RAB NY 1990) is the director of the Blaustein Center for Pastoral Counseling and the Dr. Paul and Trudy Steinberg Distinguished Professor in Human Relations at the New York campus of HUC-JIR.

Michele and Nancy are determined to make a difference helping future generations of leaders meet the needs of the Jewish people in the areas of illness and wellness.

The articles we have included explore a host of topics, but could not possibly cover the breadth of the field. When we speak of Judaism, health, and healing we explore the ways in which personal, collective, and global health are promoted and maintained and the ways in which healing is needed in all three spheres. While this issue explores some of these, we are cognizant of what is absent and look forward to upcoming issues of the *Journal* that might address the political and economic dimensions of healthcare and the responsibilities we have as committed Jews to address them. We also encourage our colleagues to write more extensively about Jewish chaplaincy and the diversity of ways clergy offer care to others in and outside Judaism while continuing to care for themselves.

Volumes have been written on Jews and medicine, and in the Jewish popular imagination, Maimonides serves as the model of a Jewish Renaissance man—physician, scholar, and philosopher. "My son (daughter), the doctor" has long held a position as a well-known comedic trope. The first two articles offer us an opportunity to expand our notions of ways that Jews are contributing to the medical professions in new and exciting ways. Sam Karff's article, "Spirituality and Religion in Health Care," presents significant changes in medical training and offers us a model of how clergy can work with medical schools and healthcare facilities to humanize the patients' experience and to help medical professionals understand the deep-seated questions of meaning and purpose that medical crises evoke. Ellen Olshansky's article, "My Daughter (or even Son) the Nurse: Jews in Nursing and the Healing Role of Nurses," traces the history of Jews in nursing in the West and highlights the ways in which Jewish nurses have contributed to the development of the field in the United States and Israel. She links Jewish nurses' commitments to public health and to caring for the whole person to Jewish concepts and teachings of *tikkun olam* and *b'tzelem Elohim*.

Michele Prince offers a big picture view of the conception and development of the nascent field of Judaism, health, and healing in her article, "The Kalsman Institute Research Roundtable: Building a Field of Judaism and Health." By sharing the findings of a research roundtable sponsored by the Kalsman Institute, she illuminates the interdisciplinary, collaborative efforts that are contributing to building a field that is transforming the landscape of contemporary Jewish life.

Carol and Richard Levy, in "Of Teachers and Angels: Jewish Insights on Transforming the Relationship between Patient and Health Professional," remind us of the need for collaborations, not only among professionals of different disciplines in the service of health and healing, but the collaboration that can and must exist between caregivers and patients for healing of the whole person to occur. They offer important observations about how the disempowerment many patients experience while receiving medical care runs counter to seminal teachings of Buber and Heschel. They suggest ways that medical professionals and patients can work together to empower patients through honoring their full personhood. Jo Hirschmann's article, "Standing in the Doorway: Pastoral Perspectives on In-Home Chaplaincy," draws on her professional experiences as a home hospice chaplain and her recent experience as a patient convalescing at home. She reflects on the ways that Jewish teachings about *bikur cholim* and *hachnasat orchim* underscore how being a host to visitors can give a patient and those with whom she lives a sense of agency and empowerment. The power of home care for both hosts and home health provider reinforces the importance of nursing services that Olshansky mentioned in her article.

How we retain our sense of agency, our sense of self, our sense of belonging in the face of illness begs the question of how we foster these core pieces of a healthy identity throughout our lives. In her article, "Beyond Membership to True Belonging: Jewish Responses to an Unchanging Need for Deep Attachment and Meaning in an Ever-Changing World," Edythe Held Mencher, a social worker and rabbi, utilizes findings from psychology to demonstrates how religious communities can create and offer individuals opportunities to meet their need to form deep and enduring attachments. Experiencing a true and deep sense of belonging will serve them through life's joys and challenges. Eleanor Steinman, in "The Stigma of Infertility," raises the question of what happens to those people whose issues with infertility engender a sense of no longer fully belonging to the Jewish community. Drawing on biblical narratives, she offers new frames and possibilities for providing healing and "re-membering" to those on the margins. This is the first of several articles discussing typically taboo or stigmatized topics in the Jewish and larger community, such as infertility and mental illness. Elliot Kukla's article, "The Torah of Despair," addresses the desire of caregivers to alleviate pain and the challenge and potential that exist in accompanying people in their darkness. Kukla draws on key biblical figures who experienced despair and suggests that their presence in our canon can serve a healing function for all of us.

Ruth Gais's article, "Ruth, Naomi, and Levinas's Other: Asymmetrical Pastoral Care," also focuses on individuals who perceive themselves and are regularly perceived by others as not belonging, the institutionalized mentally ill. Her reflections on Levinas and the Book of Ruth present new frames and theological insights into the stranger, the "other," and what it is to offer care. In "On Illness," Doug Kohn challenges us to consider the theological and practical implications of the ways that illness is depicted in our tradition. He encourages us to consider how our understandings about illness influence our understandings of ourselves, our relationship to God, and our sense of well-being.

As we consider the work we do as clergy in the area of Judaism, health, and healing, Barbara Breitman, Mychal Springer, and Nancy Wiener's article, "*P'tach Libi B'Toratecha* (Open My Heart to Your Torah): Jewish Pastoral Theology in Process," raises questions that are central to the ways in which clergy are trained for their work as pastoral caregivers. Explicating a "master class" they offered to students from three seminaries, they propose a radical reframing of pastoral work as a fertile ground for identifying, articulating, and appreciating theology that emerges and develops from practice. Harriet Rosen and Marlene Levenson explore the ways that we are training clergy to work with older couples who are remarrying in "Rabbis' Support of Older Couples' Second Marriages." Drawing on a study they conducted on couples and rabbis in the field and reflecting on current curricula at HUC-JIR/LA, they suggest ways that we can better train clergy to gain greater knowledge about issues unique to this cohort so they can feel more comfortable supporting, offering counsel, and building community with couples during premarital counseling.

As we look at ways to integrate the many roles clergy have, Geri Newburge's article, "A New Ritual for Healing and Well-Being," reminds us of the ways that we can promote health and healing after trauma when we combine counseling and appropriate rituals. Jeffrey Ableser writes about ways we can utilize the *Amidah* as a Jewish frame for recovery from addictions in "The Intermediate

Blessings of the *Amidah* as the Model for a Personal Twelve-Step Program." In "A Very Personal Reflection: Debbie Friedman's Setting of *Mi Shebeirach* as a Sonata," Evan Kent utilizes Debbie Friedman's iconic *Mi Shebeirach* to illustrate the way that music and text work together. He raises important issues related to the power of prayers for healing in a congregational context.

Congregation as a venue for promoting health and healing is the central focus of Richard Address, Richard Steinberg, and Marion Lev-Cohen's articles. In "Standing in Life before God: Report and Reflection on One Congregation's First Steps for Creating a Congregation-Based Program on Health and Wellness," Address shares the details of a newly initiated process in which his congregation participated to create an environment where healing and wholeness are central to a congregation's identity. In contrast, "Experiencing Judaism through Thematic Temple Programming" offers Steinberg's reflections on his congregation's conception and development of unified programming on topics related to health and healing. Lev-Cohen's article, "Sacred Communities: The Potential for Synagogues to Be Communities of Caring and Meaning in the Older Population," discusses ways that the needs of baby boomers can be addressed through psycho-educational support groups, classes, and pastoral support.

Marcus Freed challenges us in "The Rabbi Does Handstands: An Exploration of the Emerging Field of Jewish Yoga in North American Synagogues and Beyond" to think beyond the bounds of congregations to consider the ways health and healing goals can be met through meditative and reflective practices that are Jewishly informed.

Finally, we end with Bob Tabak's piece, "Verbatim with God," which helps us, in a humorous manner, to remember that ultimately, as our morning liturgy reminds us, our bodies and souls are given to us by God. The questions and concerns we have related to our Judaism, our health, and healing ultimately lead us back to conversation with God.

Spirituality and Religion in Health Care: A Rabbi's Personal Journey

Samuel E. Karff

For forty years I was a congregational rabbi. For ten of those years I also taught in the Divinity School of the University of Chicago and for twenty-two years, in the Religious Studies department of Rice University. In the religious story that defines me, God is the source of our being, the giver of the way we are intended to live, and God is active in our lives and in history to fulfill the divine goal for creation. I fulfill God's purpose for me by faithfulness to my people's covenant with God and by striving to repair the brokenness in that tiny corner of God's world entrusted to my care.

While God has given me the power to heal, God is the ultimate Healer. God's healing is mediated through the health caregiver, the clergy who comforts our troubled spirits, the scientist who discovers healing substances in the laboratory, and the healing powers implanted within our minds and bodies. Sometimes God mysteriously heals in God's own way, which we call a miracle. In my religious narrative, disease is not inflicted by God as punishment for our sins but is, as Maimonides insisted, the price we pay for the privilege of being sensitive, embodied persons.[1]

This is a pastoral theology that has informed my preaching and my life. Twelve years ago, when I retired, I was asked to spend time at the Texas Medical Center, not to visit congregants in the hospital, but to teach future physicians and nurses. Dr. David Low, then president of the UT Health Science Center, himself a physician trained in neuroscience, invited me to teach caregivers the non-biomedical knowledge and skills involved in healing.

SAMUEL E. KARFF, D.H.L. (C56) served as a congregational rabbi for forty years, and he has since created and taught a curriculum in Health and the Human Spirit at the University of Texas Medical School, Houston.

The assignment was so compelling that I accepted before even pondering "Why me?" Once I did ask that question, the answer was apparent. As a rabbi, I would not pray with my ill congregants before I elicited and listened to their story. I discovered that to be listened to by another person who is caring and empathetic can be a healing balm to a patient's aching spirit. Dr. Low invited me to help future physicians appreciate the non-biomedical dimension of being a healing physician—including the healing effect of truly listening to the patient's story.

That summer I read much and learned that medical education was in the early stages of a significant change. Twenty-five hundred years ago, in his *Precepts,* the Greek physician Hippocrates taught that "where there is love of man [sic] there is also love of the art [of medicine]. Some patients, though conscious that their condition is perilous, recover their health simply through contentment with the goodness of the physician."[2] This sense that there is healing power embodied in the doctor-patient relationship remained conventional wisdom through the centuries.

In the years following World War II, impressive advances in medicine, including the availability of powerful antibiotics, initiated a new understanding of the goals of medical education. With the emergence of sophisticated diagnostic tests, pharmaceutical magic bullets, and new surgical techniques, the old-fashioned family doctor seemed hopelessly unarmed, largely limited to placebos and a "good bedside manner." Medical educators in the postwar period of the 1950s and 1960s focused almost entirely on the biomedicine—believing that its knowledge and application was the only determinant of medical outcome.

In those years, I would not have been asked to teach in a medical school. But within the last thirty years a new model of education has emerged. The physician must still master the biomedicine. We are exceedingly grateful for the physician's increasing curative power. However, it is not sufficient simply to address the disease. The effective clinician will connect to the patient as a person, and, because of the mind-body interconnection, the quality of the doctor-patient relationship can affect the medical outcome. This claim, intuitively understood by Hippocrates, can now be demonstrated scientifically. We can now track the weakening effect of uncontrolled stress on the immune system[3] and the effect of meditation in lowering blood pressure.[4]

In 1977, George Engel, a distinguished physician and psychiatrist, published a seminal article in the journal *Science* that argued effectively that the biomedical model was seriously inadequate and should be supplanted by the bio-psycho-social model.[5] Engel contended that "even with the application of rational therapies, the behavior of the physician and the relationship between patient and physician powerfully influence therapeutic outcome for better or for worse."[6] He noted that the "insulin requirements of a diabetic patient may fluctuate significantly depending on how the patient perceives his relationship with his doctor."[7]

The new paradigm of medical education became official when The American Association of Medical Colleges, which grants medical schools their accreditation, issued the following guidelines in 1999: "Patients have a fundamental right to considerate care that safeguards and respects their cultural, psychosocial, and spiritual values."[8] In response, today at least 100 of the 126 medical schools in this country have programs in medical humanities or "spirituality in medicine."[9]

Defining Spirituality

As a person of faith and a teacher of Judaism my religious beliefs and practices are the deepest expression of my human spirit. But what could spirit or spirituality mean for a program at a state-sponsored medical school? To address such questions and to approve the contours of our program, I formed a faculty committee. Its members agreed with this core principle of the new paradigm: *There is healing power in the doctor-patient relationship.* We called our initiative Health and the Human Spirit and agreed that its curriculum should teach the art of practicing what I came to call a *relational medicine.*

Spirit, as we defined it, refers to a person's inner world of beliefs, passions, values, and goals—all that gives meaning to that person's life. We are meaning-seeking creatures. Meaning is the sense that my life is worth living; I have a purpose to live for—even in the midst of life's darker side, including serious economic loss, the death of a loved one, or serious illness. In humans the will to live is not instinctive. It can be lost. Meaning sustains the will to live and to strive for wellness.[10]

The sources of meaning in a human life are multiple and not mutually exclusive. Surely, a primary source is love. A loveless existence is essentially meaningless. Such love can be present not only in relation to our spouse, children, extended family, and friends, but also in the quality of the relationship between a doctor and his patient.

In the 1990s the American College of Physicians sponsored a number of workshops that invited physicians to write personal narratives about a patient encounter that reaffirmed the meaning of their medical practice. Eighty-three narratives were collected and analyzed. Surprisingly, far from describing an occasion of dramatic biomedical triumph, the narratives generally recorded a time when "these doctors discovered and were deeply gratified by the intrinsic healing capacity of simply being present . . . In the absence of curative options they sought other ways to help their patients: by appreciating them, maintaining their dignity and comfort, and even expressing love to them."[11]

If love is a primary source of meaning, so is work that gives a person the sense of being needed and useful. Job loss can result in a crisis of identity and meaning.[12] In my experience those who do best during their years of retirement have a double strategy: they allow themselves to do more of the things they enjoyed but could never do often or long enough before retiring, and they find some work outside the home that gives them the sense of being needed and useful—whether it consists of visiting patients in a hospital or mentoring young persons just entering the business world.

Patients whose illness removes them from their normal work schedule for a long period of time, or who fear they will no longer be able to do their work or have a job to return to, may experience a crisis of meaning. A sensitive physician who understands and validates those feelings and who can give them some hope for an eventual return to the job is likely to increase the probability of the patient's compliance and be a more effective healer.

A third source of meaning in a human life is to feel some intimations of our earthly immortality—some basis for hoping that though we must die, we will leave footprints through the children we have reared, the persons we have influenced, and the causes we have served. An important source of meaning is to feel that our life has made a difference, that we will be remembered and missed.

Dr. Christina Puchalski, a leading figure in the spirituality and medicine movement, writes of helping a terminally ill patient feel intimations of immortality: "A patient is dying of breast and ovarian cancer in her early 30's and she was depressed. Anti-depressants weren't helping. Through talking with her I understood the cause of her suffering: a fear that her 2 year old daughter would not remember her. I suggested that she keep a journal to leave her daughter; the hospice nurses videotaped her messages to her children. These activities helped resolve her depression."[13]

For many Americans, the ultimate source of meaning, hope, and comfort in difficult times is their religious faith. In a session devoted to the role of the physician in end-of-life care, we show a video interview with a patient at MD Anderson Hospital. When asked about her important sources of support at this stage of her life, she spoke of family and friends and concluded, "My faith is my Rock. I don't see how anyone can walk this path without it."[14]

Creating a Program for a State-Sponsored Medical School

As a rabbi teaching in a state-sponsored medical school I felt the need to craft a program that addresses the quest for meaning in both those physicians and patients who are nonreligious and those who define themselves as persons of faith. Some critics have complained about the ambiguity, inconsistency, and vagueness of the term "spirituality" in a medical context. Harold Koenig, one of the pioneers in the spirituality and health movement, acknowledges that although the research correlating spirituality with positive health outcomes has been essentially limited to the effect of religious practice (prayer and public worship), he has often used the terms "religion" and "spirituality" interchangeably. Koenig then suggests that when doctors speak to patients they should use the term "spirituality" because some may feel alienated from institutional religion and the "term spiritual is vague enough to allow patients themselves to define the playing field."[15]

Such comments have led psychiatrist Neil Scheurich to conclude that "spirituality is a fundamentally ambiguous and flawed term [that] cannot be used in a precise manner because . . . its use raises the specter of its original link with the supernatural." Scheurich would therefore substitute "value" as "the best possible protection of both secular and non-secular worldviews."[16]

In contrast with both Koenig and Scheurich I am proposing that (1) a religious and nonreligious spirituality are clearly distinguishable; (2) that, significantly, the introduction of the term "spirituality in medicine" has coincided with the recovery of a healing model that is relational and meaning-centered; (3) that a nonreligious spirituality may be defined as the practice and teaching of this relational medicine; and (4) that a religious spirituality should be attributed to all who seek to affirm and relate to a divine source of power and love—whether such persons are identified with institutional religion or are unaffiliated spiritual seekers. It should also be applied to those devotees of Eastern religions, like Buddhism, whose concepts of religious experience and spiritual fulfillment differ from the West.

In a state-sponsored medical school, we should accommodate, respect, and address the spiritual needs of all, but a nonreligious spirituality is our default mode. We have already identified three nonreligious sources of meaning that sustain the human spirit and the will to live (the experience of love, a sense of being needed and useful, and intimations of an earthly immortality). Arthur Kleinman, a leader in the movement to recover a patient-centered medicine, contends that illness always interrupts and threatens a life's meaning. The sensitive physician can play a significant role in the patient's recovery of the will to live, especially in the face of chronic or disabling illness.

This recovery of meaning requires the physician "to be with the sick person and to facilitate his or her building of an illness narrative that will make sense of and give value to the experience."[17] The caring, empathetic physician who witnesses and validates the patient's sense of deep loss may, in time, help the patient frame a narrative that declares: "In spite of my present disabilities, I am a person of worth." Reassurance by a physician you admire that you still possess considerable gifts that will help you rebuild your life may restore meaning and strengthen the will to live.

Eric Cassell, a pioneer in the field of humanistic medicine, agrees that "directly experiencing within ourselves [the patient's]…feelings of desperation and disintegration…teaches us that transcendence— reaching beyond our physical boundaries—is not confined to a religious experience but is part of the everyday world."[18] Elsewhere, he concludes that "such experiences need not involve religion in any formal sense; however in its transpersonal dimension it is deeply spiritual."[19]

The same nonreligious spirituality is to be found in those physicians who were asked to describe an encounter that reaffirmed the meaning of their vocation. The following is a particularly poignant example:

> A home visit to GG, a 4 year old with retinoblastoma: smells, staleness, roaches climbing walls. [The mother] one eyed, dignified, needy and grasping/clinging. But allowing one angry plea—'can't you do something?' The agony of 'nothing more to do' other than help her son die comfortably. Survivor's guilt. Utter isolation—abandoned by family, needed by kids. Why is she not broken? She has no resources I'd fall back on—no education, family, friends, spiritual framework. Watching (and smelling) her son's head rot . . . helping his wasted little body stand up to pee. Why is she not crushed/why am I not crushed seeing her? . . . After a visit like that, you could draw two conclusions about the world. First is that it is a capricious, horrifying place where tragedy ultimately beats us down. Or, that in the face of tragedy there can be heroic, even victorious love.[20]

The Focus and Implementation of the Curriculum

When I learned that the curriculum committee planned to make our third-year program elective, I respectfully declined to participate because it signaled that only the biomedical is essential. Fortunately, the majority agreed and our classes became an integral part of the required curriculum. Forewarned to expect resistance from faculty and students, I was pleasantly surprised by the high degree of faculty support. In time, I realized they and their families were also patients who, more than occasionally, experienced relational insensitivity from physicians. Moreover, as my active partners in each discussion, the faculty not only provided biomedical credibility but found meaning in sharing the kinds of experiences they didn't discuss in their biomedically focused classes.

While a few students contended that relational skills could not be taught, most realized that a case-based curriculum, which simulated doctor-patient encounters they will soon be responding to in real time, may be useful. Each session focused on a different relational challenge: how to give potentially life transforming news without prematurely snuffing out hope; how to address cultural barriers to the doctor-patient relationship (an Islamic family does not want their daughter's baby delivered by a male resident, but no female residents are available); how to deal appropriately with the religious requests of patients and their families; at what point does persuading a patient to undergo a necessary procedure violate patient autonomy, and when is the failure to persuade the patient, arguably, a sign of inadequate caring?

The issue of patient autonomy and its limits was illustrated by a third-year student who wrote of accompanying his resident on rounds. In one room, the resident told the patient she had an abscess that was potentially life threatening and required timely treatment. The woman declined, insisting that she just wanted to go home. When the resident reiterated the seriousness of the situation she remained unmoved. Whereupon, the resident said, "If you change your mind let us know" and he left the room. Later in the day, the third-year student returned to the room. He sat by the patient's bed, held her hand, and asked earnestly, "Tell me Mrs. Matthews, why won't you let us treat you?" She began to sob and declared, "I've been HIV positive for ten years. I don't deserve to be treated." The student responded, "You deserve to be treated as much as any of us and you owe it to yourself and your family to do so. Mrs. Matthews, please let us treat you." She agreed and was healed.

In leading these sessions, I would tell students that even as my physician partner brought biomedical credibility, I brought forty years as a congregational rabbi/pastor who was invited into people's lives at times of peak joy and great suffering. If relevant, I did not hesitate to share my rabbinic experience. When students expressed fears of burnout if they allowed themselves to empathize with the pain of their patients, I replied that it was possible for me to be fully present and emotionally engaged when I responded to a death in a family. I made an effort to share their sorrow and was often personally moved by their loss. Often my empathy was palpably evident to the family, but even in cases of a tragic death, when I returned from the cemetery, freshly reminded of life's fragility and of our mortality, I embraced my loved ones more passionately and usually ate a hearty meal. Still, it is possible to be over-engaged. I told my students that if you return daily from the hospital, unable to connect to your wife or play with your children, you are over-engaged and should seek help.

In the third-year rotations, students see patients in the clinic. These patients may wait as long as two hours before being seen. Generally, the student physician would proceed directly to clinical matters. Instead, we suggest they ask the patient how long they have waited. Then respond: "I'm sorry, I wouldn't want to wait that long and your time is as valuable to you as mine is to me but, unfortunately, there are more of you than of us. We do the best we can. Now, how can I help you today?" In an exchange that took no more than thirty seconds the student physician showed respect for the patient as a person and revealed the person in herself ("I wouldn't want to wait . . . "). The doctor-patient encounter has been "person-alized."

I teach that in virtually every patient encounter, physicians have the power to heal. Sometimes they may heal the body by skillfully employing biomedical tools and knowledge. In many encounters, the physician is also potentially a healer of the patient's spirit—by being fully present, really listening to her story, trying to understand how the medical symptoms are experienced by the patient, and being careful not to prematurely snuff out hope. Such a relationship makes the doctor an advocate rather than only a detached dispenser of medical skills for compensation. In the optimal doctor-patient encounter the biomedical and relational modes function synergistically.

When a Patient's Faith Is Her Deepest Source of Meaning

Although in a state-sponsored medical school our default mode is a nonreligious spirituality, at times of serious illness many patients regard religious faith as their ultimate comfort and support.[21] Those who predicted that as scientific medicine advanced religion would become an anachronism have not been vindicated.

Franz Kafka's story "The Country Doctor" laments that his patients expect him to produce that perfect and ultimate healing for which they used to petition God. The doctor reflects bitterly, "This is typical of the people in my district, always asking the impossible of the doctor. They have lost their old faith . . . but the doctor is expected to fix everything with his surgical hands. Well, if it pleases them—I haven't foisted myself upon them. If they misuse me for sacred ends. I'll let that pass too."[22]

Although our age is far more technically advanced than Kafka's medical world of the 1920s, the physician still functions with limited tools to achieve limited goals. To be sure, now as ever, not all petitions for God's healing intervention are satisfactorily answered. Religious faith still requires living with the darker side of life and trusting that beyond the mystery there is meaning. As long as there is chronic and disabling disease, as long as we must confront our mortality (as long as there are those who experience intimations of a divine presence within and beyond them), many will seek in religion's sacred texts and spiritual disciplines their ultimate source of meaning and hope. A Mayo Clinic publication reflects this awareness: "When people consult physicians to determine the cause and treatment of a disease, they may also seek answers to existential questions that medical science cannot answer . . . Many patients rely on religious or spiritual care to help answer these questions."[23]

In my previous life as congregational pastor, when I visited a patient in the hospital or counseled a troubled soul in my study, I realized they came to me precisely because a nonreligious restoration of meaning was not sufficient for them. They needed me to help them draw on the narratives of our tradition and its spiritual disciplines. They yearned to wrestle with and pray to a God whose healing power and love were with them.

The physicians I teach cannot claim to truly practice a relational medicine if they fail to help connect patients of faith with chaplains or congregational clergy who can address their religious needs. They are challenged to do so in a way that also respects those patients whose spirituality is manifestly nonreligious.

Much has been written about the need to ascertain a patient's spiritual needs through a "spiritual assessment."[24] A physician or nurse can discern the form of a patient's spirituality by asking this non-obtrusive question: "I know this must be a difficult time in your life. At such times, what are your sources of support and comfort?" If the patient responds by pointing only to a nonreligious support system (family, friends, music, or the beauty of nature) physicians should not proselytize or advocate for a religious alternative. If, however, the patient intimates that his faith is important to him, the physician should validate the patient's religious life. Any words or gestures that denigrate the patient's beliefs may constitute a form of malpractice. Respect for the patient requires us to honor what is important to the patient—unless it poses a certifiable medical danger.

If the physician shares the patient's religious sentiments and the patient asks the doctor to pray with her, it is appropriate to do so. If the physician is uncomfortable praying (if it's against her religion) she should not be expected to violate her conscience but should respond, if possible, in a way that does not create a barrier between them. To say, "Why don't you lead the prayer and I will stand with you hand in hand" is more relationally supportive than "I don't believe in prayer, I'll get you a chaplain."

We teach that if a patient has not asked you to pray with him, the general rule is not to pray with him, but algorithms are not always adequate substitutes for personal judgment in the situation. When Bruce Feldstein, an M.D. and a chaplain, told Mrs. Martinez that her cancer had spread to her brain she showed signs of great agitation. Dr. Feldstein, who is Jewish, noticed a crucifix around her neck. "Are you a prayerful person?" he asked. She nodded affirmatively. "Well, would you like to pray together?" "Yes, I would." Given the disparity in religious backgrounds, the doctor waited for the patient to begin; he soon realized she expected him to lead. Hesitantly, Dr. Feldstein began with a generic prayer. After each sentence, Mrs. Martinez would repeat his words. When he concluded with Amen, she still held his hand, and with her eyes still closed, she recited the Lord's prayer. Then she proceeded to pray to St. Jude in Spanish. When she opened her eyes Mrs. Martinez appeared much calmer, and with teary eyes, she said "Thank you."[25]

As a congregational rabbi I made regular visits to patients in the hospital. Not uncommonly, our session was interrupted by a knock on the door. By tacit understanding, if it was the patient's doctor making rounds, I would immediately excuse myself. When I present this situation to our medical school classes today, they invariably respond, "I would excuse myself and see another patient before I return." Obviously, there will be circumstances that dictate an immediate meeting of doctor and patient, but the students make clear their default response would be to excuse themselves and return after seeing another patient.

I believe programs such as ours have raised medical students' consciousness that at times of serious illness and upcoming surgery, when the risks are real and the outcome uncertain, many patients want the best biomedicine and the best surgeon—but they may also need and welcome visiting with a chaplain. In my experience, even if such patients were avowedly nonreligious, when I said "You will be in my prayers," none yet has responded, "Thanks, but please don't."

The Bridge between Two Vocations

During four decades as a congregational rabbi, I was a teacher and defender of the Jewish faith. During the past decade I have taught, primarily, the nonreligious spirituality of relational medicine. Martin Buber provides a bridge between a religious and nonreligious spirituality.

In his slender classic, *I and Thou*, Buber describes two modes of living in this world.[26] He labels one *I-It* and the other *I-Thou*. The *I-It* mode is detached, impersonal, and functional. It is the mode of problem solving and analyzing. It views things and people as useful in our pursuit of some further goal. To develop the technology for space travel or to chop down a tree for firewood the scientist and the lumberjack labor primarily in the mode of *I-It*.

By contrast, when an astronaut, awed by viewing planet Earth from space, reads verses from the biblical creation story, or when the nature lover views the tree not as potential firewood but as an awesome expression of the beauty and grandeur of the natural world, they have entered the *I-Thou* mode. Buber also taught that we come to know persons best, not by studying them as objects but by being fully present to them in love as an I to a Thou.

Buber believes both modes are essential for human life. At their best, physicians alternate between the *I-It* and *I-Thou* modes. The surgeon in the operating room and the cardiologist studying a patient's electrocardiogram are appropriately in an *I-It* mode. However, when that surgeon emerges from the operating room to convey heartbreaking news to the anxious family, the surgeon's tools are not clinical knowledge and skill but empathy and compassion. Her most healing gesture is a hug—or its emotional equivalent.

Buber's two modes of being provide a way to view the relationship between treating the patient biomedically and relating to the patient as person. Buber also provides the best language to understand relational medicine as a nonreligious spirituality. For Buber, treating the patient as a person rather than as simply an embodiment of disease is a sacred act of transcendent significance even when the physician is not "religious."

In Buber's view, that sacred act becomes "religious" when a person perceives the drive to act as a divine call ("Where are you?") and the act itself as a response to that call ("Here I am"). To Buber,

God is "the Eternal Thou" whom we may glimpse only in, through, and beyond our *I-Thou* relationships to God's world.[27]

Creating Programs That Are Friendly to the Religious and Nonreligious

Ideally, any curriculum in relational medicine should be user friendly to both religious and nonreligious patients and physicians. A brief description of one of our signature programs should clarify how we strive to walk that line. The Sacred Vocation Program (SVP) is an integral part of the internal medicine residency at the University of Texas Medical School. We define "sacred" as did cultural anthropologist Barbara Meyerhoff. It is "that which has authority over our lives because it comes closest to what makes us human."[28] As we have seen, being human is closely linked to our being meaning seekers. Since residents are subjected to many stressors and must combat the threat of cynicism and burnout, SVP aims to nourish their spirit and help them reclaim their work as a sacred vocation.

Residents meet in small groups with a trained facilitator. They meet twice a week during lunch over a period of a month. They pledge to honor the confidentiality of these meetings, to listen nonjudgmentally to each other, and trust each other enough to share their thoughts, feelings, and experiences at work. Some would define themselves as spiritual but not religious; others see their power to heal as a divine gift and their medical practice as a way of serving God in the world.

In one session, the residents are asked to reflect upon a patient encounter when they healed the person by the biomedical skill and knowledge they deployed and by the relational skill they displayed (listening, validating, encouraging). They also consider situations when, even if they cannot cure, they can be healers of the patient's spirit. By sharing these accounts of their power to heal, they realize their work is intrinsically life validating. Whether we are religious or not (unless we are sociopaths) we know we are on earth to heal and not to harm, to relieve and not ignore suffering, to love and be loved. Therefore, many rediscover that their work of healing can be a sacred vocation—part of what gives meaning to their lives.

In the second phase of the program, representatives of each group meet with a facilitator to address this question: What changes would you like to see in the work environment that would make you feel better about working here and better able to serve your patients? These recommendations are considered by management and, wherever feasible, accepted and implemented. Because the residents' response to the program was overwhelmingly positive the directors decided to make SVP an integral part of the Internal Medicine Residency.

The Importance of Validating Nonreligious Spirituality

As a believing Jew, mine is a religious spirituality. My religious heritage is the primary lens through which I view the world. But in the Texas Medical Center, I work with many persons who do not embrace my view or perhaps any religious story. They may have found meaning in their power to love and be loved, in work that uses the fruits of their knowledge and skill to heal and allay human suffering. They too nourish the hope that by the quality of their lives they will be remembered and missed. To their patients, they express compassion, empathy—even love. They share many of those values that unite decent persons in our medical center and elsewhere. They teach and practice a relational medicine. Theirs is a nonreligious spirituality.

But what of those physicians who are religious? Must they conceal their religious identification when they practice or teach in a medical center? Daniel Hall and Farr Curlin, avowedly Christian physicians, reject Neil Scheurich's call for them to bracket their religious sentiments and speak only in secular terms in the medical center. To do so, they contend, is not to foster neutrality but only to privilege the agnostic or atheistic perspective.[29]

I would concur that religious caregivers need not conceal their identity. However, given the status of the physician as authority figure and the extreme vulnerability of the patient, such "bearing witness" should not even appear to convey a proselytizing intent. Before he was tapped to head the National Cancer Institute and later, the FDA, Andrew von Eschenbach was a urologist at MD Anderson Hospital. He is a believing Catholic who witnesses to his faith in a way his patients can comfortably accept. He told me that after he gave a patient a potentially life-threatening diagnosis, he would say, "I promise to be with you through this journey, to give you the benefit of the latest and best medical knowledge available anywhere in this world, and, since I'm a believer, I'll be praying for a positive outcome."[30] Religious doctors should not, however, impugn the adequacy or validity of a nonreligious spirituality.

For me, a religious perspective on life is the most profound and most adequate response to the glory and pathos of the human condition. But in a world where religious zealots may discount even the religious spirituality of other faith brands, and, when politically dominant, even deny others religious freedom, it is all the more desirable that a medical center and the world at large respect and validate both a religious and nonreligious spirituality.

A Final Thought

Before the reemergence of relational healing in medical education, physicians were known by their "fight" or "flight" syndrome. When their aggressive medical intervention proved inadequate and the patient was "terminal," the physician quickly fled the scene. Noting this phenomenon, Dr. Sherwin Nuland explains that, according to a number of studies, those who choose medicine as a profession "have a greater fear of death than in any other profession. One of the reasons we deal so badly with end of life issues is because it brings back all these primitive fears."[31]

In part, doctors may choose medicine to gain significant victories over death. If, however, that becomes their only criterion of success as a healer, each time they cannot save a life is regarded as a personal failure, which impels them to retreat to the next battleground in the war of life against death. As a distinguished champion of relational medicine, Nuland reminds his colleagues that when you cannot cure you can still care. Indeed, thanks to the now prevailing paradigm of medical education and practice, many physicians have discovered that being present in non-curative situations with empathy and love may not only heal the patient's spirit; it may also imbue their medical practice with deeper meaning. This is perhaps the most precious fruit of spirituality in medicine.

Notes

1. M. Maimonides, *The Guide for the Perplexed*, trans. S. Pines, (Chicago: University of Chicago Press, 1963), 43-44.
2. Hippocrates, *Precepts* VI, cited in S. J. Reiser, A. J. Dyck, and W. J. Curran, eds., *Ethics in Medicine: Historical Perspectives and Contemporary Concerns* (Cambridge, MA: MIT Press, 1977).

3. M. R. Irwin, E. V. Yang, and R. Glaser, "Stress Induced Immunomodulation: Impact on Immune Defenses against Infectious Diseases," *Biomedical Pharmacotherapy* 54, no. 5 (June, 2000): 245–50.

4. J. W. Anderson, C. Liu, and R. J. Kryscio, "Blood Pressure Response to Transcendental Meditation: A Meta Analysis," *American Journal of Hypertension* (March 2008): 310–16.

5. G. L. Engel, "The Need for a New Medical Model: a Challenge for Biomedicine," *Science,* April 8, 1977, 129–30.

6. Ibid., 132.

7. Ibid.

8. The American Association of Medical Colleges, "Guidelines for Accreditation," 1999.

9. Cited in S. L. Prolho, "The Role of Spirituality in Medical School Psychiatry Residency Education," *International Journal of Applied Psychoanalytic Studies* 17 (June 2010): 180–92.

10. H. M. Chochinov, T. Hack, and J. Hassard, "Understanding the Will to Live in Patients nearing Death," *Psychosomatic*s 46 (February 2005): 7–10.

11. C. Horowitz, A. Suchman, and W. Branch, "What Do Doctors Find Meaningful in Their Work?" *Annals of Internal Medicine* 138, no. 9 (2003): 174.

12. L. Joelson and L. Wahlquist, "The Psychological Meaning of Job Insecurity and Job Loss," *Journal of Sociology, Science and Medicine* 25, no. 2 (1987): 179–82.

13. C. Puchalski, "The Role of Spirituality in Healthcare," *BUMC Proceeding* 14 (2001): 352–57.

14. Video produced by MD Anderson Hospital and used with permission.

15. H. Koenig, *Medical Journal of Australia* 186, no. 10 (supplement on "Spirituality and Health") (May 2007): 21.

16. N. Scheurich, "Reconsidering Spirituality in Medicine," *Academic Medicine* 178, no. 4 (April 2003): 356–60.

17. A. Kleinman, *The Illness Narratives: Suffering, Healing, and the Human Condition* (New York: Basic Books, 1988), 54.

18. E. Cassell, "The Nature of Suffering: Physical, Psychological, Social, and Spiritual Aspects," in *The Hidden Dimensions of Illness*, ed. P. Starck and J. P. McGovern (New York: Oxford University Press, 1991), 1–10.

19. E. Cassell, *The Nature of Suffering and the Goals of Medicine* (New York: Oxford University Press, 1991), 45.

20. Horowitz, Suchman, and Branch, "What Do Doctors Find Meaningful in Their Work?" 772.

21. C. Washauer, "Helping Patients by Including Spirituality in Discussion," *Oncology Times*, July 10, 2009, 14–19.

22. F. Kafka, "A Country Doctor," trans. Blahut (Prague: Twisted Spoon Press, 1997), 174.

23. Mayo Clinic Proceedings, 2001, 1225–35.

24. C. Puchalski and A. L Romer, "Taking a Spiritual Assessment Allows Clinician to Understand Patients More Fully," *Journal of Palliative Medicine* 3, no. 1 (March 2000): 129–37.

25. B. Feldstein, "Toward Meaning (A Piece of My Mind)," *Journal of the American Medical Association* 286, no. 11 (2001): 1291–92.

26. M. Buber, *I and Thou*, trans. R. G. Smith (New York: Charles Scribner's, 1937), 6–8.

27. Ibid. 75.

28. B. Meyerhoff, *Stories as Equipment for Living*, ed. M. Kaminsky and M. Weiss (Ann Arbor: University of Michigan Press, 2007).

29. D. E. Hill and F. Curlin, "Can Physicians Be Neutral Regarding Religion," *Academic Medicine* 79 (July 2004): 677–79.

30. As told in personal conversation with Dr. Andrew von Eschenbach.

31. S. Nuland, quoted in the *New York Times*, "A Doctor's Look at Life and Death," November 16, 1997.

My Daughter or Son the Nurse: Jews in Nursing and the Healing Role of Nurses

Ellen Olshansky

It is rare that we hear a Jewish parent talk about "my daughter the nurse" and even more rare to hear "my son the nurse." The nursing profession is not typically thought of as a career for Jewish women, let alone for Jewish men. Despite this, nursing embraces many of Judaism's central precepts and is consistent with Jewish text. Nursing is also synergistic with Reform Judaism's emphasis on social justice and social action, particularly seen in public health nursing. A core value of nursing is caring and compassion. Nursing practice is rooted in the central tenet of caring for patients, creating an environment for optimal healing and helping patients achieve the highest quality of life possible within their particular context. Two major precepts of Judaism are *bikur cholim* (visiting the sick) and *tikkun olam* (repairing the world). In this article I discuss the relevance of nursing to these precepts and present important aspects of the history of Jews in nursing, with a particular focus on public health nursing.[1]

Nursing: A Jewish Profession?

There are legitimate reasons that nursing does not appear to be a profession for Jews, since nursing is often described as having its roots in Christianity. Up until the middle of the twentieth century, it was common for nurse training programs in the United States to require students to attend Mass even if they were not Christian.

DR. ELLEN OLSHANSKY is professor and director of the Program in Nursing Science at the University of California, Irvine. She is a women's health nurse practitioner and a fellow in the American Academy of Nursing, co-chairing the Expert Panel on Women's Health. She holds a doctorate in nursing science from the University of California, San Francisco School of Nursing.

In addition there were serious obstacles placed before Jews who wanted to pursue a career in nursing. A compact in Massachusetts was created when the New England Hospital for Women and Children opened in 1862 with a quota of one Jewish nurse and one African American nurse. Some training programs required a letter from the clergy, attesting to the nurse trainee's Christianity.[2] These barriers to Jews entering nursing created formidable challenges, leading to an unfavorable context for nursing as a career for Jews. While it was common for Jewish women to enter fields of teaching and social work, the field of nursing was viewed differently. Many parents of Jewish women were reluctant about their daughters pursuing nursing as a career because they viewed it as "dirty work." Jewish families often discouraged their daughters from entering nursing because it was considered "secondary" in the sense of serving doctors and not being a career in which one could advance.[3]

Women's issues, too, contributed to some of the notions related to Jewish women in nursing. In the first half of the twentieth century, women having careers was antithetical to "women's roles" (with the notable exception of World War II, when women filled jobs that were vacant because men were at war, symbolized by Rosie the Riveter). In the latter part of the twentieth century, with the second wave of feminism, an additional set of obstacles appeared. With more doors open to women, Jewish women began to choose medical school and "my daughter, the doctor" became more common within the lingo of Jewish parents. Nursing was often viewed as "traditional women's work," conjuring a subservient role and negative stereotypes.

While nursing in the twentieth century presented its own set of issues for women who did not fit the inherited stereotypes and perceptions of nurses, in the twenty-first century the increase in male nurses in the United States and Israel raises new questions of what it means to be a nurse who is both Jewish and male. This past decade has witnessed an increasing number of men in nursing. It is not clear how many Jewish men select nursing as a career. Romem and Anson,[4] citing the Ministry of Health Report from 2001, noted that in the year 2000 the proportion of male nurses in Israel was 8.5 percent, which included Israeli Arabs. In the United States it is estimated that males consist of 5 percent to 10 percent of the nurses in the civilian sector, but in the military there is much less discrepancy between the genders, and the Assembly for Men in Nursing is instrumental in increasing the numbers of men who choose nursing as a career.[5] Despite the increase in males entering the nursing profession, there is often a high attrition rate of males due to difficulties they face in this female dominated field. More data are necessary in order to more accurately assess the increase in males in nursing and to more effectively support males in nursing.

Caring: A Central Precept of the Profession of Nursing

Nursing practice is centered on the concept of caring. Nursing as a caring profession conveys a discipline informed by scientific principles within a humanistic approach to patient care. Prominent nurse theorists have emphasized the interconnectedness of all beings,[6] transpersonal caring-healing as joined consciousness,[7] the reciprocal nature of intuitive reflexive responses in caring,[8] and the understanding that nursing as a caring practice comes from being available for the experience of shared humanity.[9]

Relevancy of Jewish Teachings and Nursing:
Bikur Cholim and *Tikkun Olam*

Bikur cholim and *tikkun olam* are two key tenets in Judaism that embody community, caring for others, and creating a healthy society.[10] *Bikur cholim* is a mitzvah that encompasses both the care of an individual as well as the care of the community. *Tikkun olam* reflects a responsibility to work for the betterment of community. *Bikur cholim* first appears in the Torah in Genesis (17:26–18:1), when God visits Abraham to check on him and care for him after his circumcision. *Bikur cholim*, caring for others, and loving our neighbors as we would ourselves (Lev. 19:18) are mitzvot that reflect a strong emphasis on interpersonal relationships and community.

Bikur cholim is concerned with care and healing of individuals, as in visiting an ill person. This is evident in nursing care of individuals, whether in the hospital or at home. Another way of viewing *bikur cholim* is through a community lens. Caring for the health of communities is done by promoting wellness through community efforts and education, such as stop-smoking campaigns or increasing awareness of healthy lifestyles to prevent cardiac disease. *Tikkun olam* is related to this mitzvah, since one way of repairing the world is to provide healthcare and health education at a community level.

Nursing's focus on caring for individuals and families as well as communities is relevant to the Jewish precepts of *bikur cholim* and *tikkun olam*. This is true of nursing in general and is particularly true for public health nursing. Public health nurses frequently make home visits to patients and, in fact, the Visiting Nurse Association (VNA) was created in the early 1900s to formalize the work of nurses caring for patients in their homes. Although the VNA was not created solely by Jewish nurses, the precept of *bikur cholim* can be interpreted by Jewish nurses as being integral to the VNA. Viewing health and illness within a social context, emphasizing the social determinants of health, is a key part of nursing and fits with a focus on repairing the world. By repairing the world, we contribute to the health of the public.

The role of midwives is prominent in the Torah, and midwives today comprise an important group of nurses with a strong public health focus. Shifrah and Puah, who were Jochebed and Miriam (the mother and sister of Moses according to midrash) defied Pharaoh by attending the births of babies born to Jewish women; rather than kill baby boys, as Pharaoh demanded, Shifrah and Puah let them live.[11] Today, nurse midwives deliver babies in various communities, often working in underserved communities. The focus of community that is a strong thread in Jewish text is mirrored in public health nursing.

Jewish Nurses' Influence on Public Health Nursing: An Historical Overview

The notion that individual health is promoted by creating and maintaining healthy communities is central to public health nursing. Public health nurses work on behalf of the public by becoming engaged in social change that leads to increased quality and access to healthcare. Social activism is a part of public health nursing, which can be conceptualized as similar to the Jewish precept of *tikkun olam*.

Historically Jewish nurses have played a major role in the public health movement. Lillian Wald, a Jewish nurse, who coined the term "public health nursing," is considered its founder.[12] She cared for immigrants as a visiting nurse and eventually started the Nurses' Settlement of Henry Street, just before the turn of the twentieth century, which provided visiting nursing services and healthcare to poor and needy immigrants.

Public health nursing seeks to improve the health of the public by encouraging policies such as offering vaccinations to all and educating citizens about how to prevent illnesses. In order to do such work, social activism and community organizing are necessary to initiate appropriate policies. As a social activist, Lillian Wald overcame many barriers to create public health nursing. For example, she worked actively for the enactment of the Sheppard Towner Act in 1921 to provide federal funds for maternal-child care and later for its continuation when the American Medical Association lobbied (successfully) for its repeal.[13]

Other Jewish nurses were leaders in public health and social activism. Emma Goldman worked as a nurse for ten years in the 1890s, beginning as a practical nurse when she was in prison. She later studied in Vienna to become a midwife and practiced midwifery in the Lower East Side of New York City. Hanna Sandusky learned to be a midwife from her mother in Eastern Europe. This was not formal training, but after attending the births of many immigrant Jewish women in Pittsburgh's predominantly Jewish Hill District in the mid-1800s (where she was nicknamed Bobba Hanna because it was common for grandmothers to attend births), a physician supported her to travel to Germany to attain formal training. She then returned to Pittsburgh and continued to provide midwifery services free of charge until she was eighty-two years old.[14] Naomi Deutsch was a public health nurse who worked with Lillian Wald. After moving to San Francisco she become director of the Visiting Nurse Association in 1925, and later served as assistant professor of Public Health at U.C. Berkeley. In 1935 she became director of Public Health Nursing in the U.S. Children's Bureau and then worked with international public health programs. After retiring, she taught part time at Columbia University Teachers College, where many nurses enrolled for higher education before nursing doctoral degrees were established.

Many immigrant Jews functioned informally as caregivers to the sick. My own grandmother was referred to as the "public health nurse of the Bronx" because she was always the person upon whom people depended for assistance and she frequently visited neighbors in the 1920s and 1930s. Chicken soup was a community-based remedy well before the famous Chicken Soup for the Soul series was published!

Israel is home to Hadassah Hospital School of Nursing, which was started in 1918 on Mount Scopus by Henrietta Szold, the founder of Hadassah, who was not a nurse, but a social worker who saw the need for high quality nursing education in order to promote quality healthcare. Szold was born in the United States, but traveled to Palestine and was so distressed about the poor living conditions and health problems there that she was determined to improve the situation. Highly influenced by the work of Lillian Wald, Szold planned to create a public health nursing system in Palestine. In order to do this, she invited two Jewish nurses from the United States to join her in Palestine. In 1913 Rose Kaplan and Rae Landy traveled to Palestine, where they began a public health nursing service and midwifery service and, specifically, they started the American Daughters of Zion Nurses Settlement Hadassah. This was a nurse-managed public health center, something well before its time.[15] (Today, in the United States there is an organization referred to as The Institute for Nursing Centers, whose mission is to promote nurse-managed clinics in the United States, providing primary care to the community.)

A famous Jewish nurse in Palestine (before the creation of the State of Israel) and then later in Israel (after statehood was achieved) was Raquela Prywes. She was born in 1924 and was trained at Hadassah Hospital School of Nursing, where she became a nurse midwife.[16] She attended the births of thousands of women in internment camps in Cyprus after the Holocaust, while they were waiting to be allowed into Palestine. Her unwavering commitment to the health of these mothers and babies was a significant contribution and, metaphorically, attending these births can be compared to attending the birth of Israel as a Jewish state. She actually saved Sarah, Golda Meir's daughter, who had eclampsia, a life-threatening condition, in childbirth.[17]

Contemporary Contributions of Jewish Nursing

Nursing has an important role in contemporary Jewish society. The Kalsman Institute describes the Jewish Healing Movement as encompassing the intersection among Judaism, health, and healing.[18] Jewish nurses are in key positions to contribute to this movement and are fulfilling an important role in this area, specifically within synagogues and within public policy arenas.

Congregational nurses play important roles in caring for members of the synagogue, a central part of Jewish life for affiliated Jews.[19] Nurses play key roles in Caring or Chesed Committees in synagogues, and it would be ideal to further develop and expand these committees to provide care for those in need, as well as to provide education and support for health promoting activities. (Rabbi Richard Steinberg wrote an article for this special issue about a health-themed project initiated at his congregation, Shir Ha-Ma'alot, and articles on congregational health programming are also included from Rabbis Richard Address, Marion Lev-Cohen, and Edythe Mencher.)

Jewish nurses also play important roles outside of congregations, including nursing leadership positions nationally and internationally.[20] Thelma Schorr served as editor of the *American Journal of Nursing* in the 1970s. Claire Fagin was dean of the School of Nursing at the University of Pennsylvania from 1977 to 1992, and she was also interim president of the University of Pennsylvania from 1993 to 1994. Pearl Moore began the Oncology Nursing Society and served as its chief executive officer from 1983 to 2007. In these leadership roles, these nurses represent and are responsible to the nursing profession, across all ethnicities, cultures, and religious affiliations. However, while it is important that Jews have a voice in the mainstream of the profession, we also have a role in maintaining our Jewish identity. Jewish nurses comprise a minority of nurses and our voices are important within the profession.

Recently increased emphasis has been put on the importance of integrating spirituality into healthcare.[21] Nurses have always emphasized holistic health, recognizing the interrelationships among mind, body, emotions, spirituality, and social context. Spirituality may mean different things to different people and nurses need to respect their patients' views of spirituality. Jewish nurses can play an important role in adding to the religious and cultural diversity of the nursing workforce and in adding diverse points of view and education to offer patients culturally competent spiritual care and assessment.

Summary

In sum, nursing as a profession fits closely with Jewish precepts found in the Torah and reflected in the history of Jewish nursing.

Jewish nursing has a strong record of focusing on social justice and social activism. The stereotypes of the nursing profession create challenges for nurses in general, and for Jewish nurses in unique ways. The stereotypical view of nursing as perpetuating a woman's subservient role is countered by the evidence presented by social activists such as Lillian Wald; the view that nursing is rooted in Christianity is countered by the work of Henrietta Szold in starting Hadassah Hospital and later the Hadassah Nurses Councils. To actively struggle against these stereotypes is consistent with the core of Judaism. The essence of how we find meaning and truth is to struggle with ideas, just as Jacob wrestled with the angels and Abraham struggled with God. It is this very struggle that leads us to understanding, meaning, and purpose in our lives and our careers. For me, being a Jew and a nurse provides challenges and rewards, allowing me to perform mitzvot and find meaning in my work.

Notes

1. Evelyn Rose Benson, *As We See Ourselves: Jewish Women in Nursing* (Indianapolis: Center Nursing Publishing, 2001). Evelyn Rose Benson has written eloquently on Jews in nursing and this article builds on her work.

2. Susan L. Meyer, *Jewish Women's Archives*, http://jwa.org/encyclopedia/article/nursing-in-united-states (accessed October 20, 2011).

3. Rabbi Douglas Kohn, personal communication based on his conversation with Dr. Jacob Rader Marcus (circa 1986–1987).

4. Pnina Romen and Ofra Anson, "Israeli Men in Nursing: Social and Personal Motives," *Journal of Nursing Management* 13 (2005): 173–78.

5. William T. Lecher, "Men in Nursing Are Taking Action to Improve Gender Diversity and Inclusion," http://championnursing.org/blog/Lechermen-nursing-diversity-and-inclusion (accessed October 25, 2011).

6. Martha Rogers, "The Science of Unitary Human Beings: Current Perspectives," *Nursing Science Quarterly* 7, no. 1 (1994): 33–35; J. Watson and M. Smith, "Caring Science and the Science of Unitary Human Beings: A Trans-Theoretical Discourse for Nursing Knowledge Development," *Journal of Advanced Nursing* 37, no. 5 (2002): 452–61.

7. Jean Watson, "New Dimensions of Human Caring Theory," *Nursing Science Quarterly* 1, no. 4 (1998): 175–81.

8. Janice M. Morse, Jean Bottorff, Gwen Anderson, Beverly O'Brien, and Shirley Solberg, "Beyond Empathy: Expanding Expressions of Caring," *Journal of Advanced Nursing* 53, no. 1 (2006): 75–87.

9. K. Wilkin and E. Slevin, "The Meaning of Caring to Nurses: An Investigation into the Nature of Caring Work in an Intensive Care Unit," *Journal of Clinical Nursing* 13, no. 1 (2004): 50–59.

10. Isaac N. Trainin, Jewish Board of Family and Children's Services New York, http://www.bikurcholimcc.org/whatisbc.html; Janet Offel, "A Model for Building Community in Contemporary Synagogues," (paper as a project of the National Jewish Healing Movement, with funding from Nathan Cummings Foundations, SeRaF [Senior Resource Faculty], National Center for Jewish Healing, The Kalsman Institute).

11 Women in Judaism, http://www.torah.org/learning/women/class45.html (accessed October 23, 2011).

12. Joyce Antler, "Feminism in the United States," http://jwa.org/encyclopedia/article/feminism-in-united-states (accessed December 12, 2011).

13. Jone Johnson Lewis, "Sheppard Towner Act of 1921," http://womenshistory.about.com/od/laws/a/sheppard-towner.htm (accessed October 24, 2011).

14. Meyer, *Jewish Women's Archive.*

15. Benson, *As We See Ourselves.*

17. Ruth Gruber, *Raquela: A Woman of Israel* (New York: Three Rivers Press, 1978).

18. Michele Prince, "Preface" to *Midrash and Medicine: Healing Body and Soul in the Interpretive Jewish Tradition,* ed. William Cutter (Woodstock, VT: Jewish Lights Publishing, 2011), ix–xv.

19. Karen Kosarin Frank, "Bringing Caring to the Synagogue with Jewish Congregational Nursing," http://huc.edu/kalsman/articles/Karen.pdf.

20. Meyer, *Jewish Women's Archives.*

21. Benson, *As We See Ourselves.*

The Kalsman Institute Research Roundtable: Building a Field of Judaism and Health

Michele Prince

Introduction

The Kalsman Institute is an academic center for training, collaboration, and dialogue at the intersection of Judaism and health. The institute convenes programming, educational events, and scholarship on themes in pastoral education, spirituality and healing, bioethics, illness and wellness, and healthcare practice. The Institute developed the Kalsman Roundtable on Judaism and Health Research, a project designed to promote and support basic and applied research on all of these themes. The Research Roundtable project was initiated in 2008 to begin a systematic discussion of scholarship on Judaism, health, healing, and medicine. The overarching goal of the Roundtable project and of building the field of Judaism and health is to better understand the health of the Jewish people and to improve health and well-being in the Jewish community.

The Roundtable project was funded by the John Templeton Foundation, and brought thirty Jewish leaders together across religious streams and professional disciplines to build the field of Judaism and health.[1] Rabbis, researchers, and medical professionals assembled from universities, medical centers, synagogues, and Jewish community organizations to launch new projects, research concepts, and partnerships to build a scholarly foundation for work in Judaism, health, healing, and medicine. This assembly of scholars composed an enthusiastic and vibrant community and promises to be an enduring network.

MICHELE PRINCE, MSW, LCSW, MAJCS (LA02) is the director of the Kalsman Institute on Judaism and Health of HUC-JIR. She is a licensed clinical social worker, specializing in oncology, and is co-founder of the Jewish Bereavement Project.

The first phase of the Roundtable resulted in numerous products. Outputs included field building through program assessment to document the scope of Jewish congregational and communal efforts related to health and healing, creation of an online Archive on Judaism and Health Research (www.ajhr.org), and writing, reporting, and presentations.

This paper summarizes the efforts of the project, including a culminating Roundtable Retreat held in January 2011 and meetings before and after, to delve into the priorities for emerging scholarship in this field. Dozens of research ideas and project themes, and hundreds of questions, surfaced during the retreat, ranging from interest in the efficacy of Jewish rituals for healing to attempts to obtain a snapshot of the overall health of North American Jewry. The Roundtable will continue scholarly deliberations in focused areas across the spectrum of Jewish life and practice to make a uniquely Jewish contribution to two decades of study in the field of religion, spirituality, and health built primarily from an interfaith or Christian point of view.

The Kalsman Institute charged Roundtable participants with raising as many questions as possible during retreat meetings. Participants considered the questions, issues, and problems to which the community and thus research and scholarship need to respond. What are the conditions that face the Jewish people today? What are the recurring constants and life's inherent difficulties? How might Jewish community leadership meet those conditions with responses from the field of Judaism, health, healing, and medicine?

Participants want to know how Jewish religious practice and Jewish spirituality—acknowledging the full continuum of practice and belief—are beneficial for physical and mental health, spiritual well-being, and psychosocial functioning and support. Jewish texts, rituals, and resiliency can address the continuum of illness and wellness to draw on Judaism's rich and distinctively multifaceted resources in religion, spirituality, culture, and peoplehood.

Why Build a Field?

What is a field and how is one built? The John D. and Catherine T. MacArthur Foundation supported research that defined a field as a "multidisciplinary area of specialized practice that engages diverse stakeholders."[2] The Foundation's notion of working to "advance new concepts or activities in a previously unheralded way"[3] is an important part of field building. Kalsman Roundtable efforts do not include *creating* a field but rather bringing together previously fragmented players to build a field. Attributes of field building connected to the Roundtable efforts include "seeking attention and legitimacy" for the field of Judaism and health, reducing "inefficiencies and duplicate activities," and providing incentives or opportunities for collaboration that may not have happened organically. The Roundtable project is managing the "challenges of integrating divergent sectors and fostering collaboration" to move the field forward.[4]

Kalsman Roundtable participants discussed whether field building is or should be a goal of the Kalsman Institute and the Roundtable project. Participant Doug Kohn, rabbi of Congregation Emanu El, in Redlands, California, asked, "Is the benefit of building a field to develop authenticity and validity for the activities, programs, and research under way and to be undertaken? Will field building advance professional and lay communication in this widely diverse field—linking the varied practitioners and users across disciplines?"

Participants agreed that field-building exercises would set definitions and parameters and provide baselines for those in the field, in terms of variety, quality, and quantity of research and programming.

Design Principles of Field Building

Design principles of field building draw from research by the W. K. Kellogg Foundation.[5] Principles most relevant to the field-building exercise of convening a Judaism and health roundtable include the following steps that have begun to solidify: (1) recognizing the opportunity; (2) prioritizing sets of leadership, participants, and networks; (3) building a network infrastructure to establish networks among practitioners, researchers, and/or advocates; and (4) sharing knowledge and providing vehicles for collecting, analyzing, and disseminating information and knowledge.[6] Roundtable members compose an enthusiastic and vibrant network. The MacArthur Foundation report indicated a "complex web of relationships and joint projects has many benefits." Participants agree that the Roundtable project is catalyzing new ideas and bringing together bases of support through complex interdisciplinary and interdenominational collaboration.

Some of the design principles that indicate the direction of the second phase of this project are: (5) discerning how and where to set boundaries for what is inherently included and excluded from the field of Judaism and health; (6) establishing a research base, critical for such a cross-disciplinary and cross-institutional collaborative effort, as described in the discussion above of the five areas of focus; and (7) developing and adopting the standards for practice, which will include defining common terminology (such as health, healing, and Jewish spirituality).[7] Another element of the field building will be providing access to opportunities for education, which is where the Kalsman Institute will disseminate the work and ideas of the Roundtable to congregational and community circles.

The Larger Field of Religion and Health

To successfully build a field of Judaism and health, Roundtable members reviewed the history of the larger field of Judaism and health. A two-decade investment has been made in the study of spirituality, religion, and health.[8] Study in the field of religion and health includes the health effects of public religion and private spirituality and ranges from debates on religion's effects on health, including research on mental and physical health, to use of health services and clinical applications.[9] Researchers, healthcare clinicians, and scientists largely conducted research focused almost exclusively on Christians.[10] Jewish community scholars and researchers are asking, How well do the findings and methods generalize to other groups, particularly Jews? Roundtable participants explore areas of commonality and areas of distinctiveness.

The task now is to expand research efforts focused more explicitly on specific faith traditions, such as Judaism, and to disseminate findings both to other researchers and to the general public. The Jewish community cannot read itself into the thousands of interfaith or Christian studies correlating religion and spirituality with rates and experiences of illness and wellness and into the innumerable conceptual and theoretical models, measurement indices for religious assessment, and efforts at program development that constitute scholarship in the larger religion, spirituality, and health field.[11]

Jewish religious belief, spiritual practice, and community involvement are conceptually distinct, and assessment of these constructs cannot rely on measures developed for existing studies of religion and health in other religious groups. Religion-specific limitations in prior research will be addressed.

Insights from Building the Field of Religion and Health

Two Roundtable advisors are Dr. Jeff Levin and Dr. Ken Pargament.[12] Both pioneered the study of religion, spirituality, and health. To launch the Roundtable, they shared insights from their history in the field of religion and health. Pargament stated at the Roundtable Retreat that "no one is neutral about religion."[13] The emotional power of religion makes it a very difficult topic to study systematically. Levin and several of the researchers described the difficulty and resistance they experienced in focusing their primary research on religion and health, sharing anecdotes about the early years of religion and health research. Levin remembered his dissertation advisor telling him that a focus on religion and health would ruin his career.

An initial Roundtable exploration posed the question "Is religion good for your health?" Pargament made the point that whether religion is good for health depends on a number of factors: why people are religious, how people are religious, when people are religious, and who and where the people are.[14] He said, "The question whether religion is good for your health is giving way to a tougher but more appropriate question: 'How helpful or harmful are particular kinds of religious expressions for particular people dealing with particular situations in particular social contexts according to particular criteria of helpfulness and harmfulness.'" Pargament explained that a critical attitude in this work, as in other basic and applied research, is a willingness and openness to be surprised; stating, "It is critical to consider the degree to which we are in fact open to what research may have to teach us."[15]

Levin shared that one of his primary goals in building the field of Judaism and health is to systematically review existing population health surveys to discern possible trends and needs for further study. The Roundtable community needs a snapshot of the overall health of North American Jewry. He imagines mounting a significant Jewish population health study to lay the groundwork for understanding the impact of religion on health, and health on religion, in Jewish life. Since the Roundtable Retreat, Levin has examined three bodies of data to study Jewish religious indicators as predictors of well-being and distress, and the health impact of Jewish religious observance.[16]

Background on Judaism, Health, Healing, and Medicine

When the Roundtable advisors gathered to discern goals and objectives for research and field-building efforts, they discussed Judaism's long history of attention to illness and wellness. The interconnections among Judaism, health, healing, and medicine have been a longstanding focus of rabbinic and scholarly discourse.[17] From the earliest Jewish scholars, the obligation to heal and the harmony of body and mind have been tenets of Jewish life. Our greatest historical and modern figures, including rabbis, were often physicians and scientists.[18] The Jewish community offers a model for how the complex relations among religion, personal and public health, and the scientific practice of medicine can be successfully understood through interdependent concepts of God, peoplehood, and daily life.

In contemporary times, health, healing, healthcare, and public health have become increasingly relevant to all Jewish organizations and institutions, particularly as health needs continue to grow, as the population ages, and as public and private-sector resources shrink. Health is not a side issue in Jewish life; it affects the other domains of Jewish life and is itself affected by those domains.

Twenty years ago, a handful of Jewish services existed related to health and healing. A few Jewish hospital chaplains, rabbinic visitation to hospitalized or home-bound patients, and the traditional practices of *bikur cholim* (visiting the sick) were the practices and services that defined the extent of organized spiritual care available for Jews in need at that time.

Twenty years later, the more robust, diverse, and far-reaching offerings became the focus of a special study conducted by the Kalsman Institute to build on the scholarship that began contemporary research and reflection on Judaism and health.[19]

Divergent Sectors—Or Common Areas of Focus— In Judaism and Health

As the Kalsman Institute discerned and described its own work in the field of Judaism and health, it identified five broad areas of focus:

1. Pastoral Education
2. Jewish Bioethics
3. The Healthcare System
4. Spirituality and Healing
5. Response to Illness and Wellness

This framework can ground and reinforce conversations and understanding of the field of Judaism and health and can assist in setting the boundaries for what is included and what is excluded from the field. These five areas have natural points of connectivity and remain at times disparate sectors of work and study in Jewish communal life. Roundtable field-building activities better integrated and reinforced efficiencies and collaboration, as well as sparked new ideas and support.

There are multiple ways to visualize the field. The Kalsman Institute and the Roundtable participants have chosen to look at the field from a systems perspective. Many in the Jewish community look at a model that begins with self, home, and family, broadens out to immediate community, such as congregation, agency, or school, then moves farther out from the central core to geographical area, peoplehood, and a larger sociological circle or ecosystem. These interdependent systems are considered in a concentric circular model that fits both a long-established Jewish communal tradition and a contemporary organizing model.[20]

Field building will be designed to reinforce the idea that these areas of focus are not independent silos but instead interconnected areas of study and work. Foundational research and academic pursuits cross over all five areas of focus. Two of the areas, Jewish bioethics and Jewish chaplaincy, have each developed into separate and scholarly subfields.

The subfield of Jewish bioethics engages the Jewish community in considering biomedical dilemmas, many of which emerge from the encounter between technology and spiritual values. While recognizing that any coherent Jewish bioethics rests on the legacy of inherited norms, values, and experience, the Jewish community desires to develop a variety of methodologies that bring clarity and authenticity to difficult life choices. The community strives to broaden and deepen biomedical conversation in Jewish life and to create pluralistic models of cooperation, across a spectrum of Jewish practice.[21]

The subfield of Jewish chaplaincy organizes chaplains who span the denominational spectrum and serve the Jewish community in hospitals, geriatric centers, nursing homes, assisted-living facilities, mental health facilities, hospices, correctional institutions, healing centers, community chaplaincies, the military, and college campuses. Jewish chaplains answer to standards of professional training, practice, and certification. Jewish chaplaincy also seeks to create pluralistic models of cooperation across a spectrum of Jewish practice.[22]

Select Roundtable Retreat Presentation Themes and Topics

Roundtable members considered the recurring constants and inherent difficulties that face the Jewish people today and explored how the field of Judaism and health might respond to those conditions.[23] Suggestions drawn from a speech by Rabbi Eric Yoffie, former president of the URJ, included that some of the primary trends affecting current Jewish life include assimilation and intermarriage. Radically different family and marriage patterns and radically different living patterns for young adults also impact contemporary living. Jewish leaders describe trying to find Jewish wisdom to help their constituents thrive in this period of turmoil and transition in Jewish life.[24] The burgeoning field of Judaism and health has made contributions to Jewish life, particularly addressing some of those very conditions that impact individual, family, and social health—assimilation, family and marriage patterns, and spiritual distress—by providing sensitive and effective resources, services, and support. The field has also modeled how professionals and lay leaders from varied disciplines, denominations, even different "sides of the aisle," can collaborate. A level of maturity and gravitas must now be brought to the work of the field of Judaism and health.[25]

Dr. David Rosmarin[26] described to the Roundtable gathering one of his projects, JPSYCH (www.jpsych.com), which is an online laboratory to investigate the role of Jewish religiousness in psychological well-being. He shared several studies and provided a scale created to measure trust and mistrust in God. The scale assessed "frequency of prayer, synagogue attendance, religious study, and grace after meals" to explore religion as a predictor of psychological distress in two religious communities. [27]

Rosmarin's work led to evaluation of a spiritually integrated treatment for subclinical anxiety in the Jewish community, delivered through the Internet. He described not only the study but also the strong response his team experienced from eager participants. The study found a decrease in spiritual distress and a decrease in mistrust in God. Rosmarin's work will continue to examine community attitudes and stigma toward mental health and to consider intrinsic religiosity as a buffer from physical illness and depressive symptoms among Jews. His team hopes future work allows for, among other things, longitudinal designs over multiple waves and years to track trust/mistrust and coping with religious observance and mental health.

Dr. Donna Spruijt-Metz and Dr. Marc Weigensberg[28] shared their desire to synthesize their professional and Jewish lives, providing descriptions of their projects and the questions they have asked. Both are involved in research and clinical care related to integrative medicine as well as pediatric obesity.

Spruijt-Metz discussed youth behavioral choices and suggested that religion is a protective factor against substance abuse, suicide, emotional problems, school drop out, and promiscuity. She described a comparative study of innovative street-youth programs in Los Angeles, Mumbai, and Nairobi to explore how faith-based organizations use faith and religion for intervention. Like many of the presenters, Spruijt-Metz met the request to raise as many questions as findings. She described the need for consistent definitions across settings, asking, "When is an institution faith-based and how can we define faith and religion so that the language resonates for all participants?" She asked the group to consider, "What are the working ingredients that we will need to measure, including religiosity, spirituality, and particular behaviors or practices?" She explored holistic approaches to health in minority youth and suggested that "Judaism offers so many doors to making healthy meaning—if we can find them."[29]

Weigensberg described two of his team's studies that examined integrative medicine interventions, including guided imagery and

Council, and both had positive outcomes. He offered the examples as potential interventions, which include health and healing modalities to help envision other integrative health interventions that might be adapted and explored within the Jewish community. In a study examining the effects of a twelve-week lifestyle and guided imagery intervention in obese Latino adolescents, guided imagery reduced the stress hormone cortisol and increased physical activity.[30]

A second study examined Council, which Weigensberg taught is a facilitated group relational process based on Native American tradition used for building, decision making, and group communication. He demonstrated an effective use of Council during the final Roundtable retreat discussion circle to assist dialogue about a challenge that came up during one of the evening meetings.

Weigensberg explored with the group whether "an authentic, integrated system of Jewish healing can be reclaimed, characterized and applied," and he asked, "What are its core principles and practices? Can Jewish healing be studied scientifically? What research studies can we envision to obtain solid health outcomes using this system, such as for Guided Imagery Council with Jewish content, for Jewish meditation and chanting, or herbal remedies and energy work?"[31]

Dr. Pargament also discussed "Judaism as a living religion, with religious struggle as a central concern." He defined struggles as "tensions, strains and conflicts about sacred matters with God, with others, and within oneself." He has been involved in conducting studies that link religious struggles to declines in mental and physical health, declines in spiritual well-being, and greater risk of mortality. He also suspects that "religious struggles are tied to religious disengagement."[32]

These findings appear to hold across religious groups: Hindu, Christian, Buddhist, and Muslim. His teams have wondered "whether struggles would be as problematic for Jews—we have more of a history of conflict and struggle as a pathway to growth— but initial findings suggest that Jews are also vulnerable to effects of struggle."

"To assist people in their quest for the sacred, their spiritual journey," he offered, "I think we need to take a closer look at those times in life that push people to their limits, the times when they might choose to abandon their search for spirituality without support and help. These are critical periods—critical for us as individuals and critical for Judaism as a whole. They deserve our careful attention."[33] Pargament emphasized that Judaism is a questioning tradition: debate is the norm.

Like several other Roundtable scholars, Pargament, Weigensberg, and Spruijt-Metz each described the importance of identifying and exploring distinctive features and rituals in Judaism for study and examination. They pointed to behaviors, practices, and prayer related to the Jewish calendar, for parts of each day, for Shabbat, and for holidays, as well as specific customs and prayers related to life-cycle events and age-related rituals, such as *bikur cholim* and mourning practices and bar and bat mitzvah celebrations.

Diversity and Community Building in Judaism and Health

Another consideration in field building in Judaism and health is the broad spectrum of Jewish practice and belief. Roundtable members desire to explore the interdisciplinary and interdenominational sectors of Judaism and health and to explore key issues in health and key issues in Judaism separately to see where they might intersect for each movement or denomination. The field building is strengthening knowledge and resources to serve the Jewish population and to educate others who are not Jewish across faiths and health professions.

Nancy Epstein[34] suggests that field-building efforts will target three populations: "We are creating a field to (1) serve Jewish individuals (including patients) to help them find sources/resources; to (2) serve Jewish professionals to help them find sources/resources, and for some, find meaning in their work; and (3) educate non-Jewish professionals on how to best meet the needs of Jews."[35]

Several of the Roundtable participants are pastoral educators at the Jewish seminaries, training future Jewish clergy through a combination of academic, spiritual, and professional development. Roundtable participants who discussed the subfield of Jewish Pastoral Education demonstrated existing synergies and the potential for collaboration across the Jewish denominations. All of the participating educational institutions share common components of their approach to pastoral education, including classes, fieldwork, and reflection. One participant and presenter, Michelle Friedman,[36] articulating the approach shared by pastoral educators at all of the seminaries, described that future leaders must be skilled at *bikur cholim* (visiting the sick), have a basic understanding of how to assess family and marital issues, and how to be sensitive to issues that arise around life-cycle events. "Pastoral arts of yesteryear were honed through mentorship and example. As is true in all areas, some rabbis are more talented than others in the raw skills of listening and advising."[37] Preparing future rabbis for work as pastoral counselors includes specific counseling techniques and sensitivity training, as clergy need to consider the impact of their work and relationships on the lives of their congregants and community members, and the impact of the rabbinate on their personal lives.

In addition to the attention paid to interdenominational relations and collaboration, other Roundtable members focused on the interdisciplinary nature of the group. One of the members, Gila Silverman,[38] noted that one of the greatest challenges in this work is that "we are dealing with multiple Judaisms and multiple perspectives on health, healing and research. In many ways, this interdisciplinary group of scholars is much like the blind men and the elephant. The epidemiologist analyzed data from population surveys to identify links between Jewish practice and health. The psychologists, social workers, and chaplains are interested in evaluating the impact of programs and practice on biopsychosocial-spiritual health; the rabbis seek to understand the theologies of health and healing and to find new ways to meet the needs of their congregants."[39] This construction of professional identities, agendas, and boundaries allows for the field building through the broadest lens and embraces shared and opposing points of view.

Framing Questions to Build the Field of Judaism and Health

The initial phase of the Roundtable participants' work considered priorities for research. Several underlying questions emerged from the Roundtable retreat, advisor meetings, and review of materials, and these questions map out the Roundtable's scope of inquiry for its next phases:

1. Is Jewish religious practice and Jewish spirituality—acknowledging the full continuum of practice and belief—beneficial for physical and mental health, spiritual well-being, and psychosocial functioning and support?

2. How can we apply the results of systematic research to improve the competence of Jewish and interfaith professionals and institutions to address the health and healthcare needs of Jewish people across the life span?

3. Why has the Jewish community, a heavily self-studied community, neglected to document and study the health and well-being of Jews, and how can we catalyze this exploration?

4. How can programmatic and liturgical efforts to address health and well-being in the lives of Jews who are in congregations, clinical settings, Jewish organizations, and communities be used as means to strengthen Jewish engagement: involvement in Jewish activities, commitment to Jewish causes, and participation in Judaism?

During the Roundtable retreat and follow-up dialogue, participants raised many research ideas and project themes. Members want to study patterns and determinants of the physical and mental health and well-being of the Jewish population. They also want to develop and validate assessment instruments for use in research on Judaism and health. Research is needed on the care, course of treatment, and medical or psychosocial outcomes of Jewish patients in clinical settings. Research in Judaism and Health can also study religion and use of health services

To further the work of the Roundtable's Program Assessment,[40] the group is interested in gathering information on and evaluating programs addressing special health needs of subgroups of the Jewish population, including (but not limited to) geriatric, adolescent, childbearing, disabled, immigrant, and ethnic-minority populations. Ethnographic and other qualitative studies of innovative health-related congregational or denominational programming are needed. Small groups of Roundtable members are particularly interested in outcomes research related to Jewish chaplaincy, Jewish pastoral care, and Jewish psychology, and others want to describe and evaluate Jewish healing traditions and how they might translate to use with non-Jews.

Goals and Next Steps

The Kalsman Institute Research Roundtable project was and continues to be a natural outgrowth of the need for scholarship and grounded practical application around Judaism and health, a venerated theme in Jewish life. The overarching goal of the Roundtable project and of building the field of Judaism and health is to better understand the health of the Jewish people and to improve health and well-being in the Jewish community. Continued work in field building through research, assessment, and community building will foster innovative studies and resource sharing among a burgeoning leadership of multidisciplinary scholars and clinicians working in the field of Judaism and health. Their work fuels Jewish thinking and communal life. The Kalsman Roundtable will continue to try to bring the emerging field of Judaism and health to full academic maturity.

Participants aspire to encompass efforts that will both catalyze research and inform and improve clinical practice, curricular design, and congregational and communal programming. Establishing research and services to explore these issues will solidify investigators, clinicians, and clergy, respectively, as emerging leaders of this new field. This network will serve to support work spanning both the disciplinary spectrum and the Jewish identity and practice spectrum.

Roundtable members identified the importance of exploring distinctively Jewish rituals in Judaism. They pointed to behaviors, practices, and prayer related to the Jewish calendar, for parts of each day, for Shabbat, and for holidays, as well as specific customs and prayers related to life-cycle events and age-related rituals, such as *bikur cholim* and mourning practices and bar and bat mitzvah celebrations.

A significant strategic promise of this field building is the potential of this work to enhance Jewish life through validating and promoting the Jewish value of participation in communal and religious life. Judaism is characteristically pragmatic and values action and relevance. The Kalsman Institute and Roundtable participants committed to making sure that all studies, scholarly works, programs, and services will apply to real-world problems and issues central to the lives of Jewish people and communities. All conferences, publications, and studies will be required to focus on their implications on matters of direct concern to genuinely pressing issues related to health and well-being among Jews.

Collaborative partnerships to continue building the field of Judaism and health are particularly important for those professionals and organizations for whom the economic down-turn has hindered growth. The recession stifled programmatic efforts and leaders that might have emerged in the last five years, as energies shifted to focus on meeting basic needs among constituents, such as service provision for economic assistance, employment development, and food and housing sources. Lead-ers especially yearn to add time for more scholarly endeavors while continuing to help constituents meet basic needs. Round-table participants also identified a strategic promise to focus on young and emerging leadership in the field of Judaism and health. New professionals, scholars, and lay leaders need to be mentored and provided education and growth opportunities, including opportunities for research and scholarship.

Roundtable members will continue to engage in a variety of short-term next steps: (1) search for and review Judaism and health research and programs across disciplines and across streams of Jewish life; (2) publish about these diverse Judaism and health dis-ciplines and streams; (3) educate seminary and graduate students about the field building; (4) use the Kalsman Institute and the on-line archive as a clearinghouse for materials and resources; and (5) catalyze new research to validate and solidify new thinking. For example, Roundtable members are now submitting new 2012 research proposals on the use of healing prayer in a Jewish context and on assessment, intervention, and efficacy in Jewish chaplaincy in the area of palliative medicine. There will continue to be the "real world" emphasis discussed above.

The Roundtable members continue to need a snapshot of the overall health of North American Jewry. Longer-term next steps include (1) launching a national Jewish population study; (2) co-ordinating and attending additional large and small regional and national gatherings and conferences on Judaism and health, with follow-up time for leaders to pursue scholarly endeavors; (3) con-tinued collaboration for study and projects across disciplines and agencies, and across the streams of Jewish life—leading to the creation of congregational and community programs, education, studies, and services in Judaism, health, healing, and medicine; and (4) creation of systematic support to train and support the next generation of investigators, clinicians, clergy, and lay leadership to raise awareness of the connections among Judaism, health, heal-ing, and medicine within the Jewish community and beyond.

Through these efforts and others, field building will continue beyond the life of the Templeton Foundation–funded Roundtable efforts. There is every reason to believe that the enthusiastic and vibrant Roundtable network will be an enduring community. Its work will disseminate Jewish texts, rituals, and sources for resiliency that address the continuum of illness and wellness, and draw on Judaism's rich and distinctively multifaceted resources in religion, spirituality, culture, and peoplehood.

Notes

1. The field of Judaism and health is comprised of several subfields, described later in this article.
2. Lucy Bernholz, Stephanie Linden Seale, and Tony Wang, *Building to Last: Field Building as Philanthropic Strategy* (2009), 3, http://www.blueprintrd.com/data/wp-content/uploads/2010/02/building-to-last.pdf (accessed October 5, 2011).
3. Ibid, 2.
4. Ibid.
5. Research from the W. K. Kellogg Foundation describes building blocks and design principles of field building, reflecting on the field of service-learning. It is notable that much research on field building is drawn from systematic dialogue and learning about the field of service-learning. Other field building efforts that informed this author's research were centered in end-of-life care through work funded by the Robert Wood Johnson Foundation. For more information on field building, go to a report available here: http://www.blueprintrd.com/data/wp-content/uploads/2010/02/building-to-last.pdf.
6. Brien McHugh, *Formative Years: Lessons from a Decade in the Service-Learning Field* (Battle Creek, MI: W. K. Kellogg Foundation, 2003), 10–12.
7. Ibid.
8. Harold Koenig, Michael McCullough, and David Larson, *Handbook of Religion and Health* (New York: Oxford University Press, 2001).
9. Ibid.
10. Jeff Levin, *God, Faith, and Health: Exploring the Spirituality-Healing Connection* (New York: John Wiley & Sons, 2001).
11. Jeff Levin and Michele Prince, "Judaism and Health: Reflections on an Emerging Scholarly Field," *Journal of Religion and Health* (published online first: 10 May 2010). http://www.springerlink.com/content/j82022x21p6236w1/

12. Levin is university professor of Epidemiology and Population Health, professor of Medical Humanities, and director of the Program on Religion and Population Health at the Institute for Studies of Religion at Baylor University. Pargament is professor of Psychology at Bowling Green State University.

13. Kenneth Pargament, "Is Religion Good for Your Health? It Depends" (presentation to Kalsman Institute Roundtable on Judaism and Health Research Retreat, Simi Valley, CA, January 31, 2011).

14. Ibid.

15. Ibid.

16. Jeff Levin, "Religion and Positive Well-Being Among Israeli and Diaspora Jews: Findings from the World Values Survey," *Mental Health, Religion & Culture* (published online first: Sept. 21, 2011), http://www.tandfonline.com/doi/abs/10.1080/13674676.2011.617002#preview; Jeff Levin, "Health Impact of Jewish Religious Observance in the USA: Findings from the 2000–01 National Jewish Population Survey," *Journal of Religion and Health* (published online first: April 19, 2011).

17. Natalia Berger, ed., *Jews and Medicine: Religion, Culture, Science* (Philadelphia: Jewish Publication Society, 1995); Frank Heynick, *Jews and Medicine: An Epic Saga* (Hoboken: KTAV Publishing House, 2002); David Freeman and Judith Abrams, *Illness and Health in the Jewish Tradition: Writings from the Bible to Today* (Philadelphia: Jewish Publication Society, 1999).

18. Fred Rosner and Samuel Kottek, eds., *Moses Maimonides: Physician, Scientist, and Philosopher* (Northvale, NJ: Jason Aronson, 1993).

19. Michele Prince and Adina Bodenstein, "A Program Assessment: Exploration of the Field of Judaism, Health, and Healing through Program Review and Key Stakeholder Interviews" (a report by the Kalsman Institute on Judaism and Health, presented at the Kalsman Roundtable on Judaism and Health Research Retreat, Simi Valley, CA, January 31, 2011).

20. Michele Prince, "Opening Remarks: Building a Field of Judaism and Health" (presentation to Kalsman Institute Roundtable on Judaism and Health Research Retreat, Simi Valley, CA, January 31, 2011).

21. David Teutsch, *Why the "Jewish" in Bioethics?* http://huc.edu/kalsman/bioethics/ (accessed October 5, 2011).

22. National Association for Jewish Chaplains, "Our Mission," http://www.najc.org/about/mission (accessed October 5, 2011).

23. Prince, "Opening Remarks."

24. Eric Yoffie, "Opening Remarks: Reform Jewish Think Tank" (Los Angeles, CA, November 21, 2010).

25. Prince, "Opening Remarks."

26. Dr. David Rosmarin is an instructor in the Department of Psychiatry at Harvard Medical School and assistant in Psychology at McLean Hospital, Belmont, Massachusetts.

27. David Rosmarin, "The JPSYCH Laboratory for Research on Judaism and Mental Health" (presentation to Kalsman Institute Roundtable on Judaism and Health Research Retreat, Simi Valley, CA, January 31, 2011).

28. Two Roundtable researchers came from the University of Southern California's Keck School of Medicine. Dr. Donna Spruijt-Metz is from the Department of Preventive Medicine and Institute of Health Promotion and Disease Prevention, Adolescent Health/Medical Ethics, and Dr. Marc Weigensberg is a physician and is director of Pediatric Endocrinology, LAC+USC Medical Center, and associate professor of Clinical Pediatrics.

29. Donna Spruijt-Metz, "Religion and Spirituality in Health Research" (presentation to Kalsman Institute Roundtable on Judaism and Health Research Retreat, Simi Valley, CA, January 31, 2011).

30. Marc Weigensberg, "Imagine HEALTH: Guided Imagery and its Relevance to Jewish Healing" (presentation to Kalsman Institute Roundtable on Judaism and Health Research Retreat, Simi Valley, CA, January 31, 2011).

31. Ibid.

32. Pargament, "Is Religion Good for Your Health."

33. Ibid.

34. Rabbi Nancy Epstein, MPH, MAHL, is associate professor of Community Health and Prevention at the Drexel University School of Public Health.

35. Nancy Epstein, remarks during Kalsman Institute Roundtable on Judaism and Health Research Retreat (Simi Valley, CA, January 31, 2011).

36. Michelle Friedman, MD, is a psychiatrist and is the founder and chair of the Department of Pastoral Counseling at Yeshivat Chovevei Torah.

37. Michelle Friedman, "Pastoral Counseling at YCT Rabbinical School (a report by Yeshivat Chovevei Torah, 2006).

38. Gila Silverman, MPH, is doctoral candidate in Medical Anthropology at the University of Arizona.

39. Gila Silverman, remarks during Kalsman Institute Roundtable on Judaism and Health Research Retreat (Simi Valley, CA, February 1, 2011).

40. The Kalsman Institute's Program Assessment is an exploration of the field of Judaism, health, and healing through a combination of program review and key stakeholder interviews. Provided is a review and general appraisal of programs offered to the Jewish

community through congregations, social service agencies, centers for healthcare, educational centers, and other Jewish communal organizations. There were 155 programs reviewed and 30 stakeholders were interviewed. The programmatic review and key stakeholder interviews unearthed the strengths, weaknesses, opportunities, and challenges of the field of Judaism, health and healing, and revealed how programmatic offerings have both deepened and broadened in the past twenty-five years.

Of Teachers and Angels: Jewish Insights on Transforming the Relationship between Patient and Health Professional

Carol Levy and Richard N. Levy

The doctor strides into the room wearing his white coat, the stethoscope of office around his neck. The patient lies on the examining table, draped in a hospital gown completely open in the back, no signs of her professional life anywhere, her husband secluded behind an opaque curtain, invisible. The doctor offers a cheery greeting, asks some questions and proceeds to examine the patient. When he is done, he offers a brief, positive diagnosis, instructs her to get dressed, and he departs.

A professional woman invites a physician to coffee to discuss a community issue of mutual concern. The professional stands to greet the doctor, dressed in the same sort of business attire as she. They embrace, talk about family matters, place their order, and then the professional turns to the matter at hand. After their discussion, the professional thanks the doctor for shared insights, picks up the bill, and they walk out of the restaurant arm in arm.

These separate scenarios take place every day. But they seldom take place together in a hospital room, where the person in bed is hardly ever perceived by the professionals at the bedside as anyone other than a patient with an illness. The only ones in the room perceived to possess worthwhile professional knowledge are the medical team.

CAROL LEVY is a senior vice president of the Jewish Federation of Greater Los Angeles, formerly executive director of the Los Angeles chapter of the American Jewish Congress, and a recipient of many awards for community leadership.

RICHARD N. LEVY is rabbi of the synagogue and director of spiritual growth at the Jack H. Skirball (Los Angeles) Campus of HUC-JIR, formerly director of the School of Rabbinic Studies at the LA campus, and a past president of the CCAR.

The two of us argue that the isolation of the hospital room from every other place where professionals gather can slow down the healing process for the patient who is a professional and not only alienates the medical professionals from important parts of their personalities, but also hampers them from giving the most effective, holistic, treatment of which they are capable. The isolated interactions of the hospital room can dehumanize both the patient and the medical professional and in the process exercise a negative effect on the healer's professional capacities and the patient's openness to the healing process.

Who are we to argue such a position (although we are hardly the first to do so)? Carol holds a senior management position in our local Federation campaign department; Richard is a rabbi and teacher of rabbis and other future Jewish professionals at Hebrew Union College. During the five years of her treatment for a recurrence of ovarian cancer, Carol has undergone chemotherapy and blood transfusions and has participated in ongoing clinical trials—all the while working fulltime at her Federation position. Her husband has accompanied her to most of her treatment sessions. During these five years Carol has developed a philosophy of relating to those involved in her treatment that is based significantly on a number of principles of Jewish thought that have enabled her to move beyond the traditional role of patient—an object of the health professionals' ministrations and the anonymous host of an infected organ—to a partner in a mutual relationship in which both patient and health professional experience growth and caring.

Among the principles that have informed this work are Martin Buber's philosophy of I and Thou; the Biblical teaching that human beings are created *b'tzelem Elohim*, in the image of God; and the ability to convey that essential Jewish quality of hope.

I-Thou and the Healing Experience

Martin Buber argued in his seminal work *I and Thou* that all life revolves around human beings "meeting" each other in relationship. There are two basic kinds of relationship, or "primary words," he argues: I-It, in which both parties regard the other as an object, to be acted upon, and I-Thou, in which both parties interact as subjects to be addressed by the intimate second person singular (today this is possible only in languages like French and German, etc., but centuries ago it existed in English in the form of Thou). Buber believed that the mutual respect and intimacy of a relationship symbolized by this form of address was so profound, so all-encompassing, that it enabled both parties to feel the presence of the source of all "Thou-ness," which he called the Eternal Thou, which is as close as Buber comes in this book to speaking of God. Buber argues that in each of these relationships the two words (I-Thou; I-It) influence each other: "The I of the primary word I-Thou is a different I from that of the primary word I-It."[1]

The trappings of the hospital room typically make it a textbook site for I-It relationships. Everyone wears the clothing of their place in the healing equation: the doctor's white coat, the nurse's scrubs, the patient's undignified gown—intended not, like most clothing, to reveal the best parts and hide the unflattering parts of a person, but rather to emphasize the weakest part of a person, facilitating easy access to the organs or limbs that the medical staff is there to treat. Typically the patient addresses the doctor, and sometimes the nurses, by a title, while they address the patient (if at all) by her first name. Speech also revolves around the affected organ. While the medical person may ask, "How are you today?" the "you" in question is typically not the Thou of the Buberian query, but the "you" that is the vessel for the diseased organ. "How are you today?" is usually a euphemism for, "What symptoms of your disease or your treatment are you experiencing today?" The medical personnel, believing that the patient's interest in them is only in relation to their ("It") ability to treat her disease, typically comport themselves in a way to maximize the patient's confidence in their professional skills. The patient, who has dressed in a way that most efficiently exposes her affected organs to examination, often organizes her responses in the same way: to tell the medical professional all she thinks they need to know to treat her effectively. Talk about the doctor's or nurse's family or research, or the patient's accomplishments at work, is seen as "wasting the time" of both parties in this I-It construct.

Transforming I-It

From the beginning of her treatment, Carol set out to transform these objectified relationships. She noticed that most nurses (and many doctors), though they all wear tags identifying their name and degrees, still will enter a hospital room without introducing themselves, a violation of most norms of polite social interaction. While we have not interviewed nurses about this practice, it felt to us as though the nurse believed that the patient only wanted to relate to her as Nurse—that is, someone instrumental to the patient's healing. The normal convention of introduction, "Hi, I'm ___," inviting the patient to respond with her own introduction, seemed not relevant if the nurse's role was only instrumental. The patient typically falls into the same pattern: "I'm just an organ bearer to them; the nurse isn't interested in me as a person; she has my chart with more information about me than I may know about myself. To introduce myself feels impertinent."

Carol refused to play into this scenario. "Hi, I'm Carol Levy," she says cheerfully when a nurse enters. Despite the name tags, she invariably asks, "What's your name?" If she feels, given the obviousness of the nurse's name tag, that the question is redundant, she will say, "Hi, Ann, I'm Carol Levy." This simple comment is an announcement that she is not a cipher—or an ovarian cavity.

We are both aware that naming is an important part of the process whereby an indistinguishable mass acquires an identity ("And God called the light Day, and the darkness Night" [Gen. 1:5]). Whether or not the nurse is busy with her charts, Carol will ask personal questions: "How long have you worked here? Where are you from?" If the nurse responds in monosyllables, or seems interested only in doing her assigned task so she can get to the next protocol, Carol is undeterred. If the nurse is grumpy, Carol is cheerful.

This is more than a tactic. Carol has great respect for the medical profession—her late uncle was a doctor; some of her cousins are doctors and nurses; her brother is a highly acclaimed professor in a medical school. She knows how long these individuals have studied, the long hours they work, the stresses under which they labor. She knows that the monosyllables and the grumpiness hide the compassion, care, and skill these nurses carry with them. She is determined to help them bring those qualities out of hiding, both because it will put them more in touch with the Nurse in their soul, and because the more Carol becomes a person to them, the more the "Nurse-ness" in their soul will enter into a relationship with the person Carol is and enable both of them to work together more effectively for healing. As Buber notes, "Through the *Thou*, a person becomes I."[2]

Isn't there something manipulative in this? A little I-Itness creeping in? Buber himself acknowledges that true I-Thou relationships are rare: "Without *It* a person cannot live. But one who lives with *It* alone is not a person."[3] Thus for someone to strive to be a person and not a "patient" with the other, and to help the other be as much as possible the full person who went to nursing school and struggles with her family, her supervisor, her ideals, and her reality, is to approach more of an I-Thou state than is the case in most hospitals.

And we have seen this happen, week after week, nurse after nurse. When a nurse was unable to find a vein in which to insert a chemo line and stuck Carol again and again, flustered, embarrassed, feeling that her whole professionalism was being judged, Carol would smile, reassure her, and say, when it looked like a vein was about to be tapped, "You go, girl!"—and the nurse would relax, a smile crossing her own blushing face. "I am not just a person who has been hurt," Carol would say to herself. "I am a person who needs this nurse to succeed, who wants this nurse to understand that I too have looked in vain for other kinds of veins to tap, and we are both people who make it sometimes and fail sometimes."

Unfortunately not all patients can respond in this way, and so those who can, become recipients of appreciation. A patient who responds to a nurse empathetically inspires trust, and if the patient shares stories of her family and, where appropriate, her work, then nurses, seeing her as a person, will share more and more of their personhood as well, allowing the patient, on subsequent visits, to ask follow-up questions that can deepen the relationship. The relationship should normally begin and end in the hospital room, except on mutual agreement, but these exchanges can turn the hospital room into a place of human mutuality rather than a transaction between characters of vastly unequal status.

For a while, one medical clerk seemed to challenge all of Carol's good humor. Visit after visit this woman would glower at us (and at other patients we observed), and even Carol's cheerful, "How're you doing today?" would be met by nothing more than a grunt. She would ignore call buttons, and in many ways indicate that she was much too busy to be bothered. Imagine Carol's surprise, therefore, when after months of such exchanges, the clerk said to her out of the blue, "You are such a nice person; you're always so cheerful!" After that, it didn't matter what this woman said—there was an unspoken understanding that both she and Carol were persons to each other.

Another nurse also wore a scowl on her face, and to Carol's friendly questions she would respond with one cynical comment after another. Time after time Carol would turn the cynicism aside with a positive spin on the issue that was irritating the nurse. Eventually her scowl started to melt, and almost against her will the hint of a smile began to cross her face. We sensed that she had started to become aware of the negative qualities she was projecting, and her smile revealed that she was starting to hear herself, while also expressing grudging appreciation for Carol's upbeat attitude, as hard as it seemed for her to believe that there was anything positive to say about the world she inhabited. Her growing self-realization also made the experience of treatment more pleasant for us. Patients, outsiders to the convoluted universe of the hospital, bring a new perspective that can remind the nurses who they really want to be.

The attitude of this nurse is a reminder that some patients are afflicted with the same characteristics. Because they sometimes define themselves as "someone who has been hurt" (an object, I-It, rather than a subject) the world seems an endless source of pain, and everything, every deed, every comment becomes a source of complaint. It is clear that if one defines oneself as Pained, one's pains will only increase, and a loved one or a health professional needs—often at great peril—to help the patient recognize the gifts others give her—a kind smile, a speedy response to a call button, an attempt at a joke. The model for this is found over and over again in Psalms, where the Psalmist complains endlessly of afflictions, enemies, trials—until the Psalmist realizes that God has heard and that new feelings of strength and confidence can be understood as gifts of God.

Patients whose upbeat attitude reflects a deep reservoir of gratitude can also find themselves visited by nurses or volunteers not officially assigned to them, seeking them out not so much to offer treatment but almost to receive it. With encouragement, a nurse will talk about issues in a relationship, or with a child at home. Without giving formal advice, an empathetic patient can ask questions that help the nurse reflect differently on the situation and come to see that the hospital can become a place to receive help as well as to offer it. And we see why this is appreciated. Many patients are obviously, visibly ill, and their concern about their own condition leaves them little room to think about others' needs. They receive excellent treatment—but they give back very little. The machines show that they are getting the medicines prescribed; their passive attitude indicates that they are being made comfortable. But the cheerfulness, the banter, the interest in the nurses' lives that an upbeat patient offers is lacking. Just as Jewish law requires even a poor person to dig deeply into their meager resources and give *tzedakah*, an ill person receiving care needs to dig into the well of their own empathy to offer some to their caregivers—empathy for others is an important part of healing. The nurses give of their skill and compassion unceasingly—but it helps if there is some reciprocity. Patients who are able do need to work harder in communicating—even if it is only on the level of their own pain. But when a patient relates to a nurse as a person and not just as a caregiver, it helps refill the nurse's reservoir of caring and self-respect. It also reminds them that as a result of their ministrations, a sensitive and wise patient is being kept alive to help others on this planet for at least a few years more.

Some of Carol's caregivers have stood out as remarkable human beings. They would often share some personal details of their lives with us, stemming from their growing trust in two people who seem to have proven themselves good listeners, who they thought might be able to provide some wisdom on the issues they had shared with us. We have offered prayers for ill people in their families, listened as they shared concerns about relationships, and have sought out resources to assist them with issues they were facing—and then Carol's blood test results would come back, with numbers dropping or rising, or a glitch in administrative procedures would develop, and the women who had been sharing their lives with us would hone in on Carol's problem with laser-like focus. They never sacrificed their professionalism in their pursuit of a dialogic relationship, and Carol too was able to turn quickly from counselor to responsive patient. None of the standards of the hospital room had been compromised—indeed, they had been heightened by the caregivers' determination to protect this person who had come to mean so much to them.

Rabbis are used to such multifaceted relationships, where dialogue is the norm. Medical professionals are often trained in a more objective fashion—and most patients are acculturated to accept it. But an emotionally healthy, intelligent, patient can break through these barriers, and help Buber's ideal come to pass. And what if patients lack the strength or personality to help create an I-Thou relationship? I-It relationships, as we have tried to demonstrate, can also facilitate the patient's healing—and they are certainly better than an I-Nothing relationship.

This is perhaps the heart of the issue: when a patient can bring into the hospital room the best elements of her life, personality, wisdom, and training, she inspires the caregivers to do the same. The health care professional is no longer just the instrument for the patient's healing; she is a partner in a mutually healing, growthful relationship.

I-Thou with Physicians

To what extent is this partnership possible between a patient and a physician? The frequent comment that the doctor "is a god (or God)" often stems from the sense that doctors may look upon themselves that way—founts of mysterious knowledge that they measure out to patients in doses they feel the patient can handle, commanding an obedient, sometimes awestruck, entourage of nurses and interns, all the while maintaining a distant, sometimes formal, attitude that comports with so many people's images of God. Often patients will impute God-like qualities to doctors out of the yearning that what is causing them pain and suffering can be removed or reversed. With the exception of one brief encounter with a surgeon, though, Carol has not experienced doctors who act like gods.

She has been fortunate to have been treated by physicians who have responded to her positive, inviting nature, with an openness on their own part. They never wear white coats in her examining room, and rather than enter with a weariness that cries out for energizing, their own positive attitudes energize us. They ask about Carol's work and our children, they speak to both of us, which serves to acknowledge that Carol is a patient and a professional and a person with a family. They speak about their own work, their research, and their own families. While Carol is very deferential to them, this stems more from her respect for the profession than from any expectations on their part. She also believes that though they have encouraged her to call them by their first names, to call them "doctor" is to acknowledge her respect for a profession about which she knows a great deal. It also reflects her understanding that however schmoozy the conversation, she will not let them abandon their "doctor-ness." They return the favor to Richard, who also repeatedly requests that they call him by his first name—always in vain. Perhaps if there were still a workable "thou" in English, this remaining impediment to I-Thouness might be overcome.

While Carol has often been sought out as an informal counselor to nurses, her relationship with physicians has been more limited—not I-It, but not quite I-Thou. When one of her regular physicians mentioned her own upcoming surgery, Carol asked her Hebrew name so that she might be included in our *Mi Shebeirach* list. On another occasion, while giving Carol a very thorough pelvic examination, she asked Carol whether almonds and raisins were permitted on Pesach—a juxtaposition that took Carol somewhat by surprise (most physicians are silent during these invasive examinations)—but it clearly indicated that while the doctor's hands were aware of what they were exploring in the area under examination, her mind was on Carol as a potential source of information in another area of concern to her. (One might even paraphrase Isaac confronting his camouflaged son: "The hands are the hands of It while the voice is the voice of Thou.")

One of the frequent explanations for the "Doctor is God" syndrome is the wide gap of knowledge between the physician and the patient, but the doctor who asked Carol to *paskin a shailah* (answer a question of religious practice) during the pelvic clearly had regard for the knowledge she knew Carol possessed in an area where she did not. Many patients possess all kinds of wisdom and information which, if they would only share them, could also help narrow the knowledge gap between doctor and patient. None of these encounters we have experienced would have been possible had not both Carol and the physician worked to shatter the "Doctor is God" aura—the doctor by expressing fondness for Carol as a person and Carol by overcoming some of her own awe for physicians with which she had grown up. The nonmedical conversations the two of them have had with each other made these changes of attitude possible—and have turned the physician into a fierce advocate in the cause of keeping Carol alive.

Manifestations of *Tzelem Elohim* in the Hospital Room

Buber believed that God is present in the relationship between an I and a Thou. The Bible holds (Gen. 1:26) that God created human beings *b'tzelem Elohim*, in the image of God. What that means has been argued for millennia, but many Jews have understood it to constitute a moral imperative: Look for the image of God in the human beings around you. This is particularly important when a person has a difficult personality, which pushes negative qualities to the fore. In such cases it is also important to remember the teaching in Exodus 28:36 that the High Priest was to wear a gold headband inscribed *Kodesh L'Adonai* (holy to God). Imagine if every person wore such an inscription on their forehead—how we would feel impelled to search for the holiness of that person, to look for aspects of their life that helped us feel in the presence of the God who had shared the divine *tzelem* (image) with them.

Some nurses we have encountered in the past five years, serious Christians, believe that they function as God's hands. We prefer the less anthropomorphic Jewish view that the work they do is in the image of God—that as God, the source of healing, drew from that Godly source to heal Miriam (Num. 12:13), King Hezekiah (Isa. 38:1–8), and the child of the Shunemite woman in the time of the prophet Elisha (II Kings 4:8–37), so does God do that today. In the first two cases, God was responding to prayers—Moses', for his sister; Hezekiah's, for himself. Contemporary patients also pray to God, as do their loved ones and their congregations, and we too may experience the care given by our nurses and physicians as manifesting the image of God.

Another way to understand the health professional as working *b'tzelem Elohim* is to see him or her as an *eved Adonai* (a servant of God). Moses and David were each called by this title, and while "servant" can be a humiliating title in the human sphere, it is a noble one in the divine sphere, for it indicates that the servant's work is inspired, even commanded, by God. Secular health professionals may feel uncomfortable if we tell them we perceive God's image in them or in their ministrations—some liberal Jews may feel uncomfortable too! But to see the image of God in our caregivers, to see them as God's servants, is really to add to the person's nobility, to elevate her skills and caring to a transcendent plane, helping fulfill God's desire to overcome the chaos present in the world. For the patient to share that belief with the nurse can remind her that she is not merely administering chemical infusions a drop at a time, but she is doing God's work in the hospital room. On a monotonous day, or a day when all the patients seem to be getting sicker, to tell a nurse that she is acting *b'tzelem Elohim* can remind her that God is frustrated with the slowness of healing, too, but that drop by drop she is helping to further the presence of order and harmony in the world.

Is illness a sign of the disorder in the world? And if so, why has God afflicted this patient with this disorder? This ancient question prompts another: are hurricanes, tornados, and earthquakes "disorders"?

The Rabbis understood Genesis 1:2 to mean that God first created chaos (*tohu/bohu*, "formlessness/void"; darkness and the great deeps) and out of chaos God created the ordered world we know (*B'reishit Rabbah* 1:9). But the chaos never went away; it lurks always in the background of order. As the earth moves to settle itself (moving toward order) earthquakes occur (the rumblings of chaos); as hot and cold air struggle for an orderly balance, chaos asserts itself through hurricanes and tornados. To counteract the chaos that sometimes appears in the natural world in the form of disease, God created natural remedies and human beings both to harvest them and use their intelligence to apply them to ameliorate illness. Maimonides believed that *tzelem Elohim* referred to human intelligence, which could be trained to promote healing. In the Torah, God commands Jews to bring offerings in the Temple, which over time were transformed into prayers, including prayers for health, to help God direct the power of healing to individuals in need. All these are manifestations of the *tzelem Elohim* in the healing process.

Another way to look at the healing professional is as a *malach* (literally a messenger, but often translated as "angel"). We may shrink from this title, so culturally influenced are we by the image of angels as alien beings clothed in white, with wings sprouting from their shoulders. The Bible is ambiguous in its descriptions of *malachim*— Isaiah and Ezekiel had visions of them with many wings, wrapped in flames or enmeshed in wheels. And some people—Lot, Samson's parents—saw human beings. Some (the boy Samuel, Moses at the bush) only heard voices. The lesson from these passages, we believe, is that it is up to us to perceive angels where we will—why not in the hospital room?

There are some questions we might ask: What message is the angel bringing? Does this seem to be a message God would send? Why might God choose this person to bear this message—does his or her character merit this choice? To answer these questions means that, as we have suggested earlier, we have to get to know our health professionals—and give them a chance to know us, so that we can both be assured that the message is appropriate to be delivered by this person, and that it is appropriate to be received by us—for example, "This illness is not punishment for your behavior." On the other hand, if a nurse seems to be telling a Jewish patient that her illness is the product of her refusal to accept Jesus, this is not a messenger, nor a message, that we can accept as sent by God (the Torah in fact considers a message of apostasy a sign of a false prophet).

A modest nurse will demur from the title of angel, or take it merely as a cultural metaphor—"You're an angel!" But we can take it beyond that, and gradually, without scaring the caregiver, help her to see that she may be capable of bringing truths and insights and love from the realm of God into the narrow confines of our hospital room. This brings to mind the verse from Psalm 118:5, *Min ha-metzar karati Yah, anani va-merchav Yah* ("When from the narrow place I cried out, 'O God!'—God answered me in the broad place."). In this way we can transform the distancing stereotype of "Doctor as God" into the healing idea of Doctor or Nurse as an Angel of God. As Naomi Remen wrote a decade ago, "As professionals we may not be fully connected to our lives. Distance may become a daily habit. [But] the original meaning of our work is service, [which is] a human relationship, a work of the heart and the soul."[4]

A patient who helps her caregivers see the transcendent role they play in the forces of healing in the universe can play a significant role in ennobling the healing professions, and help the caregivers to overcome their own moments of boredom or despair as they confront the depths of the calling that brought them to the bedside.

Seeking Hope in the Hospital Room: A Proposal

Perceiving our caregivers as divine servants or angels is one way to marshal the forces of healing against the dreaded enemies of despair and terror and isolation. Along with the patient's loved ones, the health professional should also be a source of hope, reassurance, or even of companionship. If the patient's prognosis is bleak, though, how can a nurse or doctor offer such qualities? And is the patient the one to teach them how to do it?

Jewishly knowledgeable patients can—along with rabbis and cantors, social workers, a wise partner, or a good friend. We can teach the nurse—and the doctor, if she is willing—that one of the names of God is *Mikveh Yisrael*, the Hope of Israel. The Rabbis recognized a profound play on words in this phrase. *Mikveh*, from Genesis 1:10, also means a gathering of waters, and it is the name given to the pool in which men and women immerse for purification. The nurse or doctor need not feel that she or he must be the source, the fountain, of hope—that is God's role. But how can the health professional who is doubtful that hope exists for this patient immerse herself in that fountain?

Literally, perhaps. The professionals might write up a list of all their sources of hope—their medical and pharmacological knowledge; their skills; their compassion; their understanding of new drugs on the horizon; the strength they give and receive from their own loved ones, mentors, and students; the love and support they see surrounding their patients; the strength they see in their patients. Then they might go to a *mikveh*, or, lacking one, to a natural body of water, and as they immerse themselves, imagine that the waters are surrounding them with all the sources of hope they have written down—and when they emerge, vow that they will try to channel these sources to the patient so desperate for signs of hope.

The patient's loved ones might make their own lists, her clergy might compile verses from Psalms and other texts which speak lyrically of God as the giver of hope, and they all might undergo their own immersions. If the patient is able, she might invite her caregivers, clergy, and loved ones to accompany her to the *mikveh*, and as she immerses, they can call out all the sources of hope they have discovered, until the patient joins them, over and over, and emerges with a new vocabulary on her lips and a new freshness in her soul. If the patient is unable or unwilling to go to a *mikveh*, the caregivers and loved ones might surround her hospital bed, reach out their hands to her and call out the sources of hope that they have found, until the patient, silently or audibly, joins in. Carol, concerned that some rituals and gestures may invade a patient's privacy, is less enthusiastic about this rite than Richard is.

In any case, one cannot engage in such a dramatic ritual very often. As hope waxes and wanes within the patient, as ordinary people become weary of offering compassion day after day, perhaps the best gift they can offer is their presence. They too were created in the image of God, and just to sit by the bedside and smile or nod, rehearse family tales, or offer occasional prayers and comforting psalms help to remind the patient who she is and how much she is loved. All these reenact God's role as *m'vaker cholim,* the Visitor to the Sick, a role the Rabbis believed God first performed as Abraham recovered from his circumcision (Gen. 17:23–18:1). A silent presence, especially if the patient cannot speak, is also a visitation—as the Israelites showed while Miriam recovered from her leprosy attack outside the camp, and the people, usually eager to get on with their journey to the Promised Land, waited patiently—praying for her, we imagine—until she was declared healed.

Eventually the patient, like Miriam, is freed to go on with her journey, or to realize that her journey is coming to an end. In either case, the patient-teacher leaves behind a professional staff who are wiser and more caring as a result of her presence, and who may well manifest their newfound insights and increased self-esteem for the benefit of other patients. In either instance, the patient-teacher will have been the model of a teacher of *torah lishmah,* for its own intrinsic worth, since she will seldom know the effects of her teaching once she leaves the hospital. What the patient-teacher should know, however, is that the health care professionals under her tutelage will have had at least one experience of encountering the presence of God at the bedside. And that, the two of us believe, may change them forever.

Notes

1. Martin Buber, *I and Thou,* 2nd ed., trans. Ronald Gregor Smith (New York: Charles Scribner's Sons), 3.
2. Ibid., 28.
3. Ibid., 34.
4. Naomi Remen, "Recapturing the Soul of Medicine," *Western Journal of Medicine* 174, no. 1 (January 2001): 4–5.

Standing in the Doorway: Pastoral Perspectives on In-Home Chaplaincy

Jo Hirschmann

Opening Stories

Chapters 17 and 18 of the book of Genesis tell two seemingly unrelated stories. The first is about the day when Abraham circumcises himself and all the males of his household, and the second is about the day when Abraham receives three visitors who bear the news that Sarah will soon give birth to a child. The Rabbis of Antiquity assumed that the juxtaposition of these two stories was purposeful and can be mined for meaning. According to the Rabbis' reading of the stories, the two events happened in close succession to each other, meaning that the three visitors arrived at Abraham's home while he was still recovering from his circumcision. Having established this chronology, the Rabbis turned the story of the three visitors' arrival at Abraham's tent into a prism that encapsulated the twin mitzvot of *hachnasat orchim* (welcoming guests) and *bikur cholim* (visiting the sick).

The part of the story that deals with *hachnasat orchim* is explicit in the biblical text. Genesis tells us that Abraham brings water to his guests and invites them to bathe their feet and rest in the shade of the trees. Abraham, Sarah, and a servant boy prepare cakes, curds and milk, and a calf for the visitors.[1] This story about Abraham's hospitality is so central to Jewish tradition that Abraham becomes the paradigm of a good host. Indeed, his tent is imagined as open on all sides so that a traveler arriving from any direction could easily enter it.[2]

Genesis 18's *bikur cholim* narrative, which is not explicit in the biblical text, grows from the fertile ground of the Rabbinic

JO HIRSCHMANN (NY09) serves as the pastoral care coordinator at Phelps Hospice in Sleepy Hollow, New York.

imagination. The Talmud tells this story about the day that Abraham received his visitors.

God appeared [to Abraham] by the oaks of Mamre as he was sitting at the entrance of the tent at the hottest part of the day (Gen. 18:1). Why does the biblical text say "at the hottest part of the day"? Rabbi Hamma the son of Rabbi Hanina said: This day was the third day after Abraham's circumcision and the Holy Blessed One came to ask after Abraham (i.e., to make a *bikur cholim* visit). The Holy Blessed One took the sun out of its sheath [to make it blaze even more hotly than usual] in order that this righteous man [i.e., Abraham] should not be troubled by guests. Abraham sent Eliezer [his servant] to go outside [to look for people to invite in as guests]. Eliezer went out but could not find [anyone]. [Abraham] said [to him], "I do not believe you." . . . [Abraham himself] went out. He saw the Holy Blessed One standing by the doorway . . . When God saw that Abraham was tying and untying [his bandages] God said, "It is not good manners to stand here."[3]

According to this midrash, God goes to great lengths to discourage guests from dropping in on Abraham who, just three days after his circumcision, is still convalescing. However, Abraham will not allow his enthusiasm for hosting to be diminished by the sun's unusually intense heat. Determined to find someone who would enjoy his hospitality, Abraham first sends his servant outside to look for prospective visitors and then goes out himself. Flesh-and-blood mortals might choose to stay inside on such a blazing day, but Abraham finds God by his doorway. Abraham thinks he has found himself a guest but God has other ideas, seeking to attend to Abraham's needs as a patient rather than put Abraham to the trouble of hosting. Seeing Abraham's discomfort as he unties and reties his bandages, God reminds Abraham to go inside and rest.

In this midrash, both Abraham and God are righteous. Abraham's custom of hosting guests is so deeply ingrained that he seeks to do it even when he is in pain. God, meanwhile, wants Abraham to rest, to be a patient, and to receive the care he needs for his recovery. Both roles are imbued with righteousness, allowing the visitor to extend *chesed* to the visited, and the visited to extend *chesed* to the visitor. Indeed, the roles of visitor and visited are interlocking and mutually dependent. In practical terms, this means that *bikur cholim* could not exist without the corresponding mitzvah of *hachnasat orchim*. In the delicate interplay between the patient and the visitor—a relationship that can be reframed as host and guest—both parties give and receive.

Overview

This article explores this interplay by drawing on the above stories, two additional biblical stories, and vignettes from contemporary pastoral care. I proceed from the understanding that the above midrash reveals important truths about our own time, inviting us to consider the content and meaning of contemporary encounters between homebound patients and their visitors. The article begins with a brief discussion of how pastoral care is similar to, and different from, the Rabbinic model of *bikur cholim*. I suggest that even though *bikur cholim* and pastoral care are not perfectly overlapping activities, Rabbinic stories about *bikur cholim* are nevertheless a rich source of material as we seek to understand and define contemporary pastoral care. I then explore the differences between in-home and hospital-based chaplaincy. I also discuss the special attention to personal and professional boundaries that in-home pastoral care requires, since any discussion of the ways in which a caregiver is "hosted" by her homebound patient must begin with a reiteration of the ethical and clinical boundaries that define the relationship.

Drawing on case material from my own work of providing pastoral care in home-based hospice settings, I describe how we might tailor the pastoral care we offer to fit the environment of the home. I then explore two biblical stories that pivot on the relationship between the visitor and the visited. Drawing on case material from my own clinical work,[4] as well as my own recent experience of being a homebound convalescent, I will show how these stories shed light on our contemporary lives and experiences. In particular, I will suggest that these stories invite us to consider how the experience of being hosted by another in his or her home—even when the host is ill—might shape and change us as caregivers and as human beings.

Bikur Cholim and the Contemporary Discipline of Pastoral Care

Some rabbis and Jewish chaplains identify *bikur cholim* as the basis of Jewish pastoral care. Rabbi Joseph Ozarowski takes this position, constructing his model of pastoral care on the halachic and aggadic dimensions of *bikur cholim*. He offers the following rationale for this:

> *Bikur cholim*, the commandment to visit the sick, offers a paradigm for the pastoral caregiver. It embodies a theological framework, and the sacred texts surrounding it provide practical guidance for our conduct with the sick. Although it has been argued that professional pastoral caregiving is different than friendly visitation, pastoral care could be considered the specialization and professionalization of this *mitzvah* . . . Moreover, the Jewish tradition's teachings on *bikur cholim* constitute the primary locus of both values and practical wisdom for the developing field of Jewish pastoral care.[5]

Conversely, others argue that because *bikur cholim* can be performed by friends, family members, and congregants who are not professional chaplains, we need to draw a line of distinction between the two activities. For my part, I tend to see *bikur cholim* as distinct from pastoral care, which is a discipline with its own standards, certification process, and codes of conduct. However, I agree with Ozarowski that the body of Jewish sacred literature provides a rich repository of teachings that help us to understand Jewish pastoral care. This article seeks to contribute to that understanding.

Hospital-Based Chaplaincy Versus In-Home Chaplaincy

Biblical stories about illness and the Rabbis' *bikur cholim* narratives take place in the homes of sick people, which makes them particularly relevant to those who provide home-based pastoral care. I work as a hospice chaplain in Westchester County, the suburban area immediately north of New York City. In the course of my daily work, I visit patients wherever they live, whether that is a house or apartment, an assisted living facility or nursing home, or a group home. (This article focuses primarily on pastoral care that takes place in patients' houses or apartments, with briefer discussion of institutional settings.) With its focus on caring rather than curing, hospice care meets the needs of people with terminal diagnoses and prognoses of less than six months. Composed of nurses, social workers, home health aides, and chaplains, hospice interdisciplinary teams provide medical, psychosocial, and spiritual care to patients, caregivers, and family members. While this article explores the dynamics of in-home chaplaincy, its broad contours are relevant to health care workers from all disciplines who deliver in-home care.

In 2008, the most recent year for which numbers are available, the National Hospice and Palliative Care Organization (NHPCO) estimates that "approximately 38.5% of all deaths in the United States were under the care of a hospice program."[6] The majority of these patients—almost 70 percent—were living in the place they called home.[7] This means that, along with other types of in-home care such as visiting nurse programs, hospice workers deliver an important slice of healthcare services in the United States. (While approximately one-fifth of hospice patients receive care in an inpatient facility,[8] this article focuses on home-based hospice care and proceeds from the assumption that there are key differences between how healthcare professionals deliver care at home as opposed to in an inpatient setting.)

In my work as a chaplain, I find myself matching my rhythm to the setting in which I work. In inpatient hospital settings, this rhythm is fast-paced and syncopated; a bedside visit can be punctuated by the arrival of nurses, doctors, social workers, aides, and technicians who provide a vast array of services to patients. Visits can also be interrupted by codes and pages from other parts of the hospital. While work on some units—oncology, for example—often affords opportunities to see the same patient multiple times over a period of months or years, many inpatient pastoral visits are onetime events. Often, a hospital pastoral care visit constitutes an infinitesimally small slice out of the long sweep of the lives of both parties.

In contrast, chaplaincy care in the home operates at a much slower pace. Once I have been ushered into someone's home, the length of the visit often settles at around one hour. During the course of a visit, I might spend time in the bedroom with the patient and then at the kitchen table with family members. On summer days, I might be invited to sit out in the garden. Although many people are on hospice for only a few days or a week, others might spend weeks, months, or even years being cared for by the same hospice team.[9] Over the course of this time, team members have the opportunity to build deep relationships with patients and family members, to enter into the narrative of a patient's end-of-life journey, and to offer evolving care that is tailored to the patient and family's changing needs.

In institutional settings, the roles of patient and chaplain are relatively clearly defined. When we enter into people's homes, on the other hand, we might find that these boundaries and relationships feel blurred. Because we are in the more intimate setting of patients' homes, both we and patients/family members may feel like a friendship is developing. We may be offered anything from a glass of water to a full meal, meaning that we need to determine what we can accept and what we must decline.[10]

Regardless of where healthcare services are delivered, there is a power imbalance between chaplains and patients that chaplains must carefully monitor.[11] Many institutions have ethical codes requiring that caregivers not receive gifts or financial compensation from patients. Sexual relationships between patients and caregivers are completely off limits and there is an expectation that the relationship will end at the completion of the period of care. In addition to whatever requirements are imposed by the institutions where chaplains work, the National Association of Jewish Chaplains requires its members to sign a Code of Professional Ethics document.[12] (Conversely, working as solo caregivers in people's homes, as opposed to in the busy setting of a hospital, requires that we pay particular attention to personal safety. This topic is beyond the scope of this article.) The following discussion is predicated on the understanding that in-home chaplaincy requires that we honor the professional boundaries between patients and chaplains, even as we tailor our care to the particular dynamics of the home setting.

Practical Chaplaincy:
Illness and the Changing Landscape of the Home

In a hospital setting, chaplaincy care often focuses on the experience of rupture—on the experience of being away from home and in a sterile, rule-bound setting. If this institutional setting represents disempowerment and loss, home represents the opposite. The houses and apartments in which we make our homes are filled with connections to family, tradition, and the narratives of our lives. In most cases, they are places of safety, autonomy, and empowerment. When we offer chaplaincy care in these settings, we have the opportunity to make creative use of the home itself in the service of healing.

Once I am invited over the threshold of a patient's home, the home setting often becomes the focus of our conversation. During the course of a visit, I might hear stories about the people in family photos, about when and how the house was built, or about a particular painting or ornament. Even while I occupy a professional, caregiving role, it is clear to me that I am a guest in another person's home. I am often offered—and generally accept—small tokens of hospitality such as a glass of water. One patient, a resident of an assisted living facility who ate all of his meals in the communal dining room, lamented that all he could offer me was a glass of the nutritional supplement Ensure. He said, "I'm such a bad host." My request for a glass of water was an opportunity for him to reclaim, and me to honor, the hosting role that still came naturally to him.

In assisted living facilities and nursing homes, I have heard residents describe how much they miss the houses and apartments in which they used to live. In addition to using the pastoral visit to explore these losses, the items that are in the patient's nursing home room or assisted living suite often hold stories that can be rich fodder for conversation. Often, I first meet a nursing home resident in the facility's common area. If appropriate, I will ask her if she is willing to show me her room and whatever mementos are in it. (As a cautionary note, I have found that leaving the familiarity of the dayroom can be disorienting for some patients with dementia.) In other cases, patients might be living with family members and facing the reality that they will never again return to their own homes. In one such case, the patient told me that what she most missed was the garden she had tended for many years. When her son joined us, we explored how the patient could spend more time in his garden. Although it was no substitute for her own garden, it was a way for her to feel more at home in her son's house, even as she mourned the loss of her own home.

During the course of an admission to home hospice, the patient, the family, and the physical space of the home all go through changes. Over time, the patient may be able to access increasingly limited areas of the house. Medical equipment might be brought in and then taken out again. When one patient's adult child acknowledged that her father was never again going to go up to the second floor of the house, she made the decision to take out the stair lift that had been installed several years earlier. Through conversation and prayer, this family member and I marked both the patient's declining health and the home's changing landscape. In another home, a piece of child's artwork that had been tacked onto the wall of an upstairs room fell down on the same day that the patient moved to a hospital bed on the first floor of the house. To their surprise, the family members found meaning and comfort in this seemingly random event, and they welcomed the opportunity to give voice to their sense that the house itself had joined them in marking their loved one's final journey.

In yet another home, one woman spent six months as a patient in our hospice's program. Initially, she was able to ambulate around her home, sit at her desk, and cook simple meals for herself. Over time, these activities became impossible until, eventually, she was bedbound. Proud and independent, this woman struggled with the apparent meaninglessness of her time at home. Once she had been the mistress of her home; now she felt like a prisoner in it. She desperately missed her work and lamented that she was no longer a productive member of society. The patient spent the months of her decline mourning this apparently meaningless loss and, eventually, finding some acceptance of the changes that had engulfed her life. Ultimately, the apartment in which she had lived for twenty years was the crucible in which this final emotional journey took place. Our visits were an opportunity for her to reflect on that journey, which included her changed relationship to her home.

In institutional settings, healthcare staff retains a level of ownership and control over the patient's or resident's room. Over the course of months or years, they see a string of people occupy the same space. Ultimately, the space belongs to the institution, not to the patient. A house or apartment, on the other hand, unequivocally belongs to the patient and/or the family. Not only is the chaplain at least in part a guest in the home, she also becomes part of the life of the home. Especially if the pastoral relationship extends over weeks or months, the chaplain and patient/family might establish a rhythm that includes how greetings are exchanged, where the chaplain sits, and what types of hospitality the host offers. If the chaplain makes a closure visit to surviving family members after the patient's death, she now enters a home characterized by disrupted and/or new rhythms. As the household goes through a period of adjustment and mourning, so too might the chaplain. Acknowledging these changes and losses with family members, co-workers, and/or supervisors can be comforting and healing for all the parties involved.

Through the course of a caregiving relationship, the patient, the family, and the home environment are in a dynamic state; all pass through a series of changes. As chaplains, we are trained to bring care, comfort, and support to patients and families. In many cases, the patient or family experiences some sort of transformation as a result of their relationship with a pastoral caregiver. This might involve expressing grief and anger, finding peace and acceptance, telling previously untold stories, or simply feeling heard and held. This article's opening stories remind us, however, that these relationships are not unidirectional. Rather, they are characterized by mutuality, meaning that chaplains are engaged with, and are integral to, the shifting dynamics that are unfolding in the home. For the purposes of this article, the question is: How is the caregiver affected, and even changed, by this? Two stories from the biblical books of First and Second Kings offer some answers to this question.

The Caregiver Crosses the Threshold

Genesis 18 is not the only place in the *Tanach* where a story-thread about visiting the sick and a story-thread about welcoming guests jostle with each other for attention. First and Second Kings record the miracles wrought by Elijah and Elisha after young boys are struck with sudden and near-fatal illnesses. In the first of these stories, God tells Elijah that a widow-woman in the town of Zarephath will provide him with sustenance during a drought. Upon his arrival at the entrance of the city, Elijah meets this widow-woman, who brings him water and bread. Sometime later, when Elijah is a guest in the widow-woman's home, her son becomes ill with a grave sickness. Elijah takes the boy to the upper chamber of the house where he is staying and remonstrates with God. Elijah demands to know, "Adonai my God, upon this widow with whom I have found hospitality will you bring evil and cause the death of her son?!" After Elijah stretches himself out over the boy (*va'yitmoded*)—literally, measures himself against the boy—God hears Elijah's prayer and restores the boy to life.[13]

The story of Elisha, the Shunammite woman, and her sick son also spins at the intersection of the themes of *hachnasat orchim* and *bikur cholim*. In this story, we learn that the Shunammite woman was in the habit of offering Elisha a bed whenever he was passing by. In time, she and her husband make an "upper wall-chamber" in their home, which becomes Elisha's room whenever he visits. They furnish the room with a bed, table, chair, and lamp stand—all the things that a weary traveler needs. Eager to repay the Shunammite woman for her hospitality, Elisha asks Gehazi, his serving lad, what they can do for her. When Gehazi tells Elisha that what the Shunammite woman most lacks is a son, Elisha prophesies to the woman that she will give birth to a son by this time next year. The boy is born according to Elisha's prophecy. Time passes and the boy grows up. One day, the boy is struck with a fatal illness and dies in his mother's lap. Desperate and distraught, the boy's mother travels to Elisha and summons him to help her son. As in the first story, Elisha lays himself out over the boy's body, placing "his mouth on his mouth and his eyes on his eyes and his hands on his hands."[14] With this act, Elisha revives the boy.[15]

In both of these stories, Elijah and Elisha perform healing miracles in the two families' times of greatest need. However, these stories are about more than the infallibility of God's prophets/messengers. They are stories about mutual indebtedness and about the reciprocity of human relationships. Long before they performed miracles over the boys' bodies, Elijah and Elisha had both been the grateful recipients of the boys' mothers' hospitality. In the first story, Elijah is a guest in the family's home when the boy is taken ill. Elijah appeals to God, protesting how unfair it is that the woman's son should be taken ill when she has worked so tirelessly as Elijah's host. In the story of the Shunammite woman, we learn significant details about the special attic room she and her husband build for Elisha. In both stories, then, the women's homes are places of support, sustenance, and rejuvenation. Ultimately, they are places where life is affirmed and sustained—not only for the sick boys but for everyone.

In both stories, Elijah and Elisha lay their bodies over those of the sick boys. In Elijah's story, the text employs the verb *va'yitmoded*,[16] which brings to mind the image of stretching out one's body over that of another person but literally means "to measure oneself against." Elijah is a powerful prophet who successfully intercedes with God to restore the boy to life. However, God does not hear Elijah's voice until after this act of measuring. In Elisha's story, this act is described in more detail; here, Elisha places his eyes, mouth, and hands over those of the boy. In the desperate moments when the boys are struggling for their lives, Elijah and Elisha give visceral, bodily expression to the humanity they share with the boys. Social status and age become irrelevant in a kinship of two bodies which, like all bodies, are both vulnerable and powerful. These bodies can fail and, with the help of another body, they can be restored again to life.

At the opening of Genesis 18, we find Abraham sitting in the doorway of his tent (*petach haohel*). While seated in this liminal space, Abraham lifts his eyes and catches sight of his divine-human visitors. According to the Rabbinic imagination, the doorway is also the space from which Abraham seeks out guests to invite into his home. A doorway is a transitory space; it is the boundary between public and private space, between a relatively fluid, open space and a space in which we must follow the host's rules. Doorways and thresholds also appear in the Elijah and Elisha stories. In the first story, Elijah meets the widow-woman at the entrance to the city (*petach ha-ir*). Later, when the widow-woman's son falls ill, Elijah takes the boy to the upper chamber. Although not explicit in the text, we know that both Elijah and the boy cross the threshold of this chamber to enter into what becomes a room for prayer and healing. Similarly, in the second story, Elisha goes into the room where the dead boy is lying and closes the door. In this way, Elisha enters and seals a space for prayer and healing.

In all three of the biblical stories explored above, the doorway is a liminal space for the patient, the host, the visitor, and the healer. When he crosses through the doorway, each party ushers in the possibility of transformation. A liminal space is one that is not fully any one thing; it is not fully public or private, it is not fully our own space or someone else's space. Instead, it is a space that emphasizes mutuality. It is a space that invites transformation because, by passing through it, we acknowledge our own malleability. It is the space that turns the visitor into the guest, the patient into the host, the prophet into the fellow human being.

The same is true in the context of contemporary pastoral care I learned this for myself in recent months after I underwent surgery and spent many weeks convalescing at home. In his landmark work *The Wounded Healer*, Henri Nouwen invites pastoral caregivers to make our own experiences of pain and suffering into "a source of healing" in our work with patients. By this, Nouwen does not mean we should engage in the "spiritual exhibitionism" of self-indulgently telling patients our own problems and stories. Rather, he describes "a constant willingness to see one's own pain and suffering as rising from the depth of the human condition which all men [*sic*] share."[17]

As I prepared for surgery with a cascade of doctors' appointments, and then as my body rebuilt itself, I learned how deeply patients' stories have entered into my being. I was now a patient and, as I adapted to this new role and began creating my own narratives, I felt strongly connected to those who have told me their stories of sickness and wellness in the course of my professional work. As I journeyed through my own health challenges, I experienced an affinity with others who have undergone surgery, waited anxiously for test results, felt the indignity and loss of control that accompany a hospitalization, and witnessed skin and muscle and bone knit themselves back together—among an endless variety of other healthcare-related experiences. It was clear to me that my story did not exist in isolation. Rather, it was one among the infinite number that fill and shape the lives of human beings.

I am grateful to those who came to hear my story or simply to sit quietly with me. I learned firsthand about the comfort and reassurance that comes when another human being reaches out and makes a *bikur cholim* visit. Some of these people had been in my home many times; others were visiting for the first time. Especially with this second group of visitors, I was aware that I was a host as well as a patient. I wanted my visitors to feel welcome and comfortable—even if they were the ones who made tea for both of us, and even if I might ask them to do a task that was beyond my capabilities. Even when I was at my most incapacitated, I took pride in my ability to be a host. As I attended to my visitors' needs in whatever ways I could, I gained a new perspective on the shifting, mutually dependent roles we play over the course of a single encounter and over the course of our lives. I gratefully acknowledged life's doorways, and the thresholds that turn a chaplain into a patient into a host and back again.

The Rabbis' reading of Genesis 18 pivots on the understanding that there is a symbiotic relationship between the one who is receiving care and the one who is giving care. In this relation-ship, it is not always clear who is the giver and who is the receiver; both parties can slip easily between the two roles. While I take very seriously that I am a paid, professional chaplain whose job is to meet patients' spiritual and emotional needs, I also understand that there is a mutuality in the roles of visitor and visited, guest and host. In this spirit, I find that my daily work with patients is a source of sustenance and rejuvenation. Humbled by my awareness of the humanity that caregivers and patients share, and having spent time in both of these roles, I know that my body is no less powerful and no more vulnerable than any other body. In my life as a chaplain and in my life as a person whose body is subject to illness, I stand in doorways and pass over thresholds and hope to be transformed by what I experience there.

Notes

1. Gen. 18:1–8.
2. See, for example, *B'reishit Rabbah* 48:9. Also see Chapter 7 of *Avot D'Rabbi Natan*. Here, Job's tent is imagined as open on all four sides. Abraham's tent is not described in this way, but his hospitality is lauded. In this midrash, we learn that, unlike Job, Abraham would leave his tent in search of prospective visitors to invite to his home.
3. BT *Bava M'tzia* 86b. Author's translation.
4. In all case material included in this article, identifying characteristics have been changed.
5. Joseph S. Ozarowski, "*Bikur Cholim*: A Paradigm for Pastoral Caring," in *Jewish Pastoral Care: A Practical Handbook from Traditional and Contemporary Sources*, ed. Dayle A. Friedman (Woodstock, VT: Jewish Lights, 2001 and 2005), 56.
6. National Hospice and Palliative Care Organization, "NHPCO Facts and Figures: Hospice Care in America, 2009 Edition," 4.
7. Ibid., 6.
8. Ibid., 6.
9. According to the NHPCO, the median length of service (i.e., number of days on a hospice program before death or discharge) was 21.3 days. Twelve percent of patients died or were discharged in 180 days or more. "NHPCO Facts and Figures," 5.
10. For a helpful discussion of boundaries see Barbara Eve Breitman, "Foundations of Jewish Pastoral Care: Skills and Techniques," in *Jewish Pastoral Care: A Practical Handbook from Traditional and*

Contemporary Sources, ed. Dayle A. Friedman (Woodstock, VT: Jewish Lights, 2001 and 2005), 109–13.

11. See Breitman, "Foundations of Jewish Pastoral Care," 113–15.

12. This document is available on the National Association of Jewish Chaplains' website at http://www.najc.org/about/ethics/

13. I Kings 17:1–24.

14. As my teacher Rabbi Nancy Wiener pointed out to me, this likely describes mouth-to-mouth resuscitation.

15. II Kings 4:8–37.

16. This is the only time in the *Tanach* that the verb appears in the *hitpael* form.

17. Henri J. M. Nouwen, *The Wounded Healer: Ministry in Contemporary Society* (Garden City, NY: Image Books, 1979), 88.

Beyond Membership to True Belonging: Jewish Responses to an Unchanging Need for Deep Attachment and Meaning in an Ever-Changing World

Edythe Held Mencher

At conferences and in studies on the future of Jewish life in North America we are presented with research and historical data indicating that many social, educational, and religious needs previously addressed by affiliation with synagogues and Jewish communal organizations are now met in other ways. Jews can rise to positions of authority, acquire Jewish or other learning, find spiritual inspiration, and develop meaningful social contacts in settings requiring less ongoing commitment. Equally compelling research and evidence suggests that while sociological, technological, and cultural developments may cause shifts in patterns of affiliation, the human need to form deep mutual and enduring attachments offering an ongoing sense of belonging does not change. Such relationships remain the bedrock of optimal emotional development and ongoing psychological, physiological, and spiritual well-being.

Of vital importance to those interested in sustaining Jewish identity and communal life is the recognition of the distinction between membership and belonging. There is a great difference between signing up or joining and becoming a part of a network of highly valued relationships. In the context of a sense of true belonging, of

RABBI EDYTHE HELD MENCHER (NY99) serves as the specialist on Caring Community and Family Concerns for the Union for Reform Judaism. She holds an MSW from Hunter College School of Social Work and received certification from the Westchester Center for the Study of Psychoanalysis and Psychotherapy where she serves on the faculty of the Psychoanalytic Training Institute. She also serves as an adjunct faculty member in the D.Min. Program of HUC-JIR/NY.

feeling personally needed, valued, known, and welcomed, membership in Jewish or other organizations becomes far more compelling, gaining in significance and increasing in perceived value. All of us will more readily give up membership than affiliations where we feel we truly belong. So far we have found no alternatives quite as effective at fulfilling human needs related to fostering emotional well-being and resilience than that which is afforded through true belonging to stable groups based on spiritual values. My premise is that these needs are not met through simple membership but are only fulfilled when enduring relationships are forged in the context of a community that fosters faith, meaning, and strength. There are actions we can take that facilitate the sense of belonging and there are actions that can inadvertently impede it.

As we seek to create positive responses that recognize changes in our culture and technology, it is important to keep aware of the elements of human life and longing that remain constant. Family constellations may change dramatically, but the wish to be part of a family endures. The form and makeup of our congregations and organizations may change, but the yearning to be a part of a collective of enduring highly meaningful relationships that inspire hope does not. We may see synagogue membership reduced, but the quest for belonging that assuages human pain and lonely anxiety continues in different venues. As we respond to perceived changes and challenges by imagining transformed Jewish settings and offerings, awareness of the centrality of the search for belonging and meaning can help us. Too heavy a reliance on strategies that create a short-lived instant sense of connection and enthusiasm may yield momentary marketing success but will fail to counter the destabilizing and impoverishing aspects of contemporary life. Crafting responses that tap into the need to belong can help us more truly fulfill the Jewish mission of helping one another to choose and sustain lives that feel worth living.

Identity is formed in the context of relationships of strong affective bonds; people remain and seek connection to individuals and groups that meet needs for companionship, meaning, hope, and comfort. People identify themselves as in relationship to other individuals and groups because there is a dynamic interdependence. Our questions ought to be about how contemporary Judaism can meet these needs just as it met these needs in the past—not so much how to hook others in and keep them, but how to create

Jewish institutions and relationships that are deep sources of belonging, meaning, and guidance.

We must not mistake the heady intoxication that people experience when they feel freed from relationships that were unsatisfying or constricting for a rejection of commitment and relationship. There are those among us who may be rejecting certain aspects of communal life and congregations much as we throw off aspects of our attachments to families in adolescence. Just as with families, however, there really is a wish to remain connected and a wish to return once we have established our freedom to leave. Let us keep in mind, if we wish our congregations to be experienced as family, that much as we may love our families, we seek distance when we hear too much about how we don't visit enough, only come for the holidays, don't share our money, or don't give enough priority to our family when we are choosing how to spend our time. Let's look at which aspects of belonging are sustainable and most vital and determine why they matter. Let's consider how to cultivate them so that we are a well-functioning family, so that we create relationships that offer both connection and the freedom to grow.

Belonging

The operative word is belonging. Belonging has at its core strong affective bonds and mutual need. It is deeply connected to a sense of meaning and pleasure in living. In *B'reishit*, God declares it is not good for human beings to be alone. Adam and Eve need one another and God. All of us need to matter deeply to others to thrive—and certainly to survive adversity. Membership to a people is often assigned, an accident of birth or adoption. In some cases, simply paying a fee, donating, or enrolling may allow us to easily acquire membership. Sometimes membership is chosen or hard-won—as in religious conversion, naturalization, election, or acceptance after competitive processes of selection. Belonging is never easily achieved and is different from membership even when obstacles to membership are great. To develop a sense of belonging, repeated experiences of significant emotional connection must occur over a fairly long period of time. We may convert to Judaism, join a synagogue, be accepted into a university, even marry into a family and still not feel that we truly belong. When membership is not coupled with a sense of belonging, membership is weaker, less personally valued, and of far less significance to us.

Let's look at historical, psychological, and physiological reasons why a sense of belonging matters so much. Let's also look at the evidence that Judaism and Jewish community still have a vital role to play in nurturing secure attachments that are the basis for resilience, for communal responsibility, for loyalty, trust, and security.

In our history—personal, communal, and religious—belonging has been linked to survival. From infancy through old age, from biblical times to the present, we need to feel that we belong to others or we may literally perish. The ancients might not have understood the neurobiology but they grasped that to be *karet* (to be cut off from the tribe, to be outside the camp) was to court psychic and physical disaster. To be cut off from such ties surely carried the danger of being without protection from predators and without reliable access to literal sustenance. But the equally great danger, then and now, is of being emotionally cut off, of existing without a sense of being rooted in relationships that engender trust and emotional security.

Attachment and sense of belonging develop in childhood as care is provided to us by people who convey enjoyment and concern, who respond empathically to our pain and to our joy and who listen to and validate our responses. Attachment is forged, as we recognize not just our need for our caretakers but also the caretakers' very real emotional need for us. The now classic research done by Rene Spitz and John Bowlby demonstrated that if these bonds of attachment and trust are broken when we are young and if no substitute equally loving relationship is developed we will protest, show extreme distress, and collapse into lethargy. This is often followed by a failure to thrive and death. Even when we survive such profound loss we are at risk of making apathetic and hollow adjustments to life, devoid of vitality and trust.

Protective Power of Belonging

Attachment and belonging are the ground on which all else is built.[1] A sense of belonging to family early in life has neurologically and physiologically protective benefits—and ongoing experiences that enhance a feeling of belonging continue to confer protective and healing effects throughout the life cycle. Attachment and sense of belonging are the basic building blocks of resilience.

When we speak of the protective power of attachment and belonging we are not merely speaking sentimentally; we are speaking of the way the brain functions and consequently the health of both body and mind. Children who are insecurely attached may respond to upsetting experiences with elevated blood pressure; increased heart rate; and physiological and psychological distress including an inability to recover, self soothe, and maintain hope. They do not have a basic sense of trust. This is not just a magical construct—their bodies and brains concretely reflect this lack of trust in catastrophic reactions to adversity. Conversely, children who have felt themselves securely attached, who sense that they belong to parents and to communities to whom they matter deeply, are able to withstand even adverse experiences because of the way their brains developed. Studies conducted by psychologist Danny Brom and his colleagues at Herzog Hospital in Jerusalem reveal that children exposed to trauma respond resiliently and recover most fully from adverse experiences when securely attached to parents who can help them process experiences.[2] Psychoanalysts Anna Freud and Dorothy Burlingham's World War II studies of children sent away from parents to the countryside versus those who remained with parents in London during bombings showed those who were exposed to danger, trauma, and even injury fared better than those who were separated but in safer surroundings.[3]

This tendency to respond poorly to stress if our attachments and sense of belonging were shaky early on persists throughout life— that is the tough news. This difficulty with managing stress, maintaining optimism, and confronting crises constructively is carried into adult life. Even in those who have had positive early experiences with belonging, later isolation and lack of support can be devastating. For some, patterns of emotional need and vulnerability remain constant throughout the lifespan; for most others, vulnerabilities will reemerge at times of stress and disorientation. We are more likely to fall ill with depression and a myriad of physical and psychological ailments when we do not feel held in a network of ongoing relationships of mutual care and connection.

Loneliness and social isolation are linked to mortality all through our lives. Vulnerable college students living far from family, friends, and community are prone to depression, suicide attempts, and addiction, particularly in the early months when meaningful relationships and new connections have not been established.

When our lives are affected by divorce, widowhood, outliving peers, living far from grown children and grandchildren, when we are separated from congregations and communities where we raised families, we crave connections that confirm our sense of being needed and cherished. With the shifting demographic in the Jewish and wider community towards older age, the challenge to sustain a sense of belonging becomes greater than ever. It comes as no surprise that depression is widespread among older adults.

Healing Attachments

The good news is that there is plasticity to the brain and to our capacity to form healing attachments. All is not said and done at the end of infancy or childhood. Even in the face of great adversity and emotional challenge, even in a rapidly changing world, new attachments that foster a sense of belonging strengthen our capacity to cope.

Viktor Frankl observed this phenomenon when he spoke of what made survival possible in concentration camps or other extremely adverse situations. He noted that the ability to recall the image and love of even one person, living or dead, to whom our survival matters, enables us to go on.[4] Our sense of hope, our values, our faith, and our will to live is dependent upon to whom we belong. Social networks—the old fashioned kind—promote resiliency and the will to go on because they give life meaning: they support existing relationships and provide ongoing opportunities to feel needed, encouraged, valued, and inspired.

While much of what we hear about the future of Judaism points to the plethora of opportunities to have needs met that were previously met by involvement in Judaism and Jewish community, the need to truly belong is one that is not often adequately met in our modern culture. Religious, value-oriented communities continue to offer unique possibilities in a world replete with opportunities for instant contact but with fewer clear pathways to truly enduring, meaningful relationships.

Belonging and the Role of Religion

Religion has always had among its many functions the cultivation and support of a sense of belonging—to God, to family, and to community. Our challenge within the Jewish community is how to more adequately and sensitively respond to this need in contemporary circumstances. Our texts and tradition offer us a template. Judaism tells a story of belonging; it encodes ways in which we belong to God and to one another and it encourages attachments that build security, meaning, and hope. Our Creation stories speak of God creating human beings to fill a void. We imagine God's loneliness and need of humanity. Whatever we may feel about "chosen-ness," we Jews have craved to see ourselves as mattering to God, and have also been sustained by the belief that God has needed us as well.

We speak of God as parent, as lover of Israel, as choosing and knowing prophets and even each of us before our birth, as nourishing us and sustaining us. First we were cared for in Eden, then again later after being freed from bondage we were fed and guided as we wandered in the desert. Our tradition tells us that it is in the context of a relationship of mutual love, care, and belonging that we received the commandments instructing us about how our lives might become holy. Only when our children, our friends, our partners, and our congregants feel certain that they belong can they hear what might be required of them to sustain such satisfying relationships and to protect the world of relationships that surrounds them. Only when we have been fed in the desert can we accept Torah—only when our congregants feel loved can they fully enter and support a community. We must become more aware of the actions and orientation that contribute to such a sense of belonging. We must become equally aware of the stumbling blocks, the impediments that block the path to a sense of belonging for some of our members and potential members.

Congregational Communities

The congregational community serves to foster a sense of belonging to God, to family, to spouse, to community. This is not accomplished primarily through sermons and commandments—it is accomplished through the encouragement of and provision of opportunities to make and sustain such ties.

In their studies detailed in *The Jew: Self, Family, and Community in America*, scholars Steven Cohen of HUC-JIR and NYU Wagner, and Arnold Eisen of Stanford and JTS offer insight into what makes those who remain involved in congregational and organizational life choose to do so. Among the reasons cited repeatedly were that congregations afforded a place to develop meaningful relationships, to meditate, and to reflect—to simply "be" in a place of deep connected-ness.[5] When congregations fulfill these functions they facilitate our being connected to others while engaged in activities and reflections that elevate our sense of meaning and purpose.

Membership vs. Belonging

But membership in our congregations and organizations in no way guarantees access to this sense of belonging. *In American Grace*, an examination of religion in America, scholars Robert Putnam of Har-vard and David Campbell of Notre Dame note that it is worse to be a worshiper with no friends than to have no membership at all. "A person who attends church regularly but has no close friends there is actually unhappier than her demographic twin who doesn't attend church at all." Putnam and Campbell continue, "Religious friends re-main very important even when we compare people with equal num-bers of friends overall and in that sense religious friendship seems supercharged (as a determiner of happiness)." There is evidence that there is special benefit to friendships forged and maintained in an atmosphere of shared spiritual search and tradition.[6] Anyone who has ever watched or been the person who has stood alone at an *Oneg* after services knows exactly how lonely it can be in purportedly sa-cred space where prayers and food are provided but fellowship is not. The person who attends services but feels she has no friends in the congregation may even be a member of the congregation but she certainly doesn't feel she belongs.

People will give up memberships when they are assessing their financial and time commitments. They will not so easily dispense with belonging. When we speak about belonging this way we are talking about the ubiquitous yearning to feel loved, needed, and con-nected to others through shared values and purpose. We are talk-ing about the answers to the questions, "Who hears my voice? Who would truly miss me as an individual if I were not here? Whose faces light up when I arrive? Who will help me when I am dejected and discouraged? Who needs what I have to offer?" We are talking about that which enables us to feel in some way at home in the world.

We must raise the question about whether congregations and Jew-ish communal organizations are currently serving sufficiently as places to nourish what Rabbi Richard Address calls sacred relation-ships. These are the relationships that offer a deep sense of belonging that engenders emotional and spiritual health. Surely it is our intention—if not, why not? We must also respond to the question of whether people actually recognize this need to belong, whether they can articulate it or whether their rejection of membership heralds a wish and reliance upon shallower forms of connection to one another. We must ask whether other social institutions meet the need for belonging, for fostering of trust and resilience, better or more easily than our Jewish institutions—and if so, why? We must address the question of whether in fact people are seeking God and some connection to the spiritual or whether religious longing and affiliation are on the wane. Do people wish to feel a sense of belonging to God or do they find it archaic and infantile; is religious faith not something they actively pursue? If they pursue it in another setting, does that other setting offer a greater sense of belonging? And what of the assertion that people do not have the patience, interest, or need for the sense of belonging that might be afforded by our congregations?

Let's look at one factor at a time. First, the need to belong is ubiquitous for optimal development—difficulty in making and sustaining attachments is another thing again. Let us not confuse the existence of a problem with a change in human nature or potential. Consider the adopted traumatized children we hear of who have difficulty making loving attachments. We meet them where they are but our goal is always to have them find special satisfactions in unique long-standing relationships. We seek to find ways to slow down their frantic quest to get needs met by people who are interchangeable; we seek to help them to attach, to value and to invest in individual cherished ties so that they can develop faith, empathy, loyalty, and concern for others.

Religious Task in an Internet World

Part of our religious task in an Internet world is to rehumanize the pace, selectivity, and depth of ties for all people. Although we may now be connected to thousands through the Internet, the yearning for in-person meaningful ongoing contact is what drives many of the searches. Of course, the Internet can be and is used for anonymous or shallow onetime encounters and, of course, for the exchange of information. Yet in the realm of human relations it is valued by most for its capacity to search out and reinforce opportunities for belonging. Dating services are used to search for spouses and committed relationships and these are offered as success stories. Skype and other video chat platforms are most often used to connect college students to their parents, close friends to close friends, romantic partners to one another, and grandparents to their grandchildren. These services are often used as bridges to connect those who already belong to one another, not as destinations. We are most constantly seeking reduced distance and isolation, not anonymity and serial short-lived connections.

We also need to ask why people are online. They are sometimes lonely, depressed, addicted, and seeking connection precisely because of the limited nature of their attachments and capacity to find relief and emotional comfort. They are seeking help with worries about health, relationships, and even faith. These concerns and hurts will never be fully assuaged by shallow relationships and short fixes. It is like the alcoholic who reaches for a drink, the overeater for a cookie, the porn addict for an image online—there is a momentary relief followed by distress and an attempt to soothe it yet again with the same inadequate means. There is anonymity, sometimes-useful information, but the result is never the same as when information and advice are offered by an empathic human being. Constant electronic and Internet overstimulation may yet be proven to produce neurological effects much in the way addictions do—our brains may come to crave something that offers short-lived sense of relief and well-being. We may find ourselves returning to a state of unsatisfied, un-soothed tension yet reach for the same something, continuing a cycle but leaving deep needs unmet.

We absolutely may learn and benefit from webinars and podcasts from people we have never actually met and whose voice and image we may see only once. Still, we continue to crave a different kind of contact and connectedness that is achieved only with repeated, sustained connection to other human beings. As we look to the future and imagine the formation of Jewish groups, congregations, organizations, and educational approaches, a clearer understanding of ways to address this deepest and most central of human longings is imperative.

It matters that strong enduring sturdy attachments of depth are psycho-physiologically protective and they can be sustained and supported by communal structures. One way in which Jewish communal organizations and programs that promote relationship offer this support is through offering sustained contact with the

same people over time. Where we succeed we are in essence training and healing brains through providing alternative experiences
to the ones that are stimulating but put us in jeopardy. Yes, the
Internet offers games, excitement, and quick results but people do
not only use the Net to play games or to surf for news. Many are
desperately searching not just to hear, "You are connected!" but to
find others with whom to have real-life, real-time relationships.
The complicating factor is that many experiences of modernity do
not provide what is needed to be able to make those connections
and sustain those attachments.

Religious communities offer an unusual opportunity in that we
needn't graduate from them when we reach a certain age or stage of
life. No other similar community institutions have emerged in which
we can remain connected throughout the life cycle and can also find
similar communities when we change geographical location.

Impediments to Belonging

But if the community is not actually fostering connections and
sense of belonging because it is inadvertently causing members
and potential members to feel like outsiders—because knowledge, beliefs, and identity are not validated; because they cannot
feel cherished as they are—then their sense of belonging will be
eroded. Then the community will not serve the function of providing unique, affirming, inspiring, and stable connections. If the
same community conveys messages that interfere with other primary attachments—such as between spouses who are intermarried, between grandparents and their grandchildren not being
raised Jewish—then they will move away to protect attachments.
They may join more welcoming faith communities, may eschew
religious affiliation, or they may live devoid of the kinds of connections that might have been meaningful. The absence may not
show up until those moments of strain and distress when the sense
of belonging that is strengthening is most needed.

If our sense of the divine and spiritual is not addressed or welcomed within a Jewish community we will search elsewhere rather
than continue to feel that we can find no sense of belonging or
comfort. The droves of people pursuing yoga, Buddhism, and pop
versions of Kabbalah all attest to longing for something spiritual
that is not so dissonant that they cannot join in. So much of what

is offered in these alternative settings is also truly part of our own spiritual tradition, but many have little access to these sources when they are truly in pain and need them.

Let's look also at the seeming paradox of the wish for religious officiation at life-cycle moments among even those who profess a lack of belief. Life-cycle moments are times of stress, change, and emotional vulnerability. One reason people may come for these life-cycle events and then leave is that the life-cycle experiences bolster and strengthen family connections in the context of tradition. This is in contrast to other experiences that may not be ones that so obviously promote and reinforce a sense of belonging to community or to one another. People will indeed come to grade Shabbats and even pet Shabbats—because they are personal and acknowledge existing attachments. They will come to healing services too—because these speak directly to powerful yearnings relating to their own well-being and that of those they love.

And what of nonbelief? There are those who say that increased rationality and lack of belief in the seemingly magical aspects of religion cause people to disconnect from Jewish community. They point to the numbers who say they do not believe. Belief is fluid and shifting, as is our concept of God and even our feelings about the people to whom we are attached. In the sickroom, on the battlefield, on a roller coaster, and when we are lost, we cry out for parents and God—even if at other moments we will say one was inadequate and the other might not exist. People need ways to belong to God and to one another that allow for the ebb and flow of feeling, the shift from a relatedness based on dependence, to defiance and even to disbelief. They need a way to belong that encompasses this often-shifting quality of relationships in a place of safety that also sustains them. Our rituals and services for some do not offer that which they need to feel a sense of belonging because the myriad, sometimes contradictory ways they experience attachments are not reflected in what is spoken and shared or sung.

People do not leave and go nowhere, they seek other places that will offer them a sense of welcome; they avoid pain and they seek acceptance. They will go to all sorts of programs to promote personal and spiritual connections that are likely to be less successful if only because they are commercial, not rooted in history, or at a franchise that may fail. They show up for programs where they can enroll in forty-five-minute classes but cannot find an ongoing community.

Are we doing all we can to promote belonging or are we too focused on membership? We may be seeking to cultivate members who are donors and who are more mainstream because we do need them and they do need us. We sometimes make the mistake of focusing mostly on those who have other places of belonging, rather than upon hearing the cries of the disenfranchised, the hurting, the marginal, the lonely—those seeking attachments to shore them up. At gay and lesbian synagogues twenty-five years ago, no one had to beg people to remain members precisely because such congregations were among the few places gay Jews could feel a true sense of acceptance and belonging. Historically it was the ones who could not belong and the ones who could not find a home where they were who set out for spiritual fulfillment who became our leaders. In our sacred stories it is Abraham who cannot belong among idol worshipers who is led to a place where he will feel secure and cherished.

Countering Despair, Loneliness, and Disconnection

So how can we use an orientation towards belonging to strengthen our Jewish organizations? It is essential to evaluate whether our current structures are addressing this need and to consider how future ones might better counter loneliness and disconnection. If some of our needs are met but we do not feel held in a network of enduring, caring relationships characterized by mutuality there will be an absence of vitality and real attachment. Paradoxically, if we feel that we don't matter, are not needed, are not known, and are not heard, and that our pain and joy are not acknowledged, reflected, and validated, then we will not develop deep attachments.

For belonging to evolve, communities must be places where we forge attachments to Jewish leaders and where we make friendships. They must be where we make marriages and partnerships, where our children make friends, where we meet other couples, other divorced people, and come into strong and constructive relationship with clergy, educators, and youth leaders and communal service workers. Let's look at each and every institution and proposed program and see where and how it promotes true attachment and belonging. Does it promote friendships? Does it promote connections to clergy and staff that are enduring? Does it involve ten meetings and contacts? Do our programs and words convey a sense of welcome and acceptance

to people as they are? Do our programs offer them voice and valida-
tion? Do we draw in those who feel they do not belong—the kids with
shaky family situations, single people, newcomers to the vicinity, the
unemployed, members of the GLBT community, those living with
disabilities, those whose children don't live close by, and those with
emotional and mental distress? Do we offer small group experiences
in which issues of deep concern and Jewish sources are explored and
where real friendships can emerge?

It is our central Jewish mission to help people connect to a sense
of the gift of life and relationship, of trust and hope and connection. This mission will be as vital in the future as when Abraham
ventured forth and welcomed wanderers into his tent, moving forward and leading others to a not-yet-known place with faith and
a sense of purpose.

Notes

1. Rene Spitz, "Hospitalism: An Inquiry Into the Genesis of Psychiatric
   Conditions in Early Childhood," *Psychoanalytic Study of the Child* 1
   (1945): 53–74; John Bowlby, *Child Care and the Growth of Love* (London: Penguin, 1965) (summary of major finding of their studies).

2. Danny Brom, Ruth Pat-Horenczyk, and Julian D. Ford, *Treating Traumatized Children: Risk, Resilience and Recovery* (London and New York:
   Routledge, 2009), 5.

3. Anna Freud and Dorothy Burlingham, *War and Children* (Westport, CT:
   Greenwood Press, 1943, 1973) (summary of conclusions of study).

4. "I understood how a man who has nothing left in this world may still
   know bliss, be it only for a brief moment, in the contemplation of his beloved. In a position of utter desolation, when man cannot express himself
   in positive action, when his only achievement may consist of enduring
   his suffering in the right way—in such a position man can, through loving contemplation of the image he carries of his beloved, achieve fulfillment." Viktor E Frankl, *Man's Search for Meaning* (New York: Washington Square Press, 1959, rev. ed. 1984), 57.

5. "They attend rather to be in palpable community, or out of family interest or obligation or to soothe and nourish the harried self, or to connection with selected elements of Jewish tradition. In this, as in all else, the
   decisive factor seems to be personal experience." Steven M. Cohen and
   Arnold M. Eisen, *The Jew: Self, Family, and Community in America*
   (Bloomington: Indiana University Press, 2000), 190.

6. Robert Putnam and David Campbell, *American Grace: How Religion
   Unites and Divides Us* (New York: Simon and Schuster, 2010), 491.

The Torah of Despair

Elliot Kukla

Save me, God, for the waters are flooding me. I have sunk in deep mire, where there is no standing; I have come into deep waters, overcome by flood. I have grown weary crying out; from pining for God my throat dried out, my eyes exhausted.

—Psalms 69:1–4

1. "Rabbi, I would like to die"

It is my job to be with people on the worst day of their life. I work as a rabbi at the Bay Area Jewish Healing Center in San Francisco tending to the spiritual needs of those struggling with grieving, illness, and dying. Someone tells me they would like to die at least once a week. I hear feelings of a loss of taste for living from the lips of those who are elderly and have lost the capacity to care for themselves or recognize their loved ones; I listen to an anguished desire to die from those living with long-term mental illness; I am often told by those who just lost a loved one that they too would like to die; people with long-term chronic pain conditions who despair of recovery often tell me that their deepest desire is to end their suffering.

Every fiber of my being longs to "fix" the situations of those who dwell in this much pain and heartbreak. Sometimes this is possible and I am able to assess the situation and offer a solution like referrals to a doctor, therapist, or psychiatrist; grieving rituals; or prayers to sustain their spirits until their anguish lifts. However, some of the people who utter these words are in situations that are "unfixable" and often the desire to die seems fair to me or at least very understandable.

This is not an article about suicide prevention, which is a worthy and important topic about which much has already been

ELLIOT KUKLA (LA06) is a rabbi at the Bay Area Jewish Healing Center in San Francisco providing spiritual care to those struggling with grieving, illness, or dying. Elliot's writing on mental illness, dying, and LGBT issues in Judaism appear in numerous journals and anthologies and he regularly speaks nationally on these topics.

written. Rather this is an article about how to stay present and spiritually engaged with people who habitually live in a place of desolation. In this article I will explore the characters in the Bible who struggle with despair and I will discuss the living Torah I learn from my clients who share their journeys through anguish with me.

I have come to the conclusion that hope is not always the best response to chronic despair. Some people need to be held in their pain until it passes and be reminded that things will change; but in some situations of intractable suffering there is no expectation of amelioration in the future and pushing hope rings empty. Releasing hope allows us to connect deeply to the reality of another person's suffering in the present and offer our companionship and comfort. And in the end, what else do we have in the face of mortality and loss but the here and now and our ability to connect to one another? When we connect to one another with whole hearts that are open to both triumph and deep despair, we bring true shalom (wholeness and peace) into the world.

2. The Torah of Despair

"I can no longer bear the burden of this people alone—it is too heavy for me. If you would deal thus with me, please kill me; if I have found favor in your sight, let me no longer see my wretchedness."
—Moses in Num. 11:14–15

The Torah is filled with voices of those who despair. When the matriarch Rebekah is pregnant she suffers from terrible pain as the twins Jacob and Esau wrestle inside of her. Rebekah says to God, "If this is what it is, why me?" These words resonate with what I hear from so many people in extreme pain—why me and why should I endure? Despite these feelings we read: "Yet she went on seeking God" (Gen. 25:22).

Job's suffering is longer term and his despair is deeper. After the deaths of his children and during numerous disfiguring illnesses he says, "I am weary of my life; my speech gives out; I will speak from the bitterness of my soul" (Job 10:1). The term "bitterness" in this passage seems apt, as so often being exhausted by life is connected to a "loss of taste" for living. Many elders reach a similar place of weariness after many illnesses and losses and sometimes they simply stop eating in order to hasten their deaths. Unlike Rebekah, Job sees no end in sight for his suffering and he is only restored to a desire to live through miraculous interventions that few of the people we serve are likely to experience.

Moses himself, the greatest leader of our people, despairs and asks to die. He is exhausted from the burdens of leadership and he says to God, "Please kill me" (Num. 11:15). Moses reminds me of those I serve who feel trapped and overwhelmed by their lives. Often the desire to die is expressed to me as the only "way out" that someone can envision.

In today's world a desire to die is often surrounded by stigma and isolation. The Torah speaks in a different voice—Rebekah, Job, and Moses are integral to the social world of the Bible. There is recognition in the Bible that while despair is painful, it is also a part of the human experience. These biblical figures are inspiring and important figures in Jewish tradition not *despite* their despair, but in part *because* their desolate states of mind are so quintessentially human. It is also what makes them such enduring characters as they offer up the wholeness of their pain and despair as well as sharing their joy with generations of readers and learners.

I do not mean to imply that despair is good. What the biblical stories teach us is that this kind of distress has been present in every Jewish society and is a natural part of human experience. We could skip over or efface these Torah portions but instead they are chanted aloud and sung melodiously from the center of our synagogues during our weekly Torah readings on Shabbat and holidays. Listening to the voices of despair without trying to "fix" these stories or encourage hope is literally a mitzvah in our tradition.

3. Hopelessness

God, please lift me from this infinite depth./The light of life and love is so far above it seems like a wisp of a dream from long ago./The sadness spreads around me reaching to every horizon./If I just lie here, eventually the lifeless air will leave me a desiccated husk of bone and skin who somehow still has the capacity for endless tears./How did I get here God? Sometimes I ask for your merciful help and implore you to fill me with your healing grace./But today I can't even seem to do that.
　　　—"Hopeless," an original prayer by Shoshana Hadassah (2011), written in response to a psychiatric hospitalization

I recently saw Susan, a client in her early sixties, whose husband and thirty-year-old son both died in the past two years. She told me with a deep, striking calm that her life is now devoted to tending their memories—she speaks to them every day and plants flowers in their honor. She told me that her siblings and friends keep urging her to hope, to let go of tending to the dead, in order to make new friends and acquire new hobbies. "I can't tell them this but I have no intention of doing that," she told me simply. "Why would I want to lose my memories and my closeness to my husband and son on top of all I have already lost? I don't want to hope for more. I have had enough. I had a life filled with love. Now I am just hanging on day by day until it is my time to die."

Susan's hopelessness was pure and simple. Well meaning encouragement to hope was leaving Susan alone in her feelings. Susan's loved ones *have* to hope for her, as their fate is bound up in hers. As her rabbi I have the opportunity to be able to companion her in her experience of hopelessness—a lonely terrain to walk alone. This is counterintuitive for most rabbis and caregivers since we have been taught to see hope as integral to religious leadership. Holding hope for someone in a short-term crisis is often extremely healing and sometimes even life saving, but holding out hope is not always helpful for someone in deep and chronic despair.

The Merriam-Webster dictionary defines "hope" as: "1) To desire with expectation of obtainment 2) To expect with confidence (archaic: to trust)." In some situations of intractable suffering there is no expectation of amelioration, and to expect change with confidence or trust actually gets in the way of fully experiencing the present moment. I define holiness as existing in what *is*—in the here and now, the real living world that God created—as opposed to what we think the world should be. Hence if we refuse to dwell in hopelessness we also miss out on moments of holiness.

Judaism has texts and traditions that refuse to turn away from the pain and the beauty of moments of utter desolation, and that honor the holiness of hopelessness as well as hope. Passover tells a purposeful story of suffering and redemption: We were once slaves but now we are free. The yearly observance of Passover reminds us that we can go from slavery into freedom and teaches us about the potential for change and redemption. On the other hand, the Book of Lamentations, which describes the destruction of ancient Jerusalem, portrays a world of chaos where mothers cannibalize their young with no glimmer in sight of restoration. This text is woven into the Jewish liturgical year through the observance of Tishah B'Av (the Jewish day of communal mourning), when it is read aloud and traditionally accompanied by wailing. We leave Tishah B'Av services that evening in silence and grief, not with words of encouragement.

Tishah B'Av eve, an observance of hopelessness, and the hope-filled Passover are *both* sacred moments in the Jewish year. Likewise, Jewish spiritual caregivers are called upon to bear witness to the holiness within both types of responses to deep suffering. Even when there is no expectation for suffering to end in the future there is still companionship and connection in the present moment. And that is often enough.

The poet T. S. Elliot says all this in another way: "I said to my soul be still, and wait without hope; for hope would be hope of the wrong thing; wait without love, for love would be love of the wrong thing; there is yet faith. But the faith, and the love, and the hope are all in the waiting."[1]

4. *N'chamah* (Comfort)

Before you know what kindness really is/you must lose things,/feel the future dissolve in a moment,/like salt in a weakened broth./What you held in your hand,/what you counted and carefully saved,/all this must go so you know how desolate the landscape can be between the regions of kindness.

—"Kindness" by Naomi Shyhbe Nye

While we can't dispel hopelessness, staying with someone *in* their hopelessness can lead to the *n'chamah* (comfort) of not suffering alone. In Jewish tradition upon a deep loss we comfort mourners by saying: "May God console you among the other mourners of Zion and Jerusalem" (*HaMakom y'nachem etchem b'toch shaar av'lei Tziyon v'Y'rushalayim*). This formula does not offer comfort through inspiring hope in an afterlife or reunion with a lost loved one; nor does it speak to the loved one being free of suffering or other encouraging sentiments. Instead it offers comfort to the individual mourner through placing the devastation of her loss within the context of divine care, Jewish history, and all the losses of our people—the loss of the city of ancient Jerusalem and the ideal of a peaceful world represented by Zion. It comforts the mourner by telling her that her loss is indeed devastating (as terrible as any national tragedy) and by reminding her that she is not alone.

We can help those who despair truly not to be alone by companioning them through their despair and by offering kindness. Kindness is the one thing human beings don't have to lose in life— eventually as we age all of us will lose objects we love, activities we enjoy, our health, our loved ones, our life. But we can be kind to each other even in death. This is what we learn in the Torah from Abraham who takes the trouble to purchase a cave to bury Sarah in, and from the way God personally buries Moses at the end of his life. It is what we reinforce every time we sit with someone in deep despair. And every time we allow someone to sit with us.

A friend of mine who has trouble with balance due to a brain injury once told me that when she falls down everyone rushes to help her get up, but in those first moments she needs to gather her thoughts and dignity and she does not want to be pulled to her feet. "I think people rush to help me up," she says, "because they are so uncomfortable with seeing an adult lying on the floor. But what I really need is for someone to get down on the ground with me." This simple teaching of what true kindness looks like is 99 percent of spiritual care—get down on the floor yourself before you drag someone to their feet!

5. The Valley of Deepest Darkness

The Eternal One is my shepherd; I lack nothing. God makes me lie down in green pastures; God leads me to waters in places of stillness; God renews my life; God guides me towards justice as befits God's name; Though I walk through a valley of deepest darkness, I fear no evil, for You are with me; Your rod and Your staff are before me— and they comfort me.

—Psalms 23:1–4

Getting down on the floor with someone who has momentarily stumbled can be anxiety provoking. But getting down on the ground with someone in deep despair can be dangerous. It is a balancing act to stay present with those who despair without being swallowed by their suffering. When we are accompanying someone in despair we are walking into the valley of deepest darkness and that takes a toll on even the strongest caregiver.

One of the ways I know to avoid getting lost in the valley is to acknowledge that I too need to be offered kindness, curiosity, and companionship when journeying with a client to painful places. This can take the form of talking to rabbinic colleagues, debriefing with a therapist, or praying to God. Rejuvenation can also come through life-nourishing physical or spiritual practices such as time in nature, time with children or animals, art, or meditation, which help release feelings of despair.

Another less talked about way that can help us is to allow those we walk with to also walk with us. Lillian is a client of mine who lives with severe and chronic emotional and physical pain. She is also a person of deep and abiding faith in God. She often tells me that she asks God every day to let her die. Last time we were together she was in a place of especially deep despair after living with intolerable daily pain for eighteen years. She begged me to offer her something that might alleviate her suffering for even a moment. I read her Psalm 23 with the prayer that she would not feel alone in the valley of her suffering and her pain. She was calmed for a moment but soon felt desperate for more and asked me to read it to her again. This time, I asked her if she would read it to me. She did and for just that moment she was strong enough to accompany *me* through the terrain of her own valley of deepest darkness—a terrain she knows well; one that is etched on her heart.

I wish this was an article with a happy ending. But it is not. Many of those we serve will continue to suffer. And many of our own hearts will be broken. All I can say is that no one is alone in this situation. Despair is part of the human soul. I believe this is what is meant by the Chasidic saying "there is nothing as whole as a broken heart." Sitting with despair is challenging, and it is a part of what it means to be "whole-hearted" with one another.

This article grew out of a workshop the author co-led with Rabbi Natan Fenner at the Bay Area Jewish Healing Center for San Francisco Bay Area Jewish chaplains. Many thanks are due to Rabbi Fenner for his collaboration, collegial support, and contributions in developing these ideas.

Note

1. T. S. Eliot, "East Coker," in *Four Quarters* (New York: Harcourt, 1943).

The Stigma of Infertility

Eleanor Steinman

On Rosh HaShanah 5771 I delivered a sermon about infertility that sparked tremendous conversation, pastoral conversations, and interest. This article is an expansion on some of the ideas contained within that sermon and seeks to go beyond it to offer suggestions as to how clergy can respond in these moments for one another and our congregants.

My friend Marisa has been married for three years. All of a sudden, people she works with started to approach her and make statements like, "*Mazal tov.* When are you due?" or "How are you feeling? You look really great." or "We have been waiting for this. We are so happy for you and your husband."

Marisa is not pregnant. These painful comments were really an unfortunate reminder that she had gained weight. I do not know when or if Marisa will have children and it is not my business. I do know that over the summer she worked out and lost over ten pounds. All of a sudden the comments returned though pointed in a different direction. "I did not know if I should share that I was worried about you" and "Oh, you look good. I thought maybe . . ." or "Is everything okay with you and your husband?"

What if she had been pregnant? What if she had a miscarriage? What if there was a story she was not ready, or willing, to share?

As a society we presume that everyone who wants to can bare children. The operating assumption in our society is that getting pregnant is easy. A lot of people get pregnant. Television commercials portray people receiving positive pregnancy test results, never is a negative result to be seen. Couples who wish to conceive think that they will be able to without any difficulty. When they start trying it comes as a surprise that it does not happen right away. This is rarely shown on television. When it is not so easy far too many people struggle in silence.

RABBI ELEANOR STEINMAN (LA08) is currently pursuing a masters degree in Jewish Education from the Rhea Hirsch School of Education at HUC-JIR in Los Angeles.

In the twenty-first century, families are presented with choices unlike those from any other time in history. The questions individuals and couples grapple with include when to have children, whether or not to have children, and even how to have children. What seems like something so easy is not. When individuals or couples decide to be conscientious about trying to reproduce suddenly it is not as easy as it seemed when we learned about the birds and the bees. "A fifth to a quarter of all first-time pregnancies yield to loss instead of life. Tens of thousands more women cannot begin or hold a pregnancy without medical intervention."[1] These are the realities. And no one seems to talk about them.

Infertility is stigmatized in our society. Even though it affects one in six couples. As a community we forget to be sensitive. We live in an era of complete openness. People post on the Internet what were once intimate details of life. However, it is so painful to speak of infertility that many choose not to and in turn, suffer in silence. At the very moment a person or a couple needs support, to know they are not alone, words cannot fill a void, and the intimate agony goes unnoticed.

The Reality Today

In 2009 the World Health Organization classified infertility as a "disease of the reproductive system defined by the failure to achieve a clinical pregnancy after 12 months or more of regular unprotected sexual intercourse."[2] We have something that our ancestors couldn't conceive of: modern medicine. Many options exist to combat infertility thanks to medical science. Surrogacy, in vitro fertilization (IVF) treatments, various prescription fertility drugs, and a myriad of other options exist; and science is advancing everyday. The challenge is, as Peggy Orenstein documents, "the descent into the world of infertility is incremental. Those early steps seem innocuous, even quaint."[3]

Peggy Orenstein was a happily married thirty-five-year-old when she decided she wanted to have a baby. While she knew it might not be easy (she had only one ovary and was heading into her late thirties), she had no idea of the troubles she'd face. First, she was diagnosed with breast cancer, fortunately treatable. After waiting the recommended recovery period, she miscarried with a dangerous partial molar pregnancy, so she had to avoid becoming pregnant for at least six months. Soon she was riding the infertility roller-coaster full-time, trying everything from acupuncture to IVF and egg donation. She endured depression and more miscarriages while spending thousands of dollars. Orenstein writes:

> Without form, there is no content. So even in this era of compulsive confession, women don't speak openly of their losses. It was only now that I'd become one of them, that I'd begun to hear the stories, spoken in confidence, almost whispered. There were so many. My aunt. My grandmother. My sister-in-law. My friends. My editors. Women I'd known for years—sometimes my whole life—who had had this happen sometimes over and over and over again but felt they couldn't, or shouldn't mention it. My shock and despair were, in part, a function of improved technology and medical care.[4]

Orenstein's very understanding husband was beginning to lose patience, when, surprisingly, she got pregnant with her daughter, Daisy.

About 10 percent to 25 percent of pregnancies spontaneously end before twenty weeks gestation according to a report by the American College of Obstetricians and Gynecologists.[5] With something so surprisingly common, we do not often hear about it, and when individuals or couples go through this painful physical and emotional process they do it alone. Orenstein writes, "Many of us choose to bear this sorrow alone. Perhaps because we do not trust our neighbors and community with our most tender feelings. Perhaps because we fear political misuse of our mourning over a potential life that has not been carried to term. Perhaps because we fear what will happen if we dare to open the gates of our bulging reservoir of pain."[6]

Let us not be naïve. Not everyone who battles infertility gets to know fertility. While the success stories are widely available in books, magazines, online, and from friends, the reality is not so. However it is described—defeat, reframing, or plan B—it is never easy to accept a new reality and come to peace with it.

In *The Motherlode Blog,* Shelagh Little writes,

> Almost two years ago, I resolved to accept that I would never have children. I was 37 and had just learned my IVF procedure had failed. Our eight-year struggle with infertility included six rounds of artificial insemination, clomid pills, hormone injec-

tions, a surgery, and countless (and sometimes painful) diagnostic procedures. Every new test and treatment carried with it the hope that this time, it would work. What I had to show for it all: a picture of three sad little clumps of cells—the embryos that didn't implant—and no real explanation of why I couldn't get pregnant.

Every woman facing infertility has to decide when she's had enough, when she has reached her ethical, emotional, and/ or financial edge. My sense of self-efficacy dictated that if I researched all the options, sought support from the right professionals and followed their instructions, I'd get what I wanted. I did all of these things to the point of obsession, but our options were running out . . . my main reason for calling it quits was that I was tired of feeling frustrated and desperate. I needed to stop trying so I could get back to living.[7]

We get to choose our partners, if we choose to have one. That is a reality today. So too are the truths that couples who choose not to have children are still families and that an infertile individual is no less of a man or a woman.

The Levels of Loss

The losses related to the inability to experience a live birth can take many forms: the inability to become pregnant, challenges carrying a pregnancy to full term, miscarriage, and neonatal losses. In some cases it might be only one partner who struggles with infertility for medical reasons; low sperm count for a male or too few eggs remaining in the ova for a female are just two possibilities. For a heterosexual couple, this puts tremendous strain on their relationship as they start to navigate medical challenges, costs, issues of masculinity or femininity, and engaging with others who have what seems impossible, a pregnancy or a child. The infertile couple may go through the levels of loss identified by Dr. Elisabeth Kübler-Ross—denial, anger, bargaining, depression, and acceptance—or an entirely different process.

Infertility does not only affect the couple, of course, but also their grandparents, parents, siblings, aunts, uncles, and cousins, who do not know what to ask or say and also do not have an outlet for their own varied feelings. It is still not culturally acceptable in North America for these extended relatives to raise their feelings. Particularly amongst their own peer group when many others might be celebrating imminent birth and their new role as grandparent, aunt, or uncle, when these expected role additions do not take place there might be a lot of questioning and fear. It is never productive to walk on eggshells.[8]

Our Tradition Speaks

For all of our discomfort, our unease, in discussing fertility issues, our Torah is loaded with such stories. When I read the Genesis stories and use the lens of fertility, I imagine the Matriarchs and Patriarchs coping with infertility in varying ways. Abraham questions his own virility until Hagar, Sarah's maid-servant, becomes pregnant. Sarah, our matriarch, turns first to surrogacy before bearing a child later in life. Rebekah's sons struggle not only in *Parashat Tol'dot*, but in utero. And Rachel might have been on the IVF rollercoaster, if that existed in biblical times.

The theology of infertility is clear: "The Torah uses barren couples as a literary device to demonstrate the miraculous nature of the conception of the patriarchs and the beneficence of God."[9] A midrash asks the obvious question, Why do all of these Matriarchs struggle to conceive? Rabbi Levi answers: Because the Holy Blessed One desired their prayers (*Shir HaShirim Rabbah*, ch. 2, 14:8). In the Torah, there is only one solution to infertility: God intervenes directly with the childless when they cry out for help.

The Torah: A Women's Commentary reminds us of the theme of the barren wife throughout: tales of the Matriarchs and of the mothers of other heroes—including Rebekah, Rachel, Samson's unnamed mother, and Hannah. The motif implies that a boy born under such circumstances is truly sent by God, his mother's condition having received special attention by the Deity. In the Bible, reproductive problems typically concern women, whereas in other traditions either parent may be regarded as infertile.[10]

Abraham lamented his own lack of procreativity when he makes the *b'rit* with God. He cries out, "O Eternal God, what can You give me, seeing that I shall die childless, and the one in charge of my household is [my servant] Eliezer . . . Since You have granted me no offspring, my steward will be my heir" (Gen. 15:2–3). When God hears Abram's cry for offspring—remember, this is the first time we hear of Abram's desire for an heir—God sends Abram outside of his tent and promises that his offspring shall be as plentiful as the stars in the sky.

Sarai our foremother is infertile. Her own answer to her struggles is to use her maidservant, Hagar.

> Sarah said to Abraham, "Look, the Eternal has kept me from bearing. Consort with my maid; perhaps I shall have a son through her." And Abraham heeded Sarah's request. So Sarah, Abraham's wife, took her maid, Hagar the Egyptian . . . and gave her to her husband Abraham as concubine. He cohabited with Hagar and she conceived; and when she saw that she had conceived, her mistress was lowered in her esteem. (Gen. 16:1–4)

Sarah gives Abraham a child the only way she knows how, through surrogacy.

However, Hagar's pregnancy is not as easy. According to Rashi, Sarai's frustration about Hagar's pregnancy in Genesis 16:5 leads Hagar to miscarry her fetus.[11] Rashi comes to this conclusion because the word ביניך typically loses the second *yod*. The text is teaching us something by keeping the second *yod* in the word. Hagar had more than one pregnancy. Rashi explains that Sarai infused the pregnancy of Hagar with the evil eye causing a miscarriage. This may be why the angel says to Hagar in 16:11 that she will conceive, referring to a second pregnancy.

Rebekah our biblical mother, Isaac's beloved, is barren. Isaac "pleaded with the Eternal on behalf of his wife, because she was barren; and the Eternal responded to his plea, and his wife Rebekah conceived. But the children struggled in her womb" (Gen. 25:21–22). This, I believe, is an early reference to the difficulty of her pregnancy. In fact, it is the only mention in all of Torah to pregnancy at all. In every other instance a woman is pregnant, we learn of conception and birth immediately follows. Rebekah is bemoaning her physical pain. According to Ibn Ezra when Rebekah inquired of other women if they experienced such pains these women all said no.[12] I believe Rebekah's fear with this pregnancy is illustrative of the reality in one of five pregnancies: miscarriage.

What must it have been like for the biblical Rachel? She is the beloved wife of Jacob yet she is barren while her sister Leah has successful pregnancy after successful pregnancy. Anita Diamant describes in *The Red Tent* that "Rachel miscarried again and again . . . she no longer hated Leah with the full force of the past, Rachel could not smile at her sister while her own body remained fruitless . . . Rachel tried every remedy, every potion, every rumored cure. She wore only red and yellow—the colors of life's blood and the talisman for healthy menstruation . . . Whenever she saw running water, she lay down in it, hoping for the life of the river to inspire life within her."[13] When she complains to Jacob, he says to her, "Can I take the place of God, who has denied you fruit of the womb?" (Gen. 30:12). Rachel masks her own pain and sends her maidservant to lie with Jacob. Bilhah bears two children.

For the rabbis, it is a woman who teaches them what it means to open those gates. Hannah becomes a model for spontaneous prayer. And what inspires her? Her own fertility struggles. Though her husband loves her more than his other wife, the Eternal closed her womb, or so says the text. Hannah was completely distraught. During the annual pilgrimage to Shiloh she couldn't eat or drink of the sacred meal. "In her wretchedness, she prayed to the Eternal, weeping all the while. And she made this vow: Adonai Tz'vaot, if You will look upon the suffering of Your maidservant, and will remember me and not forget Your maidservant, and if You will grant Your maidservant a male child, I will dedicate him to the Eternal for all the days of his life" (I Sam. 1:10–11).

It isn't only God who takes note of Hannah. Eli the priest watched Hannah's mouth. Hannah's lips moved but he could hear no sound. Making his own assumptions, Eli takes Hannah for a drunkard. He called out to her, "How long will you make a drunken spectacle of yourself? Sober up!" (I Sam. 1:14). Hannah turns to the priest, the man of God, "Oh no, my lord! I am a very unhappy woman. I have drunk no wine or other strong drink, but I have been pouring out my heart to the Eternal. Do not take your maidservant for a worthless woman; I have only been speaking all this time out of my great anguish and distress" (I Sam. 1:15–16). Eli is impressed with Hannah. He begs her to go in peace and wishes her prayers be answered. She conceives and bears a son who becomes the prophet Samuel.

Suggestions for Clergy

It is my belief—and I learned from my own experience—that raising this issue in the context of a High Holy Day sermon was extremely important for allowing people to start a conversation. Numerous congregants approached me for spiritual counseling about how to live with their current situation or to begin to uncover feelings from many years prior. Together we studied these Genesis texts more closely.

In a different congregational setting and with support from a local Jewish family service organization, I might hold ongoing support groups.

As *m'sadrei kiddushin* (wedding officiants) engaged in premarital counseling, I believe it is our responsibility to include conversations about if, when, and how many children (and combining families if there are children from other relationships), testing for genetic diseases, and what options they might consider if they have trouble giving birth to the children they desire.

There are many books about this topic that are helpful resources to have on our rabbinic bookshelves as a welcoming visual symbol in our offices. There are pamphlets from organizations that address targeted issues such as "Mourning a Miscarriage" and "Jewish Adoption: Unique Issues, Practical Solutions." Sometimes we can start an unexpected conversation by having a book on our coffee table that sparks a congregant's interests.

In the past number of years creative rituals have been produced to honor these fertility transitions. Websites like ritualwell.org, sponsored by the Reconstructionist Rabbinical College, offer rituals and prayers authored by Jews for such transitions as a "Kaddish for the end of biological fertility," meditations for using the *mikveh* when dealing with infertility, and a healing ritual after a hysterectomy. *Lifecycles*, volumes 1 and 2, published by Jewish Lights Publications, also address some of these issues. An individual or couple grappling with infertility might appreciate working with a Jewish professional in developing a ritual that will speak to them.

In order to prepare ourselves for these conversations, we must be in touch with our own experiences, of course. It may not be reasonable for us to pastor our congregants if we are struggling with infertility in our own lives. When we do not have an option, it is appropriate to consult with a counselor or therapist for our own transference and counter-transference.

With the infertility statistics as they are, it is inevitable that as a pastoral presence we will encounter individuals and families grappling with infertility. Perhaps we must only look in the mirror. The knowledge of infertility's prevalence may not bring relief, however the knowledge that an individual or couple is not alone may bring comfort. The biblical stories that detail different experiences with infertility may provide entry into conversation, learning, and community at an isolating time. May our words and deeds bring comfort to those in the throes of infertility.

Notes

1. Nina Beth Cardin, *Tears of Sorrow, Seeds of Hope* (Woodstock, VT: Jewish Lights Publishing, 1999), 14.
2. Infertility Awareness Association of Canada, http://www.iaac.ca/content/world-health-organisation-recognises-infertility-disease (accessed August 19, 2010).
3. Peggy Orenstein, *Waiting for Daisy* (New York: Bloomsbury USA, 2007), Location 1042.
4. A new not-for-profit organization founded by our colleague Rabbi Martin Lawson's daughter-in-law works to provide financial assistance for those who cannot afford the high cost(s) of surrogacy, egg donation, and IVF. The foundation is seeking donations from individuals, institutions, and/or businesses to help those who wish to apply for grants in order to have a child. The more that the foundation receives, the more it will be able to help couples and individuals achieve their dreams of having children. For more information, please visit http://www.babyquestfoundation.org/.
5. Orenstein, *Waiting for Daisy*, Location 1000.
6. American Pregnancy Association, http://www.americanpregnancy.org/pregnancycomplications/miscarriage.html (accessed January 8, 2012).
7. Orenstein, *Waiting for Daisy*, Location 2000.
8. Shelagh Little, "Life After Infertility Treatments Fail," Motherlode Blog, *New York Times*, September 10, 2009.
9. I recommend the following volume as a helpful resource: Michael Gold, *And Hannah Wept: Infertility, Adoption and the Jewish Couple* (Philadelphia: Jewish Publication Society, 1994). For information on infertility in halachah, a summary is available in Elliot N. Dorff, *Matters of Life and Death: A Jewish Approach to Modern Medical Ethics* (Philadelphia: Jewish Publication Society, 1998).
10. Valerie Lieber, "Contemporary Reflections" to *Parashat Tol'dot*, in *The Torah: A Women's Commentary*, ed. Tamara C. Eskenazi and Andrea L. Weiss (New York: URJ Press, 2008), 152.
11. Eskenazi and Weiss, eds., *The Torah: A Women's Commentary*, 71.
12. See Rashi on וביניך ביני ... תי... נתתי אנכי.
13. My understanding of Ibn Ezra on Gen. 25:22.
14. Anita Diamant, *The Red Tent* (New York: Picador USA, 1997), 46–47.

Ruth, Naomi, and Levinas's Other: Asymmetrical Pastoral Care

Ruth Gais

I found Shem Nachum, the fifth reincarnation of the Most Royal King David, hunched over the pay telephone.[1] She had asked to talk to the rabbi and so I introduced myself. His Majesty was a large, handsome African American woman, dressed in baggy sweat pants and sweatshirt, a dirty white towel draped over her head. She wanted my help; could I help find her wife, Whitney Shilah Houston, who had just given birth to ten thousand babies and needed her? Somehow the two of them had been separated and Shem Nachum had set out to find her—a journey, via bus, taxi, and train, and on foot, that took her from a Bronx group home to Newark Airport, Lakewood, Bergen County, and finally to the state psychiatric hospital where I work. When I met her, Shem Nachum was lost, angry, desperate, and in mourning.

Naomi, like Shem Nachum, at one time had what she needed: a husband, two sons, two daughters-in-law, enough food to eat, and a place to live. Then, as the Book of Ruth recounts, in quick succession almost all of this disappeared: Her husband died, then her sons, and she and her Moabite daughters-in-law found themselves in a desperate situation. What kind of life could there be for three widows in their society? So Naomi, as did Shem Nachum, set out to return home, unsure what she would find there, grieving, angry, afraid. As she said, "Do not call me Naomi [pleasant], call me *Mara* [bitter] for Shaddai has made my lot very bitter. I went away full and have returned empty" (Ruth 1:20–21).[2] The *Targum* clarifies her bitterness: "I went away full with my husband and sons, but the Lord has brought me back with no one and nothing."[3]

RUTH GAIS, Ph.D. (NY00) is rabbi of Chavurat Lamdeinu, Madison, New Jersey, a board-certified chaplain, and ACPE supervisory candidate.

Both Shem Nachum and Naomi feel forsaken, alone, and in the wrong place. They feel alienated from their surroundings, strangers in a strange land, even if a psychiatric hospital is, alas, a familiar environment for Shem Nachum, and Bethlehem, Naomi's home. In their present emotional states, they are both foreigners. Their feelings of separation and confusion are too often the norm for patients in almost any clinical setting like a hospital or nursing home. And quite often, the care our patients receive increases rather than diminishes their loss of individuality, their loss of a sense of self. Shem Nachum, viewed through the too often dispassionate eyes of the clinician, is a paranoid, delusional schizophrenic of ambiguous sexuality to be medicated and eventually dispatched to a variety of treatment programs. Rarely is she seen as anyone of worth; she is the Other in the worst sense as is the "Pancreatic Cancer in Room 311, the Kidney Failure in 1007, the Heart Attack in 706," who are no longer seen as humans but as faceless diseases. The patients themselves are strangers in their new country of suffering and sadness, a land that they might not have ever known before.[4] Our understanding of the transformation of the human into object is now almost commonplace, primarily due to Martin Buber's major work, I and Thou, which sets forth in detail the important distinction between being with the Other in an I-It relationship and being with the Other in an I-Thou relationship. The Other in an I-It relationship is seen as different, strange, an object; there can be no possibility of real connection. It is not, however, just the patient in the strange world of suffering who feels disoriented and alone, this alienation can extend to the family member, the friend, the novice chaplain intern, to anyone who goes into a hospital room for the first time; almost everyone may feel like an intruder, an Other. As a result, we might very well ask why anyone who doesn't have to enter a hospital room would ever do so? The answer comes from the refrain heard so often in our Torah, "because we were strangers in a strange land." This ethical justification for how we treat another understands the suffering that being in an unfamiliar place engenders. By forcing us again and again to remember our suffering, by virtue of being aliens, our Torah teaches that we are commanded to prevent others from experiencing the same thing.

Understanding our shared history of being the Other can perhaps lead us towards an authentic I-Thou relationship in Buber's terms because we participate in a mutual moment of reciprocal understanding. The theological basis for the possibility of such a relationship is found in the concept of our being created *b'tzelem Elohim* (in the image of God) (Gen. 1:27). It is common to use this idea to take us to the comfortable if clichéd statement that although we may appear very different, underneath differences such as race, religion, education, economic status, gender, and more, we are all really alike. This apparent identity is what seems to allow us as pastoral caregivers to enter into empathic relationship even when the Other may seem so very different.[5] There is, however, as the Jewish French philosopher Emmanuel Levinas pointed out, a real problem with basing relationships on an underlying commonality: that is, if we decide that such a proposition is not valid, that we aren't alike after all, it therefore becomes very easy to abuse or demonize or despise the Other.[6] This problem was not merely an abstraction but very real for Levinas who was interned for years as a prisoner of war during World War II and lost many family members in the Shoah. Levinas's own suffering deeply influenced his life and his work.[7]

Levinas takes *b'tzelem Elohim* as a foundational text as well but for him being created in God's image does *not* lead to seeing us as all fundamentally alike. For Levinas, when we look at the Other we do not see ourselves, we see the Other and, as a result, we are forced out of our solitude into relationship. This change occurs because, for Levinas, in the moment of being with the Other, "the dimension of the divine opens forth from the human face."[8] The face of the Other does not reveal an image of God, we do not see God in the face of the other; what is revealed is a trace of the Infinite. Every encounter with another also includes a fleeting trace of the Infinite.[9]

As a result of this recognition of the trace of the Infinite, however momentary and fleeting it may be, we cannot turn away from the face of the Other; "trace is the sign of a hidden God who imposes the neighbor on me."[10] The imposition of the Other forces us to decide how to act towards the Other, in other words the face of the Other forces us towards ethics. Ethics, for Levinas, the first philosophy, because it does not rely on any similarity between one person and another, is based on our infinite responsibility to the Other.[11]

My infinite responsibility to the Other is what compels me to act ethically towards someone like Shem Nachum who sometimes

scares me, who is so different from me in so many ways. Sometimes, as I listen to Shem Nachum or Kurt, a provocative, fervent
Messianic Jew, always dressed in white, or Elizabeth, who is Jesus, I am afraid. Would one of them hurt me? Many of them are,
after all, paranoid or delusional, with past histories of violence.
And maybe they will hurt me because to them I am the Other?
Sometimes, though, as they look at me, a person who can come
and go as she pleases, who can unlock doors, who has power, I
can see that *they* are afraid—would I mock them, would I report
them, would I hurt them? According to Levinas, this question and
the unease it engenders, unspoken but palpable in the difficult environment of the psychiatric hospital, are always present at any
encounter between one person and another, no matter what the
circumstance—hospital, supermarket, at home, everywhere—and
force us to respond ethically. The face of the Other, Levinas tells
us, cries out for justice and commands us, "You shall not commit
murder." The face commands us towards ethical behavior.[12]

I may be scared of Shem Nachum—I cannot ever understand
how it is to be her—but I am compelled to treat her ethically. I do
not know how to describe our relationship;   I do know I have not
killed Shem Nachum. I believe that I respond empathically to her
suffering and in some way she knows this and does not fear me;
she confides in me and we pray together. I know that like so many
incarcerated people she talks to me in the hope that I can help free
her. Such knowledge on my part does not diminish my empathy
for her, but suppose it did and suppose that as a result I became
cold or angry.[13] If our relationship were based solely on my need to
sense reciprocal feelings of some sort, then Shem Nachum would
be in the very danger that Levinas feared when relationships are
predicated on commonality rather than difference.

What would save Shem Nachum's life is my understanding that
even though we are not alike, we are each Other to the other, and
that, precisely as a result of our otherness, the face commands me
to act ethically even if I dislike or fear that person. Even if I cannot enter into the Other's emotional world or the Other cannot enter mine, I must act ethically towards the Other—this is Levinas's
asymmetry of the ethical relation. As Putnam puts it, "the Levina-
sian *sine qua non* for entering the ethical life—which is to say, entering *human* life in any sense that is 'worthy of the name'—involves
recognizing that one is obliged to make oneself available to the

neediness of the other *without* simultaneously regarding the other as so obliged."[14] Levinas is very close to the Torah's often repeated injunction to take care of the widow, the stranger, and the orphan. As mentioned earlier, what drives us to act justly may come from ourselves, our empathic memory of being a stranger in a strange land, perhaps, but what is paramount and trumps feelings is ethics, even if, as Levinas suggests, our fundamental obligation to the other leads to an asymmetrical relationship.

And then there is Ruth, or rather, the Moabite Woman Ruth, whose name is rarely mentioned without the adjective "Moabite" except at the beginning and the end of the story. Ruth is every bit as much the Other as my patients. Naomi upon her return to Bethlehem is no longer recognizable to herself and to others as Naomi; she has become other to herself, she is Mara, she is not the person she was. Her suffering has named her much like the "Pneumonia in 412." She is Bitterness and Bitterness, eating herself alive in her pain, cannot recognize the suffering of another. Thus Naomi cannot empathize with Ruth or Orpah but can only invalidate their own great losses: "Oh no, my daughters! My lot is far more bitter than yours" (Ruth 1:13). Bitterness cannot respond to Ruth's famous and heartfelt words of loyalty; emptiness, paradoxically, has filled Naomi instead and she falls silent.[15]

When they arrive in Bethlehem, Ruth is invisible. The townspeople are interested only in Naomi.[16] Here, I would argue, we see the workings of Levinas's asymmetrical relationship and its effect on Ruth. Ruth has acted as Levinas insists we all must act towards the Other. The irony, of course, is that it is the quintessential Other, the Moabite Woman, whose exemplary behavior is exactly how the Torah commands the Israelites to act. Even as Naomi rejects Ruth, Ruth stays with her, does not abandon her but at the cost of her own sorrow; eventually her identity is diminished and devalued. As the story continues, Ruth's identity as Ruth continues to be compromised. She is called Ruth the Moabite six times. First as brides of Naomi's sons, Ruth and Orpah are called Moabite women, immediately introducing the uncomfortable topic of intermarriage in general and of a prohibited marriage in particular.[17] After Naomi and the invisible Ruth return to Bethlehem, the narrative pointedly tells us that Naomi returned with "her daughter-in-law Ruth the Moabite" (Ruth 1:22), designations that both include and exclude relationships.[18]

From this point until finally Ruth and Boaz are wed, Ruth's name is never simply "Ruth." She is always Ruth in relation to someone: Ruth the daughter-in-law or Ruth the Moabite,[19] Ruth the handmaid (Ruth 2:9), Ruth the stranger (Ruth 2:10). And once she is simply "Ruth," when she is married and her status changes, she disappears for good. After she gives birth she is honored as the redeemer and the daughter-in-law, valued for what she gives to others but not for herself, once again she is nameless. Naomi takes the child to her breast and becomes its foster mother, its *"omenet."* The women of Bethlehem once again ignore Ruth and name the child the child of Naomi. "The women who once welcomed Naomi and heard her lament of emptiness now 'intuit' the significance of this child in restoring Naomi to her former 'maternal self' . . . They recognize that it is Naomi and not Ruth who is fulfilled by the child's birth."[20] If this is the case, then it is Ruth who is now empty, her womb usurped together with her breasts and the milk they might have contained. Naomi kills Ruth.[21]

Levinas is well aware of the heavy burden our ethical responsibility to the Other may bring. In a poignant passage that cannot but remind us of Naomi's usurpation of Ruth's maternal identity, Levinas compares our infinite ethical responsibility to that of a foster parent's care of a child:

> In proximity, the absolutely Other, the stranger whom "I have neither conceived nor given birth to," I have already in my arms, already I bear him, according to the Biblical formula, "in my breast as the foster-father (*omen*) bears the sucking child." (*Num.* 11:12). He has no other place . . . without roots, without a fatherland, not an inhabitant, exposed to the cold and the heat of the seasons. Being reduced to or having recourse to me; this is the homelessness or strangeness of the neighbor. It falls upon me, makes me incumbent.[22]

If the story of Ruth were different, we could imagine Naomi as Ruth's *omenet*, not the foster mother of Ruth's child. Ruth as Other needed Naomi. Instead, Ruth made Naomi full and left herself empty. Ruth became the foster mother to Naomi, fulfilling her ethical obligation, but at a great price. There is a bleakness in the story of Ruth.[23] R. Zeira said, "The scroll [of Ruth] tells us nothing of purity or impurity, of prohibition or permission. For what purpose was it written? To teach how great is the reward of those who do deeds of kindness [*chasadim*]."[24] I would add that her story teaches more; it can be read as a cautionary tale of the asymmetry of our infinite responsibility to the Other. There is a danger in caring for the Other, the danger of sacrifice of self to Other. As a chaplain, I am always available to the Other and do not expect that the Other, often in crisis and suffering, is necessarily capable of fulfilling his or her obligation. There is not always a mutuality of obligation. Levinas's asymmetry of relation is the norm in pastoral care where the clergy person is in some sense a professional Other. As such, the chaplain or rabbi or family member or any other caretaker runs a grave risk of becoming empty of self by engaging in the maternity of ethics. I may urge family members to eat, to take care of themselves as they tend their beloved ill or begin to mourn their dead.[25] But I, neither a saint nor a martyr, though Levinas acknowledges the possibility of that happening,[26] need another Other, equally able to fulfill his/her obligation towards me, to nourish me from him/herself when I cannot. I am all too aware of the vulnerability of the Other, perhaps not enough aware of my own. My infinite obligation to Shem Nachum and all the others, like Ruth's to Naomi, can kill me, if I let it.

Notes

1. All names of patients are pseudonyms. I am grateful to Joy Ladin and Elizabeth Denlinger for discussing this topic with me. Thanks also to David Sperling for his comments on the dating of the Book of Ruth and the meaning of *chesed* and to Henry Resnick, always a valuable bibliographical resource.

2. Unless noted otherwise all Biblical translations are from the NJPS *Tanakh* (Philadelphia: Jewish Publication Society, 1999).

3. As quoted in Tamar Cohn Eskenazi and Tikva Frymer-Kensky, *The JPS Bible Commentary: Ruth* (Philadelphia: The Jewish Publication Society, 2011), 25.

4. See also two very personal and valuable accounts of the gaps between our perceptions of the "normal" and the sick or disabled: Lawrence A. Hoffman, "Post-Colonial Liturgy in the Land of Sick," *CCAR Journal* 53, no. 3 (Summer 2006): 10–35 and Harriet McBryde Johnson, *Too Late to Die Young* (New York: Henry Holt Publishing, 2005).

5. See Edith Stein's definition of "empathy" in her important 1916 doctoral dissertation, as "acts in which foreign experience is comprehended." Edith Stein, *On the Problem of Empathy*, trans. Waltraut Stein (Washington: ICS Publications, 1989), 6. Also significant is

Heinz Kohut's definition of "empathy" as "vicarious introspection" in "Introspection, Empathy and Psychoanalysis," *Journal of the American Psychoanalytic Association* 7 (1959): 459.

6. Hilary Putnam, "Levinas and Judaism," in *The Cambridge Companion to Levinas,* ed. S. Critchley and R. Bernasconi (Cambridge: Cambridge University Press, 2002), 35.

7. "[My life and career] were dominated by the presentiment and memory of the Nazi horror." Emmanuel Levinas, *Difficult Freedom,* trans. Sean Hand (Baltimore: The Johns Hopkins University Press, 1990), 291; Putnam, "Levinas and Judaism," 33–34.

8. Emmanuel Levinas, *Totality and Infinity*, trans. Alphonso Lingis (Pittsburgh: Duquesne University Press, 1969), 78.

9. Edith Wyschogrod, "Language and Alterity in the Thought of Levinas," in *The Cambridge Companion to Levinas,* ed. S. Critchley and R. Bernasconi (Cambridge: Cambridge University Press, 2002). Wyschogrod quotes Levinas, "To be in the image of God is not to be an icon of God but to find oneself in his trace." Ibid., 197.

10. Ibid., quoting Emmanuel Levinas, *Otherwise Than Being*, trans. Alphonso Lingis (Pittsburgh: Duquesne University Press, 1998), 94.

11. Putnam, "Levinas and Judaism," 43.

12. Levinas, *Totality and Infinity*, 199. According to Putnam, "Ethics can—and must—be based on a relation to people, but a relation which is totally free of narcissism and the further emphasis that to be free of narcissism one must respect the 'alterity' of the other, the other's manifold difference. My awareness of my ethical obligation must not depend on any 'gesture' of claiming (literally or figuratively) to 'comprehend the other.'" Putnam, "Levinas and Judaism," 55.

13. Levinas does not discuss "empathy" per se but does discuss the suffering of the Other as leading us towards our ethical obligation. See, for example, Michael L. Morgan, *The Cambridge Introduction to Emmanuel Levinas* (Cambridge: Cambridge University Press, 2011), 197: Morgan quotes Levinas, "That in the evil that pursues me the evil suffered by the other man afflicts me, that it touches me, as though from the first the other was calling to me, putting into question my resting on myself and my *conatus essendi*, as though before lamenting over my evil here below, I had to answer for the other . . . the horror of the evil that aims at me becomes horror over the evil in the other man."

14. Putnam, "Levinas and Judaism," 55.

15. Eskenazi and Frymer-Kensky, *Ruth*, 22, discuss some of the interpretations of Naomi's silence. See also Laurie Zoloth-Dorfman, "An Ethics of Encounter: Public Choices and Private Acts," in *Contemporary Jewish Ethics and Morality*, eds. E. N. Dorff and L. E. Newman (Oxford: Oxford University Press, 1995), 219–45, for a

different understanding of Naomi's behavior. Aviva Zornberg's important discussion of this issue in her chapter, "Law and Narrative in the Book of Ruth," in *The Murmuring Deep*: *Reflections on the Biblical Unconscious* (New York: Schocken, 2009), 344–79, on this point and others has influenced my own thinking. See most particularly 353–61.

16. Eskenazi and Frymer-Kensky, *Ruth,* 24.

17. Ibid., 7.

18. Ibid., 26. I disagree with the comment that "by recording that Naomi has returned with Ruth, the narrator reminds the reader that even though Naomi presents herself as empty, she is not alone." I would argue that by her silence, Levinas's withdrawal into the solitude of self, Naomi is alone, refusing to look at the face of the Other.

19. Ibid., 45. "All three times that the narrator refers to Ruth as a Moabite occur in connection with Naomi (1:22; 2:2, 22) . . . This may signal the extent to which Ruth's 'Moabiteness' colors Naomi's relation to her."

20. Ibid., 92.

21. Zornberg finds that the midrash that places Ruth enthroned at the side of her royal descendant Solomon "undermined the totality of closure . . . Solomon must know himself as seen by the woman, the ultimately unknown woman, whose gaze has been acknowledged with such difficulty." Zornberg, *The Murmuring Deep*, 377. I agree but wonder if this is sufficient recompense.

22. Levinas, *Otherwise Than Being*, 91. See Lisa Guenther's discussion of the ethics of maternity in "'Like a Maternal Body': Emmanuel Levinas and the Motherhood of Moses," *Hypatia* 21, no. 1 (Winter 2006): 119–35.

23. This bleakness may come from the date of composition, which I believe to be during the postexilic period. Ruth may be a subtle polemic against the disturbing xenophobia of the time. See Eskenazi and Frymer-Kensky, *Ruth,* xvi–xvii, and Moshe Weinfeld and S. David Sperling, *Encyclopaedia Judaica*, 2nd ed., s.v. "Ruth, Book of." In a telling parallel, Levinas developed his theories of ethical obligation during a time of intense anti-Semitism and xenophobia.

24. *Ruth Rabbah* 2.14. See "*Chesed,*" in G.J. Botterweck and H. Ringren, eds., *Theological Dictionary of the Old Testament*, vol. 5, trans. D.E. Green (Grand Rapids: W.B. Eerdmans Publishing, 1986), 44–64, for a comprehensive review of the term. A summary indicates three elements involved in the concept: *Chesed* is "active, social and enduring…*Chesed* always designates not just a human attitude but the act that emerges from this attitude. It is an act that preserves or promotes life. It is intervention on behalf of someone suffering misfortune and distress. It is a demonstration of friendship or

piety. It pursues what is good and not what is evil . . . The second element . . . is its social nature. There is always someone else to whom *chesed* is shown or from whom it is expected . . . the concept lies in the realm of interpersonal relations . . . The third element, the demonstration of kindness, is heard as a divine requirement. It thus becomes extended to the sphere of humanity as a whole and becomes a mark of faith . . . kindness frequently intends mutuality." Botterweck and Ringren, eds., "*Chesed*," 51–52. See also Eskenazi and Frymer-Kensky, *Ruth*, xlviii–l.

25. See Levinas, "Judaism and the Feminine," in *Difficult Freedom*, 30–38; Susan Schept, "Feminist Ethics in Jewish Tradition," *Conservative Judaism*, 57, no. 1 (Fall 2004): 21–29; Claire Elise Katz, "Ruth: or Love and the Ethics of Fecundity," in *Levinas, Judaism and the Feminine* (Bloomington: Indiana University Press, 2003), 78–96.

26. See Guenther, "'Like a Maternal Body,'" 121.

On Illness

Douglas Kohn

Introduction: Origin of Illness

How has Jewish tradition regarded illness, itself? As the academic field of Jewish healing advances and definitions in the field are established, illness qua illness is often overlooked in a healing-centered religious perspective, and illness, itself, needs to be reconsidered in order to better understand healing and Jewish healing endeavors. It is hoped that with a better Jewish understanding of illness, we will then more ably introduce illness into discussions of Jewish healing and health.

Jewish tradition addresses the very nature of illness, itself, albeit perhaps tangentially. In a rich and fascinating discussion, *Midrash B'reishit Rabbah* raises the existential, ethical origin of illness, itself. Reflecting on Jacob's aged infirmity near the close of the Book of Genesis, the midrash describes the sources of old age, suffering, illness, and chronic illness, accounting each condition to the various needs of the elderly Patriarchs and a king of Judah (*B'reishit Rabbah* 97, *Va-y'chi*).[1] Abraham sought old age to differentiate himself from his youthful son; Isaac demanded suffering to justify his cause before eternity; and Jacob needed illness to impel him to tidy matters with his sons. According to the midrash:

> Jacob demanded illness, saying to God: "Sovereign of the Universe! A man dies without previous illness and does not settle his affairs with his children; but if he were two or three days ill, he would settle his affairs with his children." "By thy life," replied God, "Thou hast asked well, and it will commence with thee." "And one said to Joseph: behold, thy father is sick." (Gen. 48:1). Rabbi Levi said: Thus Abraham introduced old age, Isaac suffering, and Jacob illness.

DOUGLAS KOHN (C87) is rabbi of Southern California's oldest synagogue, Congregation Emanu El in Redlands. He is the editor of *Life, Faith, and Cancer* (URJ Press, 2008) and *Broken Fragments: Jewish Experiences of Alzheimer's Disease* (URJ Press, 2012).

The midrash therefore offers a handy, humanistic answer to the lofty questions of when and why illness entered the world. It began with Jacob. Illness, it teaches, is a functional apparatus to alert the human being to his or her frailty, to compel the person to arrange one's affairs before imminent death. Illness, it neatly suggests, did not exist before chapter 48 of Genesis and only entered the world when Jacob needed a timely reminder of his mortality. Illness, therefore, is not a normal, ongoing, and regular condition of life, but is a singular, checkered flag at old age that signals the end of the race.

The midrash, however, was not content with that answer. Regarding Abraham's old age and Isaac's suffering, the midrash was satisfied. But, illness bore a different, intrinsic quality: After all, a person does not overcome old age, and suffering often remains a trusty companion throughout a lifetime. But one might be fortunate to be healed from one's affliction; illness might be surmounted. Thus, the midrash continued:

> Hezekiah brought in a new thing—repeated illness. "Sovereign of the Universe!" he pleaded. "Thou hast kept man in good health until the day of his death! But if a man fell sick and recovered, fell sick and recovered, he would fully repent." Said God to him: "By thy life! Thou hast asked well, and with thee it will commence." Thus it is written, "The writing of Hezekiah king of Judah, when he had been sick, and was recovered of his sickness." (Isaiah 38:9) Rabbi Samuel ben Nachman observed: This intimates that between one sickness and another he had an illness more severe than both.

The midrash wrestles with recurring illness. What, it asks, would justify a person becoming ill repeatedly and successively recovering? Rabbi Samuel's final comment is dramatically instructive. He offers not a theological summation, such as illness is relative to repentance and misdeeds, or is divine punishment for transgressions, but rather he presents a purely observational, almost scientific comment: Illness was normal, recurrent, and existent. It was part of the human condition—the king's condition—and now it needed to be understood.

A review of classic texts and modern volumes addressing Judaism and health issues reveals much discussion of halachic instructions and ethical values attendant to healing, prevention of sickness, and maintaining general and specific wellness. Lacking, however, is a discussion of, and even a definition of illness, itself. In contrast, contemporary conventional Western medicine is largely disease-centered; fields of medicine and professional medical specialties focus on specific disease families: cardiology—heart disease, oncology—malignancies, and so on. The disease precedes healing, and healing is predicated on a definition and an understanding of the disease. In Jewish thinking, however, is illness, itself, an existentially independent condition or entity, as it is in conventional, sometimes termed allopathic medicine, as in a bacterial disease? Or is illness considered to be a variant condition commonly recognized in contrast to a general, normative state of wellness? In Jewish thought, is there a fundamental state of wellness from which illness deviates? Or is illness an ethical condition, a divine punishment for misdeed?

Illness from God: Biblical Understanding

Although present medical and Jewish thinking has advanced significantly since the biblical period, we find basic Jewish themes in the Bible's posture towards illness. In Exodus and Deuteronomy, illness is a divine tool wielded as punishment inflicted on the Egyptians and threatened as punitive recourse when Israel might stray from God's commandments (Exod. 15:26, 23:25; Deut. 7:15, 28:59, 61). Illness also is represented as a metaphor for suffering in the Book of Isaiah, in the famous "suffering servant" vignette of Isaiah 53 and in the poetic imagery of the prophet Hosea (Isa. 53:3, 10; Hosea 5:13).

But, most commonly, illness is a condition delivered by God as a quid pro quo punishment for transgressions. The Book of Kings describes Elisha ministering to a vicious king of Aram who was ill and who had implored the prophet to inquire of God if he would recover from his illness (II Kings 8:7-15). Similarly, in the Book of Kings, the illness of Abijah, the son of Jeroboam, is attributed to Jeroboam's evil ways (I Kings 14:1–14). The famous incident of Elijah laying over a stricken child and pleading, "O LORD my God, will You bring calamity upon this widow whose guest I am, and let her son die?" concludes with God hearing Elijah's cry and restoring breath to the lifeless boy. The illness of King Hezekiah, referenced in the *Midrash Rabbah* citation, above, is most striking. Isaiah came to the stricken king and said to him, "Thus said the LORD: set your affairs in order, for you are going to die; you will not get well." Thereafter, Hezekiah prayed to God, and wept profusely. Isaiah then returned to the king and reported, "Thus said the LORD, the God of your father David: I have heard your prayer, I have seen your tears. I am going to heal you" (II Kings 20:1–5). In each of these episodes, illness is neither existential nor a medical condition as we understand it today, but is a mechanism of God to mete out justice upon the deserving. Moreover, illness is not its own, defined condition, independent of the bearer's character, but is the punishment condition preceding dying and death. Only most infrequently is an illness described medically. (In I Kings 15:23, King Asa has a "foot ailment," and in II Chronicles 21:15–19, Jehoram suffers "disorders of the bowels.")

Similarly, the treatment of leprosy and other skin ailments in the Books of Leviticus and Numbers portrays the illness as punishment. The afflicted one, after presenting himself to the priest and undergoing sequestration, and ultimately being determined clean and ready for readmission to the camp, was compelled to bring sacrificial offerings, including a guilt offering, thus implying that some wrongdoing would underlie the illness. The case of Miriam's sudden affliction with leprosy—"she was white as snow" (Num. 12:10)—has been widely interpreted as a penalty for her having spoken slanderously about her brother, Moses. The sixteenth century Italian Torah commentator Ovadia Sforno would write, "This disease is a kind of punishment, designed to prompt the victim to repentance, as it is said (Job 36:10) 'He opens also their ear to discipline, and commands that they return from iniquity.'"

Illness, therefore, was not an independent, biological condition, but rather was an ethical condition wrought as a punitive instrument of God. Until later knowledge and science would open new vistas in approaches to illness, such was a reasonable and effective explanation for malady. A germ, DNA, or a virus was still invisible to the human eye, and therefore still unknowable; and, though God was just as invisible, it was however a plausible rationale for illness because God, or God's law, was deemed knowable, as it was revealed in the Torah. Illness could not be independently existent when it remained inseparable from God. Moreover, to indeed separate illness from God—to isolate that which took life from that which created life—was essentially a violent heresy, as it demanded that one posit another independent power—nature or biology—that stood equally in contrast with the power at the source of life. Recognizing illness, therefore, would require a radical new understanding that admitted limits in at least this category of theological thinking. In the biblical text, illness was a category of theodicy; God used illness as a powerful tool. Once illness became independently recognized, as would begin to occur in medieval writings, it unwittingly but essentially limited God's hand, and conversely began to elevate the human hand and that of the physician.

Rabbinic and Later Literature: Illness in the Hand of the Healer

If illness remained in the province of God, what then was the need of doctors, medicine, and healing? In the Rabbinic period, Talmud clearly assigned to the healer the privilege to heal. The Talmudic Sages employed the verses Deuteronomy 22:2, "You shall restore the lost property to him," and Leviticus 19:16, "*Lo taamod*—Do not stand idly by your neighbor's blood," as mandates to the physician to heal. Moreover, a scholar, and by extension, any Jew, was prohibited from living in a city that lacked a physician (BT *Sanhedrin* 17b). Illness, therefore, stood in opposition to the desired healthy human condition, and humans were charged to ameliorate that condition. Thus the art of healing challenged a divine authority for illness; it was reassigned to the human domain.[2]

Rashi, the eleventh century sage, offered a commentary to the biblical verse in Exodus that details damages to be paid when two men fight, and one is injured and thereafter mended of his injuries. Rashi, in his commentary to the Torah text (Exod. 21:19), indicates that he agrees with the Targum's rendering, namely, that "he [the responsible party] shall pay the fee of the physician." However, commenting on the same verse further in the Talmud (BT *Bava Kama* 85a), Rashi goes radically further, "implying that permission has been granted the physician to heal." Rashi subsequently charges that "We are not to say, 'How is it that God smites and man heals?'" Clearly, by Rashi's day, the causal relationship between illness and God was fully suspect; illness needed a new definition. That a man could heal illness implied either that God had approved consigning a special category of powers to human beings—of healing those whom God had made sick—or that illness was not really reserved to God's domain, but it existed autonomously in the natural or human province, and had been misunderstood previously to be a divine instrument. The source and nature of illness, then, became a fulcrum that teetered theology: that humans could control sickness poked holes in God's omnipotence and in God's instrumentality.

Jewish philosophers and medical ethicists have long wrestled with this issue, asking if God generates illness, then by what right would human physicians be permitted to heal? Wouldn't they thereby be tampering with divine dictates, or worse, impugning or indicting God? Commonly, their answers ignored the ontogeny of illness and rather were founded in the Torah's ethics, not only as Leviticus taught in the command, "Do not stand idly by your neighbor's blood," but also "Love your neighbor as yourself" (Lev. 19:16, 18).[3] Interpretation of these verses provided the *hechsher* to the physician to intervene therapeutically. Thus, one could treat the ill or the injured person as the fulfillment of a commandment, irrespective of the origin of the affliction. Once physicians began to ponder illness, improve their skills, and initiate early scientific inquiry into causes and possibilities of illness outside of God's hand, the genie was let out of the bottle. Thus, as physicians and medical artistry advanced, illness, disease, and injury were categorically removed from God's bucket of tricks and were rendered independent and existent. Indeed, as Rashi suggested, it already was on that trajectory by the early medieval period.

In the Rambam's View

In Rambam's brilliant *Regimen of Health* (1202), written to the Sultan Al-Malik Al-Afdhal, the eldest son of Saladin the Great,[4] and considered the Rambam's most renowned medical writing, Maimonides firstly offers a prescription for the Sultan's digestive disorders and then proceeds to outline the philosopher/physician's general understanding of a healthy life protocol. He presents a summary of medical procedures to be followed in the absence of a physician, and thereafter presents his description of a healthy mind and body and a synopsis of prescriptions for a variety of health conditions and ailments.[5] Consistent throughout his booklet, Rambam systematizes symptoms and illness phylogenetically, like a modern biologist, progressing from type of malady to type of malady and to corresponding remedies. What is notably absent in his writing, however, is an attribution of illness to God. Rather, to Maimonides illness is either resultant of human behavior, such as overeating, or was implanted in one's body from its beginning (surprisingly suggesting a modern genomic origin of illness; see also *Sefer Mada* 4:2). As well, Rambam recognized an intrinsic relationship of health and illness—that illness was a deviation from the standard and proper healthy human condition, and that management of illness would result in a return to that condition of health:

> The practice of medicine comprises three regimens: The first and most distinguished is the regimen for the healthy and that is the regimen of the existing state of health so that it is not lost. The second is the regimen for the sick and that is the following of the physician's advice and its implementation to restore the lost health. This is known as medical advice. The third is the regimen which Galen calls vivification which is the regimen for someone who is not totally healthy but who is also not ill.[6]

For the Rambam, illness is thoroughly independent of God and is a condition begging human intercession. It is plainly a deviation from the regular, healthy course of life, as the body was naturally inclined to follow. Illness is not to be endured; rather, it is to be cured. Moreover, it is to be classified and studied, and treated scientifically, with symptomatic study, empirical review, and repeatable, remedial results. Rambam, therefore, despite using what we might deem primitive treatment formulae, was thoroughly modern in his outlook and understood medicine and illness in a modern, conventional perspective, both homeopathically and allopathically; illness was the opposition to be defeated by the physician's art.

Contemporary Literature: Ambiguity

It is fascinating, then, to see a seeming regression or anachronistic reversion in the medical approach of many people in our present day. In 1981, Rabbi Harold Kushner published his landmark bestseller, *When Bad Things Happen to Good People*, written following the premature death of his son, Aaron, to progeria. In his book, Kushner proffered the seemingly radical idea that bad things—accidents, misfortune, illness—happened randomly, essentially that God was not in control of the allocation of "bad things":

> Can you accept the idea that some things happen for no reason, that there is randomness in the universe . . . Residual chaos, chance and mischance, things happening for no reason, will continue to be with us . . . In that case we will simply have to learn to live with it, sustained and comforted by the knowledge that the earthquake and the accident, like the murder and the robbery, are not the will of God, but represent that aspect of reality which stands independent of His will, and which angers and saddens God even as it angers and saddens us.[7]

Kushnerian randomness, therefore, presupposed an independent operating system that should seem self-evident to moderns who customarily doubt the personal involvement of God in daily affairs. Yet Kushner's book was written precisely because so many modern, learned, intelligent people still held tenaciously to pre-Maimonidean concepts of illness, indeed, biblical notions that illness was divinely meted-out for some unfathomable reasons. They asked, "Why me?" and sought answers from God. Unexplainable illness and loss, such as the death of Rabbi Kushner's son, could be explainable and even acceptable if one believed that God had decreed it for a reason, even an unknowable reason. In 1981 many of Kushner's readers likely still held that viewpoint, harboring a teleological and even theological approach to illness, despite protestations of a rational modernity. In Kushner's system they sought a comforting reinterpretation of the source of illness in order to counter those ideas and to empower them to live with their own misfortunes and diagnoses of illness. The great success of Kushner's book testifies to the endurance of the biblical, teleological concept of illness, and it suggests that even the most erudite and learned person today may still entertain the notion, that when facing disease, perhaps there is a (divine) reason for their illness. In my book *Life, Faith, and Cancer,*[8] a number of the contributors, thoughtful Jewish clergy, pondered the premise that perhaps God had afflicted them with their cancer, and I devoted an entire chapter to wrestling with the question, "Why me?"

A review of recent literature addressing Jewish perspectives on illness and healing reveals that questions of the nature of illness are rarely considered. Illness is either ignored or avoided, or it is addressed tangentially or relegated to the side as a mystery. In one recent book, Rabbi Kerry Olitzky, who has written widely on this and other allied themes, wrote: "There are those who understand illness as punishment for one's sins. Others see illness as a mystery, one that, like God, is beyond human comprehension. Illness just seems to be a part of life's process, an inevitable part of living. We move between sickness and health throughout our lives."[9] Olitzky is absolutely correct. Yet he fails to clearly and helpfully define illness for his reader. It is left vague; it is not the focus of his inquiry. Rather, his concern, as is the concern of most contemporary volumes in the field of Judaism and healing, is to address the spirituality of healing, to which illness, itself, is a sidelight. Similarly, Rabbi Joseph Meszler, in his new book, *Facing Illness, Finding God*, offers no other explanation of illness than it is "when something in our bodies or minds deviates from being normal,"[10] which would be quite accurate, and then proceeds to offer many vignettes and rich support to aid those facing illness.

No wonder that before Kushner's book, readers had naturally and readily embraced a biblical teleology of illness—that disease continues to emanate from divine decrees—which Rabbi Kushner sought to dispel with his explanation of randomness. There is sorely lacking an alternative and acceptable religious understanding of illness that satisfies the contemporary mind and the hurting, yearning heart. Oddly, Maimonides' understanding of the existent nature of illness as a deviation from the normative condition of healthiness, and often evolving from our own behavioral imbalance, offers greater explanation than do most contemporaneous volumes on the subject. It is easier, if not necessary, to consign illness to the sidelines if one is to seek spiritual power to transcend it.

A Hebrew Definition: A New Jewish Reframing of Illness and Health

Language is more than merely symbols and sounds that represent ideas, things, and events. Language and philology also are invested with an intrinsic philosophy or theology, the world view of a language's civilization. The most common Hebrew word for "illness" is *choleh*, with its synonyms *machalah* and *choli*.[11] Each is derived from the Hebrew root *chet-lamed-hei*, which is related to the word *chol* (*chet-lamed*), commonly translated as "profane," "common," or "regular." *Chol* is familiarly used to characterize a regular or profane day, as opposed to a sacred or Shabbat day. In the closing blessing of the *Havdalah* service marking the end of Shabbat, one praises God for distinguishing *bein kodesh l'chol*—between the sacred and the profane. The linkage of the two words for "illness" and "regular"/"profane" offers the opportunity to recontextualize the idea of illness in Jewish thinking via the parallelism: Illness is to health as profane is to Shabbat. Illness is the base, common, or profane version of the body's natural condition of health, as Maimonides also taught, while health is the ideal, the Shabbat. Continuing the Shabbat and *Havdalah* metaphor, it is interesting that the *chol* condition is six of the week's seven days.

Illness, or *choleh*, is also known through its Hebrew opposite or corollary: health, in Hebrew, is *b'riah* or *b'riut*, which is derived from the same Hebrew word for creation and creating, *boreh* (*bet-reish-hei*). Thus, health is the original, sacred condition hearkening to when the body and the human being were created, or from that pristine, first chapter of Genesis, whereas illness is the condition that follows once an improper condition is introduced to the perfectly created body, causing it to deviate from the condition of health. Furthermore, richly implicit in the two Hebrew words for illness and health is a variant Genesis theology from that seen in the other biblical texts, above: namely, that the juxtaposition of health and illness is rooted in the concept of a pure and perfect creation as reflected in the first chapter of Genesis. Humans, in their healthy state of creation, are created in God's image (Gen. 1:26). The state of illness, therefore, is the contrast, the imperfect state. And the process of healing or health is the endeavor to return from the profane or base state back to that which is akin to the state of health in creation.

Understanding of illness in Jewish thinking can be articulated. Following a midrashic discussion of the origin of illness, the common biblical understanding of illness as punishment for transgressions dissolved firstly with Rabbinic empowerment of physicians, which reassigned illness to the human and not the divine domain, and later with greater understanding of illness gained by physicians in the medieval period. The Rambam clearly identified illness as a deviation from the natural condition of healthiness, which he argued was the natural balance of the human being. Today, despite some who persistently hold to the idea that illness is God's doing, the conventional Western medical perspective of illness as pathogenic or genetic disease is normative. Yet, for most Jews, a Jewish definition or understanding of illness, itself, is usually left to the sidelines.

However, throughout the eras and the various Jewish theologies of illness, the Hebrew language offers a profound understanding of illness—and of health. Illness is *chol*; health is *b'riah*. Illness is the human in a base or common condition; health is the human in the ideal condition established from creation.

Health is the condition associated with sacredness and God's intention for human living; illness is the experience of life when life is other than perfect. Health is the ideal; but illness, oddly and counterintuitively, is the real, the regular, the *chol*.

Notes

1. The midrash also appears in a varied form in BT *Bava M'tzia* 87a.
2. See Elliot N. Dorff, *Matters of Life and Death* (Philadelphia: Jewish Publication Society, 2003), ch. 2.
3. See also works on Jewish medical ethics by J. David Bleich, Fred Rosner, Moshe Tendler, Immanuel Jakobovits, and Elliot Dorff, as well as Maimonides, *Mishneh Torah, Hilchot N'darim* 6:8, *Shulchan Aruch Yoreh Dei-ah* 336:1
4. Al-Malik Al-Afdhal (c. 1169–1225) "was a frivolous and pleasure-seeking man of thirty, subject to fits of melancholy or depression due to his excessive indulgences in wine and women, and his warlike adventures against his own relatives and in the Crusades. He complained to his physician of constipation, dejection, bad thoughts and indigestion." See Maimonides, *Medical Writings: Three Treatises on Health*, trans. Fred Rosner (Haifa: The Maimonides Research Institute, 1990), 10, 19, 31.
5. Maimonides, *Medical Writings.*
6. Ibid., 40 (*Regimen of Health*, 2:1).
7. Harold S. Kushner, *When Bad Things Happen to Good People* (New York: Schocken Books, 1981), 46, 55.
8. Douglas Kohn, ed., *Life, Faith, and Cancer* (New York: URJ Press, 2008).
9. Kerry Olitzky, *Jewish Paths toward Healing and Wholeness: A Personal Guide to Dealing with Suffering* (Woodstock, VT: Jewish Lights Publishing, 2000), 24.
10. Joseph Meszler, *Facing Illness, Finding God* (Woodstock, VT: Jewish Lights, 2010), 3.
11. See also article by David Zucker, "The Chaplain's Gift: The Present of Presence," *The Jewish Chaplain* [NAJC Journal] 4, no. 1 (Spring 1999): 22–23, in which he offered a homiletic recasting of *choleh* as being in a difficult place.

P'tach Libi B'Toratecha
(Open My Heart to Your Torah):
Jewish Pastoral Theology
in Process

Barbara E. Breitman, Mychal B. Springer,
and Nancy H. Wiener

Now you must go out into your heart
as onto a vast plain . . .

Be modest now, like a thing
ripened until it is real,
so that he who began it all
can feel you when he reaches for you.
                —Rainer Maria Rilke, *Book of Hours*, II, 1

We live at a moment when postmodern science is discovering what mystics and poets have intuited for centuries: the radical interconnectedness of all life. Relationship is not what forms between separate beings. Interrelatedness *is* the fundamental nature of reality. "It is the source of our mutual vulnerability and our fondest community."[1] It does not seem to be a reality, however, that is easily perceived. Attentiveness, openness, and receptivity

---

BARBARA E. BREITMAN (GTF, D.Min. 2006, U of Penn MSW 1978, LCSW) is assistant professor of Pastoral Care and director of training, Spiritual Direction Program at the Reconstructionist Rabbinical College in Wyncote, PA.

RABBI MYCHAL B. SPRINGER (JTS92) is associate dean and director of Field Education of the Rabbinical School at the Jewish Theological Seminary, where she holds the Helen Fried Kirshblum Goldstein Chair in Professional and Pastoral Skills.

RABBI NANCY H. WIENER (NY90) is the director of the Blaustein Center for Pastoral Counseling and the Dr. Paul and Trudy Steinberg Distinguished Professor in Human Relations at the New York campus of HUC-JIR.

are necessary, as well as a shift in focus from things to processes, from individuals to relationships; it requires practice. Attunement and empathy,[2] capacities that can be cultivated, enable us to participate knowingly in the web of interrelatedness and to sense its inherent sanctity.

Pastoral caregivers, who practice attunement, experience the transformative potential at the heart of relationship and call it holy. The mystery is that in the context of pastoral encounters, we have access to a form of relationship that has a reality, almost solidity, not accessible through abstraction or the primarily intellectual engagement that has long been the medium for creating theology. Whatever we say about God emerges from the torah we learn companioning people through times when life is most palpably uncertain and precious—birth and death, illness and healing, coming of age and partnering, grief and loss, alienation and atonement, reconciliation and celebration. While we enter regularly into theological reflection[3] on such relationships, we have barely begun to contribute to the broader field of contemporary Jewish theology. As pastoral educators interested in probing the theological dynamics of pastoral relationships and contributing to the emerging field of Jewish pastoral theology, we gathered a small group of students for an exploratory seminar. This article describes our process and reflections.

Methodology

In January 2011, we offered a two-day seminar, inviting one student from each of our seminaries, JTS, HUC-JIR, and RRC, to participate. Our primary "texts" were the verbatims of encounters between students and the people they served as chaplain and spiritual caregiver[4] in three settings: an ex-urban synagogue, the surgical intensive care unit (SICU) of an urban hospital, and a soup kitchen for homeless Jews and at-risk Jewish elders. Unlike other verbatim-focused classes we offer in our seminaries, we did not focus on skill building. We sought to unearth some of the religious and theological dynamics that are at play in pastoral interactions and to make connections to the text, myth, metaphor, ritual, and liturgy of Jewish tradition.

We worked in an improvisational, intuitive, embodied way, reenacting pastoral encounters psycho-dramatically as well as discussing verbatims reflectively. We were as interested in how students were changed through pastoral relationships as we were in how patients and congregants were changed. We sought to explore how creative process might bring forth theology. We noticed that theology is ever-evolving, resulting from the interplay between caregiver and care-receiver and the mutual becoming they experience. We observed, however, that the awareness of becoming is not always apparent, upon first reflection, by those involved in a pastoral encounter. As we focused on particular moments, some consciously recalled and others unconsciously held by the presenter, we experienced how a group's dynamic process helped students identify transformative dimensions of interaction hitherto unacknowledged and gave rise to new theological possibilities. This midrashic—nonlinear, improvisational process—felt organically Jewish as we moved associatively not between traditional texts, but between the torah of peoples' lives and Torah, as well as the broader metaphoric and mythic system of Judaism. After the two-day seminar, the authors continued our conversation, expanding on insights that arose in the group.

As has been the tradition in the field of pastoral care, we chose to work from life to text, rather than from text to life.[5] We believe that each pastoral encounter has the possibility of achieving the kind of learning Franz Rosenzweig described at the opening of Lehrhaus:

> A new "learning" is about to be born—rather, it has been born. It is a learning in reverse order—a learning that no longer starts from the Torah and leads into life, but the other way round: from life . . . back to the Torah.[6]

As pastoral educators, we bring a unique set of questions to this "new learning": How do we help students cultivate attunement, presence, and receptivity? How do we support students to enter pastoral relationships ready to hear and learn Torah from others, not only to "confer" the wisdom of Torah? How do we encourage students to open up to being transformed personally and theologically through pastoral relationships? How do we support students to discern the ways healing transformation has or has not occurred? How do we encourage students to notice the sometimes paradoxical ways they are becoming a person they aspire to be, but doubted they could become? How can we help students appreciate the mystery and power of encounters that can move a caregiver and care-receiver from an initial stance of *p'tach libi b'toratecha* to a relationship through which a living, evolving experience and understanding of the Holy can emerge? How can our students draw forth new torah and find Jewish language to express the theological insights that these lived experiences inspire? We believe, as expressed by process theologian Catherine Keller, that "because we are who we are only in our open-ended processes of interaction, we require a radically relational theology."[7]

Student Pastoral Encounters

Although we did not select verbatims with any predetermined focus, a common theme emerged from the student narratives: companioning people as they encountered grief, illness, death, or traumatic loss. It is not remarkable that this focus emerged. These are times when pastoral caregivers are on the front lines as comforters and companions. What was notable was the correlation between the degree of attunement within a pastoral relationship and whether or how we perceived God's presence in the encounter. In Hebrew, the word for musical "attunement," tuning one's voice or instrument to vibrate with everyone else's, uses the same root as *kavanah* (intention). In pastoral care, as in music and prayer, intentionality directs the heart and enhances sacred connectivity.

The Accompanist

The first encounter involved a student inexperienced in offering pastoral care. On a monthly basis, he traveled from his seminary to a congregation that once had three hundred families in a small city geographically isolated from any center of significant Jewish population. During prayer services, the "choir" (comprised of a pianist and her husband) chose to sit behind a partition, hidden from the congregation and rabbi. Though the synagogue could afford to buy copies of the movement's more recent prayer book, they chose an earlier iteration.

As we reflected on the verbatim, we were struck by how pervasive were images of distance and disconnection: the isolation of the community; the distance the student traveled; long stretches of time between rabbinic visits; the choir behind a partition, anachronistically clinging to an era when an invisible "angelic chorus" echoed through a sanctuary filled with people; the use of an out-dated siddur. Trying desperately to maintain integrity and identity, this was an aged community trying to hold onto a distant past.

We thought of God blessing the people Israel to be as numerous as the stars in heaven. We asked, "What does it mean for these people to be a remnant, *shayareet Yisrael*?" We imagined them asking, "If we have no future, did we have no merit in the past? And if we had merit, why won't we have a future?" How does the pastoral caregiver respond to the immediate losses of elder congregants in a context already pervaded by loss and yearning for God's involvement in their declining years?

The verbatim told of the death of the congregant-pianist's brother. Lois had traveled a significant distance to her brother's funeral. She did so without pastoral accompaniment, as it was not the student's responsibility to attend a relative's out-of-state funeral. The verbatim encounter occurred just prior to *Kabbalat Shabbat* on the evening the pianist and her husband returned. With an earnest and "desperate" desire to help, the student tried to offer wisdom from the tradition to his bereaved congregants:

Lois1: It's good to be getting back into routine.

Student Rabbi1: (*Okay, here we go. I've been thinking about and preparing for this conversation for a week. I'm anxious to see "how I do," and I hope to provide some comfort to Lois after the loss of her brother.*) That's very normal. Many people find it helpful to start getting back to normalcy after shivah. But, of course, it will come in stages—it won't all come at once.

L2: I know. It's very hard. [*tells me about her brother's prolonged illness*] He's at peace now. He can rest.

SR2: Yes. (*She is obviously sad, but I don't think she's having a "theological crisis." I don't know what, exactly, she "needs" from me, but I desperately want to provide it. If nothing else, though, I remind myself that simply being there with her can be helpful. I mightily hope that I'm as comforting as I'm trying to be. I'm putting on my best "non-anxious presence" face.*)

L3: I believe he's in heaven now. I know that Judaism doesn't believe in heaven, but I do. I always have. (*I sense transference here—not directed at me, but directed at her tradition. I'm afraid that she feels isolated or like a "bad Jew" for believing in heaven. I want to tell her that her beliefs are not only true but also kosher.*) Ed didn't believe—he thought that the end of life is just turning into dust. But when I was with him, I told him that I knew he was going to heaven. He didn't think so, but I told him that he was. He said [*laughing*], "Well, I hope so!" [*I join in the laughter.*] [*Lois pauses, looking at her music stand. She looks sad.*]

SR3: (*This is my moment!*) You know, actually, there are many Jewish traditions that *do* believe in heaven. There are a lot of writings about the afterlife and the world to come.

L4: [*looking relieved*] I thought I read something about that. I do believe it.

SR4: (*I feel relieved that I believe in the eternality of the soul. This would be so much harder if I didn't.*) I do too. (*I feel a connection with Lois, and I feel that my presence matters to her. I'm not a disembodied voice on the phone now—I'm a person who hears her. I feel happy to have made this connection, though I wonder what more can be done to help her with her pain.*)

[*Lois continues to tell me about her brother; I'll spare the details.*]

L5: Well, thank you, rabbi. This is hard.

SR5: Of course. It sounds like Ed has left a really wonderful legacy, and you're surrounded by love of family and friends.

L6: Yes, rabbi, that's true.

As we moved into a reenactment, using role-reversal to enable the student to "get into his congregant's shoes," the group perceived greater interpersonal distance than had been discernable from the verbatim. Lois sat at the piano facing a wall. The student stood to her side. Her husband stood silently at an opposite wall. The student had not drawn up a chair or invited Lois into a face-to-face conversation. As the role-play unfolded, the unexpressed emotion between them became more palpable. The poignant tension was the ambivalence of both congregant and student rabbi about opening to themselves or each other. Though he wanted to comfort his bereaved congregant, the rabbinic intern had not created a context where a depth of meeting could occur.

Another student volunteered to enact the role of rabbi as the original student played Lois, enabling him to sense how a different approach might have felt to her. Doubling as rabbi, she deepened the pastoral conversation and "Lois" became angry: "I don't want to be pushed." We wondered: Is this how Lois would have responded or was the student giving voice to his own fears?

We invited the student to embody Lois with more intentionality. We suggested he close his eyes and imagine himself in her body, to assume her posture in the chair. "Do you have children?" "No." Then he recalled the photograph Lois kept on top of the piano. "Yes, I do. I have children and grandchildren." Stepping away from the piano, the student realized Lois had been using a walker. Suddenly, the bereaved sister appeared older, frailer, and more disabled than initially portrayed. We sensed Lois's reluctance to share her grief, unsure if this young rabbi could comfort her.

After the role-reversal, the student revealed he had recently become very preoccupied with death. The role-play had evoked thoughts of his mother's death, though she was not ill or presently at any increased risk of dying. "I can't imagine what it will be like for me when she dies." With group support, the student was able to touch the dread that had prevented him from empathizing with Lois's grief. If our focus had been clinical supervision, we would have invited him to re-play the interaction with this new awareness. But we proceeded with theological reflection.

What makes it possible for people to draw closer to God? What creates distance from God? How does a caregiver bridge distances? Is heaven far or near? Was either the student or congregant changed by this encounter and how? What do the answers to those questions reveal about pastoral theology?

We thought about the oft-quoted saying of the Kotzker Rebbe: "God is present when we let God in." We let God in when we let in other people. We are always making choices about how much to let someone else in. In this encounter, the rabbinic intern and the congregant would only let each other in, in a limited way.

We realized how tempting it was to think that the theological question was whether Judaism includes a belief in heaven or an afterlife. Rather we saw Lois's mention of heaven as a pastoral opportunity to enter her experience. Her belief in the existence of heaven provided some comfort, enabling her to imagine a place where her brother would abide after death and from which her relationship with him could continue. If heaven were secure, she would be saved from the emptiness of the void.

This conversation led us to the thought of Rebbe Nachman of Bratzlav (1772–1810). In his theological imagination, *hallal ha panui* (the vast empty space) created through God's self-contraction (*tzimtzum*), remains always at the heart of creation. What in Lurianic Kabbalah was a cosmological feature of the created universe became, for Nachman, the existential experience of emptiness and nonbeing. Death, trauma, illness, and loss rupture our web of relationships and plunge us into the void. Lois's beloved sibling had suffered a prolonged illness, the devastation of which the student had not consciously absorbed, as he barely alluded to it through an abbreviated parenthesis. Not only losing her brother, but likely peering into the mirror of her own decline and death, Lois grabbed onto "routine" as a shaky perch in the void. She needed a spiritual caregiver willing to step into the void with her, to create a firmer place, where she could risk touching her own vulnerability.

The traditional formulation for greeting the mourner (*HaMakom yenachem etchem b'toch shaar avlei Tzion v'Y'rushalayim*) took on enriched meaning. How odd to invoke God with such a nonpersonal name, *HaMakom* (the Place), as the One to comfort mourners. But for Lois, and for all of us, after the death of a loved one, it is precisely our place in the web of interrelatedness that has been rent or lost. The empathy of a caregiver spins invisible threads of connection to hold us in the void and keep us from its yawning depths.

Havdalah offers a verse of reassurance for void-touching moments, *Hinei El Y'shuati. Evtach v'lo efchad.* (God is my Salvation. I will trust and not be afraid.) The verse is a proclamation of faith that offers theological sustenance on the edge of darkness. Faith and fear coexist in the life of the spirit. They do not cancel each other out. To willingly step into the void as caregiver we need to trust possibilities inherent in it. We have to encompass uncertainty, even emptiness, as part of God's creativity. This is the promise between God and the people and can become the aspiration of the pastoral caregiver who wants to establish trust with a congregant facing the void.

In *Parashat Ki Tisa* (Exod. 33:17–23), Moses asks if he may behold God's presence. He is told he cannot see God's face and live; but if he stands in the cleft of a rock, the Presence will be *Iti* ("There is a Place with Me") (Exod. 33:21). We behold God's presence as the place of "with," of connection: *"Here! The place of 'with' is Me."* We glimpse God in relationship, as we care for one another and become responsible and "response-able" participants in the web of interconnectedness, embracing the truth of our radical interdependence.

Vaani T'filati ("My prayer is for you"/"I am my prayer") (Ps. 69:14)

In the second verbatim we witness a healing transformation that can occur when a pastoral caregiver steps into the void. A student, serving as a hospital chaplain intern, visited the wife of a patient, a sixty-five-year-old man, born in Morocco to a religious Jewish family, who later immigrated to the United States. What was supposed to have been a brief hospitalization had turned into a three-week stay. During those weeks, the student entered into attuned relationship with the patient and his wife, evoking and listening to stories about the husband's childhood memories of Jewish life in Morocco. She also prayed with them. The verbatim encounter occurred as the patient was intubated in the SICU and likely to die. As the student chaplain entered the waiting area, the wife invited her to draw up a chair. Sensing the enormity of what was unfolding, the student stayed with the wife's experience moment to moment as she began to find words for the unspeakable. Early in the conversation, the wife said:

J6: I don't want to cry in front of my husband or in front of my kids.

Student Chaplain 6: [*calm silence*]

J7: I . . . [*starts to cry*] . . . it's in me . . .

SC7: [*more calm silence*]

J8: It feels good to cry.

SC8: You have a lot of emotions churning inside of you; it's wonderful you can let them out.

J9: I feel this lump in my throat, but I need to be strong for everyone.

SC9: You do?

J10: I don't know. Maybe I could cry with R. I want him to have hope.

SC10: Your tears would mean that there isn't any more hope.

J11: [*crying*] Yes. My dear husband. I love him.

SC11: [*I'm also teary eyed*] You have so much love for each other. (*I've seen them together and this is a true statement.*)

J12: We should go in.

[*She gathers her things and I push the chair back. We walk slowly into the SICU together.*]

A nurse asks them to return in fifteen minutes. In the intervening time, the wife continues to cry and tells the chaplain she wishes there were a prayer she could say:

SC15: [*I say softly*] What should we pray for?

J18: His healing. That my kids are okay. That we have the strength to get through this. That he'll get through this [*crying heavily*].

SC16: Dear God

J19: Dear God (*I wonder if she's going to repeat the whole prayer.*)

SC17: Be with R.

J20: Be with R. [*She adds his Hebrew name.*] (*I am not sure how to continue praying knowing that she's repeating every word; I feel like I have to be more conscious of my words and give them in small phrases.*)

SC18: Be with him and grant him calmness of mind.

J21: Be with him and grant him calmness of mind.

SC19: Support his family.

J22: Support his family. [*She adds names.*]

SC20: Bless them with the strength to get through this.

J23: Bless them with the strength to get through this. Please God. Please. Help him. Help him.

SC21: Help him, God. Help him and protect him.

J24: Help him, God, and protect him. [*crying so much that her tears are falling onto me*] (*I feel this great* k'dushah *as I feel her tears, and can sense The One between us as I hold her arms and she cries into me.*)

SC22: *Baruch atah HaShem, shomei-a t'filah*, Blessed are you God who hears prayers.

J25: Blessed are you God who hears prayers.

SC23: Amen.

J26: Amen.

J27: [*She has cried so much that her nose is running. I take out tissues for her. She wipes her eyes and nose.*] Thank you. That was so beautiful. I really do have a sense of peace. [*pointing to her chest*] It feels different now, like God heard us.

Reflecting as a group, we felt we had witnessed a moment of sanctity. Attuning to the wife's grief, her love for her husband and longing for healing, the chaplain intern found words in her own heart that resonated in the heart of the other. The divine presence seemed palpable. A transformative moment had occurred, expressed by the wife as "feeling heard by God" and by the student as a moment of "great *k'dushah*." In a state of contemplative interconnection, joined by braided words of prayer, the patient's wife and the student had found *HaMakom* (a place of divine presence) even in the midst of the void.

Yet processing after the role-play, the student expressed how unsettled she had been by the encounter; how skeptical she was about its theological significance. Her very efficacy as a caregiver was, paradoxically, the source of her distress.

The student explained her current theology: "Is it really God or is it me? They were just my words. How could 'I' have had a religious experience, felt that God heard her, just because she repeated my words? What really happened here? . . . When things go well, it is God. When things don't go well, it's my fault." She described herself as someone who feels a constant sense of God's presence, but of a God with a reality totally independent of her. She was distressed by the idea that God's presence had anything to do with her.

We had witnessed a possible dynamic of intercessory prayer: From the wife's perspective, she and God could not initially communicate. The chaplain intern made a place where she and the wife could "stand" in the void and created a scaffolding of prayer. Feeling heard and known, the wife felt assured that even in the face of looming destruction, she could be held. But attunement to the wife's anguish evoked the chaplain's desolation.

Without sharing details, the student revealed she had a history of trauma. She began to articulate her dilemma: "If God's presence depends on me, then the God who rescued me might not have been with me all the time. There might have been a time when God was not there." Perhaps she had survived trauma by blocking out memories of feeling unprotected and vulnerable. If those memories became accessible, might she remember a time when God was absent? The student was thrown into theological crisis. She had survived trauma by imagining an ever-present God, independent of human participation, with the power to rescue her. But in the pastoral interaction, she had experienced how her attunement with another had created a sense of God's presence. She began to struggle with a new and challenging idea: If God's presence depends on human capacities, then God is limited.

The student had stepped willingly into the void and encountered creativity at the heart of emptiness. She began to glimpse God working in and through her, through human beings. Our group process had begun to urge her toward a deeper understanding of divine-human partnership: perhaps a theology that envisions God as that which draws human beings toward expanding creativity through trustworthy and responsive interrelatedness with others. Perhaps this is even a God who evolves through human relationship, changing as we are changed.

Redemptive Love: *Ahavah Rabbah*

In the third verbatim, we are introduced to a relationship of trustworthy depth between a student and an eighty-year-old survivor of the Holocaust. As a student chaplain at an urban soup kitchen, the student felt immediately drawn to Saul: "It was apparent to me there was something special about him when I first came to the soup kitchen. Something about how he dressed. Always clean and stylish. I noticed how appreciative he was about everything he received. He is kind of leader-ish in the group. He is the one who makes the *Motzi*. He is a voice from the old world."

The student chaplain was moved and intrigued by Saul's capacity for gratitude after all he had suffered: "He has such an ability to be grateful. I have a hard time understanding it. He feels as though all these miracles happened to him. What about all the people who died? Where was God when he witnessed his own father's death when he was just a small child? Does theology have to be consistent?"

In the verbatim, fear about an impending surgery suddenly triggered memories of Saul's childhood trauma.

SC1: So you are having your surgery tomorrow.

S2: [*Saul immediately begins to cry and seems to be speaking under his breath; I see his lips moving but it is obviously not English. After a minute or so I take his hand and hold it as he continues crying. After a few more minutes he begins to speak.*] All these things I have done I want God to forgive me. When I was a boy when I would come home I was so tired mine mother would send me out for a pear. I'd walk ten blocks to bring it for her.

SC2: You took such good care of her . . .

S3: I was at the market with my father. I saw they took him away. I came home. I wasn't going to tell my mother but then I started crying. She asks me what is wrong. I tell her. She begins screaming. Everyone could hear it. She took the kerosene and drank it. (*I am confused. In previous conversations Saul has said that it was only him and his sister who survived the war but I had not heard how his parents were killed. Saul seemed to jump from one association to the next.*) They took her to the hospital and she came back but she always had trouble with her liver so she couldn't do anything.

SC3: You saw your father taken away. (*I am confused by the story and, at least initially, its connection to the upcoming surgery.*)

S4: We went to the market with some clothes, you know, to trade for bread and potatoes, a little food . . . They took him and tied him up. He was screaming, I was screaming. They took him to a mass grave buried him with all those other people (*I realize he doesn't actually say how his father was killed but I assume that he was witness to it*) . . . Mine sister and I were in the orphan house. I tried to do good things for my sister, for everyone. I send money twice a year to an orphanage in Israel before Pesach so people should have money to buy what they need. My sister always told me that, not to wait until the last minute. I try to be a good person. SC4: (*I think to myself: "You are a good person. God loves you. I love you." Saul is speaking so quickly that I somehow feel I can't interrupt.*)

S5: Oh, mine God, I just ask that he protect me and you and everyone. I have to go. Thank you so much. God bless you . . . you and your family.

SC5: Can we say a prayer together before you go?

S6: Yes, thank you. That would be very nice.

SC6: [*I take Saul's hand and stand close to him.*] *Y'hi ratzon milfanecha, Adonai Eloheinu v'Elohei avoteinu*, May it be your will, Lord our God and God of our ancestors to send healing of body and strength of spirit to Shlomo ben Dovid v'Malka and give him peace of mind, body, and spirit. [*I conclude with the priestly benediction in Hebrew, which Saul says along with me. We say amen and Saul begins to tear a little. I place my hand on his shoulder.*]

S7: Thank you, thank you. I pray to God that the doctors will have good news.

SC7: I will be praying for you

[*Saul hurries out the door.*]

For a few moments, Saul was a child in Romania, murmuring in his native tongue, confused, terrified, crying out to God for forgiveness. Forgiveness for what? What sin had he committed? Not saving his father? Telling his mother about his father's murder so that, in an act of despair, she drank kerosene? Feeling rage toward the mother who abandoned him at the most terrifying moment of his life? For the sin of surviving *at all*?

A complex interface between psychology and theology was discernable. The pending surgery triggered the most deeply buried of traumatic memories from Saul's Holocaust childhood: the day he became an orphan when the Nazis murdered his father and his mother made an impulsive, permanently disabling suicide attempt. So much cruelty, brutality, and terror could not be integrated by a child. Dissociation had enabled Saul's psychological survival, but prevented him from viewing these events from a more compassionate adult perspective. As surgery threatened Saul's life and bodily integrity, he was thrust back into the horror of his childhood. The fragmented memories brought with them feelings of sinfulness attached to a harsh embedded theology[8] of reward and punishment. This is the theology of most children and the theology of the Bible.

Confused by the broken narrative, the student realized she could only be a witness. She did not have to understand; she needed only to receive what was offered and hold it as sacred. She could touch his revelations with the holiness of prayer. She could hold his hands and offer the human touch his mother had failed to give him.

Reflecting on this moment, the student wrote:

"And the bush was not consumed" makes me think that even with all of the burning and all the suffering in his life—Saul was not consumed— he survived and is an amazing presence still able to be in deep relationship with God even as the burning continues. The images of crematoria and of doctors burning off cancerous lesions are right now intertwined in my head—the idea that if Saul can survive this sort of burning he can survive anything. In some ways I feel like Saul is pastoring me in this relationship more than I am pastoring him. It is Saul who is reminding me of

God's omnipresence even in this suffering. At the same time Saul is wondering how it is that he must suffer more—but he wonders this while still professing deep faith. I am both confused and awed by this.

Selecting an excerpt to reenact during the role-play, the student did not return to this traumatic moment. She chose instead an encounter when Saul spoke of the miracles he had received: how *Basherte* (meant to be) his life has been. Theologically, the student was most curious about Saul's gratitude for his life. How had he sustained hope, generosity, and a capacity to love after such unspeakable trauma?

We watched as Saul and the chaplain met in a chapel at the soup kitchen. Saul explained that his mother always spoke of the *Ganze Basherte*, how the Whole Thing is *Basherte* (everything happens for a purpose). He described how he and his sister escaped from the Nazis when they were in a line-up and everyone else was being shot; how they fled to the woods and survived by discovering carrots in the ground. Creeping past the Gestapo who never saw them, his sister recited the *Sh'ma*, the prayer Jews hope will be on their lips when they die. "It was all *Basherte*." "God has given me a miracle once. I need another miracle." The chaplain wanted a miracle for him too and told him so. Holding his hand she intoned the *Mi Shebeirach*, praying for a healing of body and soul. In a poignant moment, Saul returned the favor and spontaneously offered his young chaplain a blessing for her health.

Basherte is the theology Saul learned from his mother and carried into adult life. It is a theology that imagines God to have a plan and purpose for everything. *Basherte* was Saul's way of speaking of participating in that something beyond ourselves that organizes everything we experience. *Basherte* theology reassured him that trauma *is what it is*, but is part of something ultimately meaningful. His guilt was diminished and his survival became a miracle from God. He could live filled with gratitude and love just for being alive. The *Basherte* theology lived alongside a theology in which God punishes children for the cruelty of others, neither resolved in the other. This was a theology that didn't *explain* anything; but contained *everything*. Such a poignant example of how we must make room for contradiction inside a life of faith.

Role-playing the *Basherte* encounter, the student realized how much she loved Saul. "I couldn't tell who I was saying the prayer for more. For me or for him." She was so touched that he offered *her* a blessing: How much joy he took in all that she had; how he seemed to lack all jealousy. "I sometimes have a hard time taking joy in other peoples' joys," she confessed. She was awed that Saul could pray for her health as *he* faced surgery.

What occurred between Saul and the student illustrates how the pastoral care relationship can become one of reciprocal vulnerability and spiritual formation. Saul's resilience was that he knew how to get people to love him. He knew how to foster the love in his young chaplain that he needed to receive. In the process, the student discovered that her own capacity to love was much greater than she had known. Her love for him made it possible for Saul to come to faltering speech about the horrors of his life and finally to be witnessed. Both people experienced healing and transformation. The student participated in an awesome love that is part of the great love, *Ahavah Rabbah*. Through reflection, the student came to understand a dimension of God's redemptive love that had been inaccessible to her before she knew Saul.

As pastoral educators, we are aware of how many Jews who engage in theological discourse tone down love as a dimension of Jewish theology. But in pastoral work, as we understand it, love (*chesed*) *is* at the center. Grounded in lived relational experience, pastoral theology can point us to life-affirming ways of thinking, even about Holocaust theology. As long as Holocaust theology is an effort to intellectually explain or understand, we are stuck. We need to learn what this survivor learned: When we open our hearts in ever-widening circles, we can encompass even the horrors of the Holocaust. When we find within ourselves the capacity to break open our hearts in the midst of suffering, we can discover a love at the center of it all. As long as the Holocaust is viewed as an event separate and apart from all other horrors of human history, we remain at a theological impasse. When we break open our hearts, we discover that our individual suffering connects us to all people who suffer.

Mystery at the Heart of Relationship

As pastoral educators, a focus of our work is to support students to move from "trying to find the right thing to say" to entering deeply into the mystery at the heart of relationship where heal-ing and transformation happens. We can touch the divine in the process of mutual becoming in such relationships. Reflection on the sacredness of pastoral work in learning community is itself a dynamic religious experience.

As pastoral caregivers, we so often consider ourselves primarily as practitioners. Theological reflection is what we do to enrich our direct service to others. As the field of Jewish pastoral care evolves, we are becoming a community of practitioners who can speak of theological dynamics powerfully, authentically, and Jewishly, with appreciation for the mystery of how God moves in this broken world. We are pastoral theologians who can enrich the broader field of contemporary Jewish theology with "a radically relational theology."

Notes

1. Catherine Keller, *On the Mystery: Discerning Divinity in Process* (Minneapolis: Fortress Press, 2008), 22.

2. In the field of interpersonal neurobiology, resonance, attunement, and empathy are related but distinct concepts. *Resonance* behav-iors, triggered by mirror neuron systems, are automatic responses, such as reflexively yawning when others yawn or looking up when others look up. Resonance behaviors are thought to have evolved to synchronize group behavior for survival, like hunt-ing or fleeing. Attunement is a state of neurobiological intra and interconnectedness. As we take in signals from another person through the five senses, the mirror neuron system, by way of the insula (associated with visceral functions) alters limbic (involved with emotion) and body states to match those we are seeing in the other person, providing us with a visceral-emotional template of what the other is experiencing, allowing us to know another from the inside out. *Empathy* is actually a hypothesis we make about an-other person combining visceral, emotional, and cognitive infor-mation. To read more: Louis Cozolino, *The Neuroscience of Human Relationships* (New York: W. W. Norton & Company, 2006), ch. 14.

3. Theological reflection makes pastoral care distinct from other forms of care. We are concerned about questions of faith and meaning that are often beyond the purview of medical or psycho-logical professionals; about how people think about and practice the values that form their religious orientation and enable them to live with the challenges of mortality. Theological reflection is required by Clinical Pastoral Education (CPE) and is part of the pastoral counseling curriculum of rabbinical colleges.

4. In this article, we use the terms "spiritual caregiver" and "pastoral caregiver" interchangeably.

5. The pioneer founder of the CPE movement, Anton Boisen, taught that both the people who receive care and the givers of care are "living human documents" as complex and worthy of study as sacred text. See Anton T. Boisen, "Cooperative Inquiry in Religion," in *Vision from a Little Known Country: A Boisen Reader, ed. Glenn H. Asquith, Jr. (Decatur, GA: Journal of Pastoral Care Publications, 1992), 77.*

6. Nahum N. Glatzer, *Franz Rosenzweig: His Life and Thought (Schocken: New York, 1961), 231.*

7. Keller, *On the Mystery, 11. For recent explorations of Jewish Process Theology see Conservative Judaism: The Process Theology Issue 62, nos. 1–2. (Fall-Winter 2010–2011). The Winter issue of CCAR Journal offers articles on Process Theology.*

8. The term "embedded theology" refers to the host of associated elements—memories, early beliefs, feelings, and values—accrued over time, absorbed and formed unreflectively from childhood experience, family, and culture. "Deliberative theology," in contrast, is actively constructed through reflection on embedded theologies, evaluating beliefs, and constructing new ones. See Carrie Doehring, *The Practice of Pastoral Care: A Postmodern Approach (Louisville, KY: Westminster John Knox Press, 2006), 112ff.*

Rabbis' Support of Older Couples' Second Marriages

Harriet Rosen and Marlene Levenson

Rabbis officiating at weddings ask, or are asked, to meet with couples prior to their marriage. What academic training do rabbis receive that prepares them to engage in premarital discussion? What topics, issues, and concerns are discussed and what do rabbis and couples think should be discussed? Should rabbis ask couples to discuss difficult or sensitive issues or to seek relevant expertise? And does this interaction have the potential to start or strengthen a couple's connection to the rabbi, the synagogue, and to Jewish communal life?

This article shares highlights of a six-month Second Marriage survey project during which rabbis and couples were interviewed to discover the answers to these questions. The project's findings offer concrete recommendations to support older couples entering second marriages and to support the rabbis who officiate at their weddings.

Background

Responding to the significant social changes resulting from individuals marrying later and increased numbers of divorces and remarriages, Rabbi Eric H. Yoffie, then-president of the URJ, asked the Reform Movement leadership to consider these changes' impact on Jewish communal life. In 1999, he launched a Biennial initiative to

HARRIET ROSEN, MA, was the editor and a writer for the Participant and the Facilitator manuals for the Aleph-Bet of Marriage program and part of the group making decisions about the program's direction. She is a trustee of the URJ Board and was chair of the Jewish Family Concerns Committee.

MARLENE LEVENSON, LCSW, spent her career in the field of aging and geriatrics; she has led support groups for individuals going through divorce for more than twenty years. She is a trustee of the URJ Board and was a vice-chair of the Jewish Family Concerns Committee.

find ways synagogue communities could strengthen this primary Jewish relationship. Marriage, a recurring image of the connection between God and Israel, stresses responsibility and commitment; supporting strong marriage relationships, which create stronger family and communal connections, is clearly a Jewish value.

Under the auspices of Rabbi Richard Address, then-director of URJ's Jewish Family Concerns, Lynn Levy, CSW, was hired as director of Premarital Education to research and create what became the Aleph-Bet of Marriage program. The group she created to pilot and support the project included Rabbi Martin Weiner, then-president of the CCAR, who made it one of his projects during his term of office.

The resulting program addressed "Who are you and what skills and expectations does each partner bring to the marriage?" Key issues were examined in a seven-session program using rabbis and skilled behavioral health professionals in their areas of expertise. Couples worked through a variety of diagnostic tools and approaches to better understand individual expectations and develop skills for positive communication—all with a Jewish lens—to better navigate life's inevitable complications and stresses. The approach was practical and interactive with exercises and homework for each partner.

In a pivotal meeting in the Aleph-Bet project's development to assess the written material and early results of the first pilot programs, the decision was made to limit the program to first marriages for two reasons: (1) statistically, the success rates are far higher for first marriages;[1] and (2) the opportunity to confront potential problems before marriage was an important hedge against dysfunctional relationships. The more complicated issues and lower success rates for subsequent marriages that follow a divorce or a death would have created too many variables for a clear focus in the initial Aleph-Bet program.

The Second Marriage Project

In 2009–2010, one of the authors was involved through the Kalsman Institute in providing HUC-JIR/Los Angeles rabbinical students with an elective one-day training on conducting premarital meetings. During the sessions, which included role-playing, we noted students' responses to age and life experience differences, as well as the changes in expectations from cultural shifts. The need for rabbis to understand an older population of couples entering second marriages and to know in what areas to offer support to these couples is the impetus for this study.

The need to support second marriages became clear. These couples are a segment of any congregation and juggle many more variables in their relationships. Because those remarrying represent a diverse group, we, the authors, also made the decision to focus on one subgroup: couples fifty years old or older who have no children living with them.

We left out of the study the most complicated of these new relationships—children from previous marriages living with the couple. While there is substantial published research on the problems and complications of "blended" families,[2] there is far less focus on older adults remarrying after a divorce or a death. The Aleph-Bet project did not cover many issues that are relevant to our target group.

Methodology

We interviewed (1) forty rabbis trained by the Reform, Conservative, or Modern Orthodox movements who perform wedding consultations and ceremonies for this subgroup; and (2) forty couples who met our criteria. The rabbis were diverse in professional training, background, age, positions on Jewish marriage law, and experience and from places large and small across North America. The majority interviewed was ordained by the Reform or Conservative movements.

As a check and for insight into a wider perspective, we also interviewed Christian clergy and an ultra-Orthodox rabbi. In addition, we read books and articles that looked at marriage and shifting cultural patterns.

The couples, too, were a diverse group geographically and in age, spread across more than thirty years with the youngest in their fifties. The majority interviewed were in their mid-sixties and early seventies. The couples, either or both, had adult children, but no child lived with them; were either heterosexual or homosexual (Marriage as a legal contract is only recently and still not widely available to homosexual couples; the social changes are not marked the same.); and were either widowed or divorced. Some couples were intermarried with one partner a non-Jew, and some had wide differences in each partner's affiliation and relationship to Judaism. All had sought a rabbi for their ceremony, and both partners had been married at least once before.

The candor and willingness of both groups to discuss this subject was both welcome and deeply appreciated. Each couple and each rabbi was asked for thirty minutes and almost all gave us far more time, which was very generous considering the stress and constraints of busy schedules. Interviews were in person or by telephone, geography and time determining the option. Rabbis and couples provided their viewpoints on the benefits, limitations and frustrations of pre-marriage meetings.

Two basic questionnaires were developed: we varied slightly the rabbis' questions—asking each rabbi to self-identify as either experienced or new to learn if there are differences in training opportunities, tools and skills—while all couples were asked the same questions. Overall, we wanted to know what range of topics and types of support and guidance rabbis could offer to older, remarrying couples in their premarital meetings.

Some of the questions posed to the rabbis: What were the depth and types of premarital training rabbis received as students and in professional development opportunities? What tools do they use for meetings with couples? How do they structure a meeting? What topics are covered and problems encountered? What tools and ideas could rabbis suggest that would help both new and experienced rabbis to hone their skills?

Overview of Findings

1. Successful interchange that the couple sees as valuable and meaningful can strengthen bonds to the rabbi and the synagogue. Interviews also indicated that this interchange is important for communal involvement. Older couples are an important and often neglected population in synagogue life, and this is a rabbi's opportunity to engage them. Are there benefits for the couple, the rabbis, and the synagogues that reach beyond the ceremony?

2. Although some rabbis had formal training in psychology and counseling, most did not, and both new and experienced rabbis reported they were understandably careful about dealing with issues beyond their expertise. We looked at perceptions.

What did rabbis feel they provided spiritually and in support and guidance without venturing into areas where she or he has no training or specialized expertise?

3. Many couples said they wished that more in-depth questions and problems had been addressed in a session. Not that couples necessarily wanted or expected rabbis to supply answers. Often both the rabbis and the couples said they sensed discomfort in discussing candidly a particular topic, but in hindsight, it was clear there was a need to bring challenging topics forward.

Therefore some couples' expectations were not met. After their marriages, they regretted that their rabbis had not pursued potentially problematic issues. Although almost uniformly, partners in second marriages said they felt their expectations of this new marriage were more realistic and flexible; nevertheless issues and challenges arose that blindsided them.

The Survey Questions for Rabbis

What follows are a composite of the **questions posed to rabbis,** our observations, and *representative rabbis' responses.*

Logistics

In an average year, at how many second marriages for older couples do you officiate?
The average is about four to six a year or fewer.

Many couples hire a rabbi specifically for this occasion because they are no longer affiliated or the rabbi is associated with the former spouse. Rabbis commented that many couples live together rather than marry because it simplifies financial issues.

How much time and how many sessions?

While the range is from zero to twelve 45- to 60-minute meetings, the majority of rabbis meet with couples three or four times. Sometimes the rabbi is hired solely for the ceremony. Several rabbis stressed how unsatisfying this is to them. *"It's the flowers, the cake, and the rabbi."* When there are no premarriage meetings with the rabbi it is often because a rabbi is from a former or geographically far congregation or is a friend or relative who "comes in" for the ceremony.

"I require three meetings."

"I assign readings and then we sit and talk about them. I meet with them ten to twelve times."

"I meet them before the wedding [ceremony] and we talk about what family members will do and who will stand where."

Where are the meetings held?

Rabbis use any one or a combination of locations, such as offices, studies, and libraries of synagogues; gardens and restaurants; and the rabbi's house for Shabbat lunch or dinner.

The Differences Between First and Older-Adult Second Marriages

How do these couples differ?

Overall, rabbis talked about older couples bringing more realistic expectations to this relationship. They are less *"starry eyed than younger, first-time couples."*

"If divorced, they try harder because they don't want another failed marriage. If widowed, the challenge is to retain the memory of the deceased mate without their being the third person in the marriage."

"Often these are marriages of convenience—not deep love—and sex is not always as important a part of the relationship."

"Second marriages are simpler; they celebrate this blessing, opportunity, and privilege of a second chance. Older couples are more reality based in acceptance of one another."

What issues or questions are specific or more common to these couples?

1. The major common marker is adult children who can bless, curse, and disrupt this new relationship whether the previous marriage ended in divorce or the death of the former spouse. Couples emphasized that a rabbi's help in dealing with the emotions and often the anger of adult children is the single most important support they need and often will continue to need.

"What this new commitment means from the children's perspective is that it kills any hope of reconciliation, of recreating that former family, even if the marriage ended with a death."

2. Release from the prior spouse either literally or emotionally enters into many discussions, again whether the former spouse is alive or deceased.

"I tell couples, 'Don't try to duplicate. You need an openness to what's new so you can create new memories.'"
   "Caregiving is a serious concern if one has been a caregiver of a deceased spouse."
   "[A] previous relationship ignored, and feelings not communicated, will cause problems."

3. Finances and inheritance play a major role, as much for children as for the couple.

"Whose children get what and I want to protect my children comes up."
   "People who age that have assets have already thought about this."

Training, Experience, and Tools

What kinds of training have you received or sought?

Pulpit rabbis often lack the luxury and flexibility of spending time with couples in what is preventative work. How open to discussing any sensitive issue rests on the couple's existing relationship with the rabbi and the rabbi's comfort level. Added to this is the often continuing social interactions with the couple; several rabbis noted their discomfort with discussing subjects and learning *"more than I'm comfortable knowing."*

The first interview words by several rabbis was, to quote one of them, *"I was not trained as a counselor but feel if questions are not raised, I've lost an opportunity to engage and then it's an opportunity lost."*

The rabbi went on to say that when there was clearly a need, couples were encouraged to seek appropriate help. Many rabbis do refer or encourage the couple to seek professional help and provide either referrals or resources. Many rabbis, however, said they felt unable to venture into topics that might lead them where they felt they had no training or expertise. In difficult situations, they were often uncertain about how to handle or to suggest either delaying the marriage or to have couples seek help.

The majority of rabbis, new or experienced, said that there was little to no pastoral training in premarital discussions in their rabbinic training. Some had taken professional development sessions in Prepare/Enrich (a premarital resource and guide) and several endorsed its tools, particularly those accessible by computer, and its ability to be specific to a couple's life experiences.[3]

Many rabbis developed questionnaires that couples fill out before or after a meeting. Ideally, the couple discusses this in advance of the meeting. Some rabbis have social or mental health training and use those skills in their approach.

> "I developed my material from many sources and vary it depending on feedback from couples."
>
> "I use Rabbinic text and don't project but observe and have a listening ear."
>
> "I took workshops given by CAJE, studied with a family therapist, found a mentor, and also talked with psychologists. Basically, I'm self trained."
>
> "I had a class in human relations but very little practical preparation. I read a lot of books on marriage. There should be more training than I had."

What Is Gained?

Do these interviews strengthen the couple's bond with the synagogue?

Yes, if that bond is already in place. Couples and rabbis gave examples of when the rabbi's warm acceptance of the new partner—intermarriage, very different affiliation or commitment, connection to former partner—created a new bond.

No congregation or rabbi had any process or formal programs to draw in these couples although many rabbis invited couples to services, programs, or a Shabbat dinner.

As a rabbi, what do you offer a couple?

> "I am there in the joyous and the sorrowful times. I offer them support, guidance, trust, and honesty. I present a Jewish perspective on marriage and help them understand the sanctity of the covenant of marriage."
>
> "The spiritual aspect and sanctification of a relationship; compassion for one another; ability to forgive, the connection to a sacred community."

What do you think creates a strong relationship?

> "If it bends, it's a relationship worth working through."
>
> "Self awareness to meet challenges, ability and willingness to talk about those challenges, a sense of humor, community that supports and celebrates their lives."
>
> "To know it's a gift to find someone to marry and to work hard to deepen the gift."

The Survey Questions for Couples

What follows are a composite of the **questions posed to couples,** our observations, and *representative couples' responses*:

Logistics

Did the rabbi offer or did you request a premarital meeting?

Many rabbis required that the couple meets with them or they will not officiate. Their conviction was that it provided value opportunities for learning and interaction on many levels.

> *"We had several meetings but they only focused on the ceremony, nothing about us."*
> *"We had several meetings, two general and two on the ceremony, and the rabbi initiated them. We felt like a friend had invited us who was warm and interested in us as people and made us feel comfortable."*

How well did you know the officiating rabbi and why did you choose him or her?

> *"Never a question. She was 'our' rabbi."*
> *"We liked the rabbi and rejoined the congregation when we decided to marry."*
> *"The rabbi had celebrated my child's bat mitzvah and officiated at my mother's funeral."*

Did the rabbi make you feel comfortable?

It was clear that those who are unaffiliated or currently uninvolved felt having a rabbi to officiate was important, but the relationship often went no further. Positive interactions at premarital meetings have the potential to strengthen a couple's involvement in Jewish life.

> *"No relationship established."*
> *"Yes, open, had spoken with him before, and respected his opinions. We would be comfortable talking to him again."*
> *"Full of laughter and a very open discussion."*

The Discussion

Who initiated questions and what was discussed?

There was a wide variety of responses. In our interviews the majority of couples and rabbis came to the meetings to discuss the ceremony and "talk," but the talking expectations often were not defined. A question we did not ask was how the invitation to meet was extended; were the reasons for the meeting and its possible scope made clear?

> "No, he didn't cover practical things including how this is different from marrying in your early twenties when you didn't know what to expect or that there would be challenges. It never occurred to me to prepare my kids, and it turned out to be a problem and it took a long time to work it out."
>
> "As a gay couple, we thought we'd worked everything out but still the rabbi posed questions she thought we may not have considered."
>
> "We wanted questions and were very surprised that the only thing asked was 'What are your expectations from this marriage?' We didn't get much from the meetings and wanted an in-depth discussion about marriage and family relationships."
>
> "We were profoundly affected by the rabbi's question: 'What traits do you like the most about one another?' We had to answer one another directly. It brought the discussion to a deeper level when we spoke about our feelings for one another."
>
> "The rabbi asked had we discussed children and grandchildren and about these obligations and our abilities to put this new spouse before them."

What questions did you wish/hope the rabbi would cover?

> "The rabbi didn't talk or even suggest help in bringing our families together or even bring it up. My daughter's reaction, how she acted at the wedding, blindsided me."
>
> "That when you're dealing with adults with a different story, some kind of understanding of what's different from first marriages."
>
> "Wished she had brought up possible stumbling blocks. It's not just about love but about the down-the-road issues to deal with and to really talk about them."
>
> "Would have liked a list or reading of 'often encountered' issues and to see them in advance so we could be prepared to discuss them."
>
> "Meetings are useful when they're a catalyst that make us lay our cards on the table. Make us look at things in a way we hadn't before. Make us think about our future life."
>
> "A rabbi is someone you can trust, someone you respect enough to ask his advice on family and personal issues. A rabbi is in a good position to refer you for marriage counseling."

What Is Gained?

Did these interviews strengthen the couple's bond with the rabbi or the synagogue?

"Yes, 'Harvey' said he felt closer and the rabbi moved closer to 'Harvey.' Getting to know the rabbi enhanced the relationship."

"My bride and the rabbi brought me back to synagogue involvement."

"I joined the congregation as a result of those meetings."

"It would have if the rabbi had done something to make us feel welcome and to give us a reason to participate. We have a new rabbi who remembers our name and acknowledges our relationship."

What do you think a rabbi offers that is important to your marriage?

"Ritual and the value of rituals. The rabbi's blessing us integrated us Jewishly."

"Because it's a Jewish wedding. Because it's who I am. It reflects the way I see my family, my community, and my life."

"It models being Jewish in a ceremony in front of my children and grandchildren. We're Jewish—it's unthinkable not to have a rabbi and a Jewish wedding."

"It's the sense that God sanctifies this relationship: His seal, not the state's."

What do you think makes for a strong marriage?

"In my first marriage, peace was all that mattered, an absence of issues. You learn to change, to know that there always will be issues and our work is to be able to talk, define, respect, and learn to change."

" 'We' is a priority—a marriage needs to be nurtured and tended well. You should want the other person to be happy."

"Know you can't reshape either of you. You're not going to grow old together because you're already there."

"What did I learn? That life can be wonderful when you're with the right person. There's joy!"

Conclusions and Recommendations

This was a small sample, about 120 individuals, who we talked to about their experience with second marriages. Nonetheless, there was often consistency in opinions and impressions from both rabbis and couples, from which we compiled the following four conclusions. We noted generational differences in expectations and outlooks, which helped us better evaluate responses.

1. Rabbis have a unique opportunity to build strong relationships with couples in these meetings.

We bring ourselves to interpersonal interactions. In any exchange between a rabbi and a couple, knowing and understanding how personality, life experience, and generational differences play a role are important to the interaction. Training brings the kind of confidence that assures couples and supports a rabbi's intentions.

Meeting, or even better, exceeding a couple's expectations is its own membership retention policy. Most individuals are grateful for help and support at the critical moments in our lives, joyful or sad. Since little in life comes unmixed, finding ways to offer support matters deeply and can create strong bonds.

While trust and connection between the rabbi and the couple are a gift of time and communal involvement, this remains an ideal opportunity to begin or strengthen a strong connection.

Recommendations

- Create an environment and opportunity for in-depth discussion by sending a list of discussion points in advance. The couple then has the opportunity to talk and comes prepared to the meeting. They can decide what topics and areas they are comfortable discussing.
- Create and maintain referrals or categories for other professional help and read and recommend relevant books and articles.
- Provide programming that would be valuable to couples: adult children and their impact on new relationships, examining individual values, discussion guidelines, blended families with adult children, life stages, career-retirement conflicts, navigating obligations to children and grandchildren.
- Meet with the couple at least once, ideally more, within the first year they are married.
- Mentor newly married couples to integrate and encourage participation in synagogue life.

2. Within the curriculum at HUC-JIR teach the practical skills needed for pre-wedding meetings and premarital counseling. Develop materials for rabbis to use during their

meetings with couples at CCAR and other continuing education workshops.

Almost every rabbi we spoke with felt the absence of solid, practical, hands-on experience with any counseling techniques in their rabbinic training. More and better is needed. Many sought some kind of training on their own: classes, professional development, mentors, reading, and Prepare/Enrich. These available resources have limitations and while certainly useful, need to be approached with enough knowledge to evaluate and adapt their use.[4]

Recommendations

- Provide opportunities for reading about and observing best practices. Many rabbis said an opportunity to watch an experienced and skillful rabbi conduct a meeting would be especially useful.
- Have rabbis discuss successful, and even more important, unsuccessful exchanges with couples.

3. Train rabbis in the skills needed to raise sensitive topics.

One important area is a rabbi's observing serious problems when talking to a couple. When asked about red flags,[5] the lack of training was clear. Natural talent in this area was also clear. Some rabbis just "knew" what to say and do but like singing great opera, talent clearly matters.

Then, and most difficult, is when a rabbi feels strongly that a couple should not marry. Every rabbi remembered dealing with at least one such couple. What to do and how to handle such a situation is complicated. Rabbis told us of such couples finding another rabbi or divorcing shortly after the wedding. In the best cases, the couple delays the marriage to work out problems or decides not to marry.

Recommendations

- This is a skill that can be learned. Experienced therapists can teach a vocabulary to use so rabbis can comfortably talk about issues in a nonjudgmental and non-accusatory way. Rabbis, who are viewed with respect, with training can suggest professional help by a combination of skill and the weight of their position.

- When adult children pose a problem, meet with the children alone. Candid discussion can defuse the anger and concerns that often erupt later.
- Clearly, there are issues that need professional expertise such as financial advisors, lawyers, health professionals, and psychologists. Some rabbis recommend that couples discuss these topics with one another and seek appropriate professional guidance or resources. Rabbis should use this opportunity to address or even prevent problems by encouraging couples to seek the help they need.

4. There are challenging topics that the interviewed couples recommend marrying adults discuss with one another—and with their children.

One or both of the partners face the reality of having to deal with the other spouse's children and discussing decisions and plans in advance can prevent conflicts as well as grief.

Recommendations

- Using either a list of topics sent before a meeting or providing it at a first meeting, encourage a couple to discuss each topic and seek guidance if needed.

  Many couples expressed the wish that the rabbi had in some way asked them to consider the following:
  a. tensions and concerns in second marriages;
  b. adult children and the problems the new relationships can create;
  c. communication problems between the couple and with their children;
  d. children's and grandchildren's roles in their lives and each partner's feelings of obligation and involvement;
  e. money issues and most specifically inheritance and dividing or allotting assets;
  f. long-term planning for health issues, illness, and long-term care;
  g. decisions on living wills, health and financial powers of attorney, and burial.
- Rabbis can recommend relevant Rabbinic text and use it as a discussion starting point. There are excellent books on

weddings and marriage available to read and recommend to couples. Rabbis can provide professional recommendations or types of resources to help a couple find the right resource. Many rabbis do this and find all of these successful ways to provide help.

- Rabbis who see or strongly suspect serious problems should urge couples or individuals to seek appropriate help and follow up with the couple or individual.

Just as couples need support and guidance in their roles, rabbis need support and resources to do this important job well. Couples who seek a Jewish wedding roughly divide into those engaged Jewishly and those for whom this aspect is largely ornamental. But when we asked the question—why a Jewish wedding—it was clear that at some level it mattered deeply to at least one partner. It is an opportunity to engage, and rabbis should have the best available training and skills to make this interaction meaningful. It's good for the rabbi, the couple, and Jewish communal life. It's good for the Jews!

We are grateful for the generosity of rabbis and couples not only for their time, which was a gift, but for their willingness to share their experiences. We thank everyone who helped us gather this material and for sharing their experiences with us.

Notes

1. Center for Disease Control (cdc.gov/divorce), most current statistics: 41 percent of first marriages, 60 percent of second marriages, and 73 percent of third marriages end in divorce (accessed December 29, 2011).

2. A blended family is one that has "a role structure in which at least one parent has been previously married and which includes children from one or both of these marriages." Allan G. Johnson, *The Blackwell Dictionary of Sociology,* 2nd ed. (Malden, MA: Blackwell Publishers, Inc., 2000), 119

3. Prepare/Enrich is a well-researched couples assessment tool and program for premarital counseling, marriage enrichment, couples therapy, marriage mentoring, and marriage education, frequently used by North American clergy. The program includes adaptations for Jewish couples. Information available at www.prepareandenrich.com.

4. Current practice at the different HUC campuses includes a one-day Prepare/Enrich workshop, as well as related coursework in pastoral counseling and rabbinic practices classes, and exposure in pulpit fieldwork.
5. Red flags warn that there are serious problems or dangers to the relationship or an individual.

A New Ritual for Healing and Well-Being

Geri Newburge

On Rosh HaShanah of the year 5611 Rabbi Isaac Mayer Wise faced what must have been the greatest challenge of his personal and rabbinic life. The president of his congregation in Albany, New York, Louis Spanier, wished to damage Wise's career, culminating in Spanier's assault on him on the bimah, in front of the entire congregation. While there had been difficulties between the two men prior to Rosh HaShanah, a punch in the head is hardly something one could anticipate. Such a traumatic event brought not just physical pain to Wise, but great emotional trauma and grief.[1] As rabbis, hopefully we will never have such an egregious encounter, but certainly we have all had our individual and professional challenges.

It is the same for the people we serve. Life takes unpredictable twists and turns. Some of these unanticipated events yield joy, learning, and satisfaction, while others yield hurt, embarrassment, and existential crisis. Divorce, economic crisis, loss of a friendship, loss of health, difficulties with a child or spouse, and a demotion at work are just a few of life's challenges that many of us encounter. One can never fully know how any given situation will affect our lives or our attitude toward it or the experiences we have had.

During the Days of Awe we focus on the concept of *t'shuvah*, of turning away from our own problematic behavior or actions and seeking forgiveness for any wrongdoing. While *t'shuvah* offers a means for reframing the past, and moving toward a new, hopeful future, it sometimes does not fully speak to the emotional and spiritual difficulties that many face. Additionally, *t'shuvah* and the accompanying prayers of this liturgy, for example *Un'taneh Tokef*, address personal responsibility, and to a certain extent account for

GERI NEWBURGE (C03) is the associate rabbi at Temple Emanuel in Cherry Hill, New Jersey; she is grateful for her family's support at all times.

the unpredictability of life or our lack of control over it (with our prayers and liturgy acknowledging intentional and unintentional sins). Yet, this does not allow the individual to focus on a particularly difficult event or time. Coupled with the personal and professional trials of the rabbinate, this led me to examine various existing ceremonies and, eventually, to create a new ritual that would enable an individual who has experienced a traumatic event, beyond one's control, to acknowledge and process their anguish Jewishly and then move beyond it emotionally and spiritually.

Jewish tradition is rich enough to offer insight and wisdom through the trials and tribulations of life. The scientific community recognizes it too; there were more than twelve hundred studies published during the twentieth century that attest to the relationship between religion and mental health.[2] In fact, a majority of the studies examining the association between religious practices and behavior and indicators of psychological well-being report at least one significant positive correlation between these variables:[3] "Public and private religious practices can help to maintain mental health and prevent mental diseases. They help individuals cope with anxiety, fears, frustration, anger, anomie, inferiority feelings, despondency and isolation."[4] Or in a more positive context, "Religious involvement is correlated with: well-being, happiness, and life satisfaction; hope and optimism; purpose and meaning in life; higher self-esteem; adaptation to bereavement; greater social support and less loneliness; less anxiety, etc."[5]

With Job, who literally loses everything he has but keeps faith in God, we find a correlation with our reactions to our own life struggles. Even with his tenacious hold on faith, Job cries out, both in anguish as well as in anger to God, "Even today my speech is bitter; my wound is heavier than my sigh."[6] Like Job we are left bereft, disheartened, and broken after one of these trials. Understandably one can feel stuck when confronted by life's tests. To allow others or circumstances to control our lives or our happiness is a posture that must be rejected, and in actuality our tradition teaches us that just as we say a benediction for the good in life we must also say a benediction for the bad.[7] A significant trauma requires time for healing, whether it is of a physical, mental, or spiritual nature. According to the scholars and rabbis at the National Jewish Center for Learning and Leadership, "As we have discovered, and as our sages have long known, there is no experience in the life of a Jew that cannot be marked in Jewish ways. There are times when the available Jewish rituals just don't seem to fit well enough to use, and we need to adapt them. There are also times when there really isn't an obvious Jewish way to mark some of the events of our lives, and we work together to develop new rituals that are deeply based in tradition."[8]

Judaism has long recognized the significance of rituals, and over the course of time and circumstance many rituals have evolved. All major milestones are essentially marked by ritual: bris, bar mitzvah, weddings, funerals. If a ritual did not exist one was created—like the baby namings for females and bat mitzvah we do today, or even the use of a *mikveh* after an illness or surgery. So too in the case of marriage, the ritual has evolved over time. While Rabbinic in origin, it used to be two separate ceremonies and with no *ketubah* reading. The *ketubah* was instituted two thousand years ago; it was formulated to protect a Jewish bride from financial hardship in the event of a divorce or her husband's death, making it among the first documents conferring legal status and financial rights on women.

This historical perspective is significant; it reminds us that our religion and its traditions are malleable. Yet, "performing new rituals, even as they serve to repair, heal, and reclaim tradition, can still feel both dangerous and paradoxical to those performing them."[9] This should not inhibit us from using Jewish symbols, rituals, or objects in creative and meaningful ways when we need to do so.

In fact, when we see the positive impact it can have on our outlook and sense of well-being, we should race to embrace such ritual. Professor Judah Goldin brilliantly observes, "To change we are all subject, perhaps most profoundly when we offer greatest resistance; adaptation, on the other hand, requires genius."[10] It is when we are suffering from one of life's traumas—feeling despondent, insecure, and lost—that we are most resistant to change. We don't want to face another defeat, or suffer another loss. The most unanticipated loss we experience is the loss of ourselves, "of earlier definitions that our images of self depend upon. For the changes in our body redefine us. The events of our personal history redefine us. The ways that others perceive us redefine us. And, at several points in our life, we will have to relinquish a former self-image and move on."[11]

The void left when we abandon our self-image can be consuming. We feel frightened, confused, or despondent when the reality of our lives changes, especially when it changes unexpectedly or suddenly. I discovered, from personal and professional experience, that when we must "relinquish a former self-image" due to a challenging event, our tradition did not present an appropriate ritual, though prayers and rituals exist for some other life-changing moments; for example, a *b'rachah* for parents when their child becomes a bar/bat mitzvah or a dance for parents when their last child marries and their primary focus is no longer raising children. What *b'rachah* or prayer could ease the pain? What might be offered that could be done in a nonthreatening way, cost no money, and allow the individual to put the heartbreaking event into a spiritual and temporal framework and then walk away from it? After perusing various texts, websites, and siddurim I came up short on a rite that created a time and space for a person to address a challenging event in her or his life in a religiously meaningful way. While there are a plethora of beautiful and insightful readings and prayers available, almost none offered a ritual experience. The closest such opportunity is found in *On the Doorposts of Your House*, which contains responsive readings for two people to recite "After a Trauma."[12] The pitfalls of this ceremony lay with some of the readings as well as the conclusion. The readings make an unnecessary distinction between man and woman, suggest that the distressed individual might not be able to help others or love, and do not give space for personal thoughts or feelings; the conclusion can be fulfilling if you are at the *mikveh*, a suggested possibility, but without a *mikveh* or its equal there is no real sense of closure to the ritual. Other resources felt incomplete because they (1) failed to include a communal element, (2) failed to include an intentionality about location of prayer, (3) failed to address the specific reality of the individual, and/or (4) failed to bring about a definitive culmination of the ritual. These are really about personal preference, but ultimately that is what this creative ritual provides—a broad-based approach to acknowledge, to place into context, and to bring an end to the suffering.

In the end I was inspired by the Jewish bill of divorce, the *get*. The delivery of a *get* involves both a document as well as a ceremony that dissolves a marriage, a symbolic and literal end to a period in one's life. It prompted me to craft a "ritual of release" that would act as a divorce from the painful experience.

This ritual of release is meant for anyone suffering emotional and spiritual pain from a situation or circumstance that was beyond their control; it can be utilized at any time when the individual wants to close that particular chapter of her or his life. The section of the ritual for the individual to offer personal remarks, prayers, or reflections is critical. In his article "On Private Prayer: A Covenantal Experience" our colleague David Lieb wisely points out, "It may be that the script of the prayer book does not reflect our own identity as we come before God in the private, prayerful moments of our life…The words of prayer at such a moment should be as authentic and as personally accurate as they can be. They should say what we need to say and make us feel as if they could accomplish and articulate the task we address."[13] Of course we can offer suggestions for additional prayers or readings, but the middle, individualized section provides the kind of opportunity stressed by Lieb, whether the words are spontaneously spoken by the person or taken from readings or prayers selected by the individual. The individual enacting this ritual can conclude it in a number of ways; the document can be burned, shredded, kept on file as a reminder of the finality of the incident, or even used as the "crumbs" for *Tashlich*. Essentially, using a document with a ritual, instead of just a prayer, will allow the individual to place the traumatic event within a time and space that brings a conclusion to the distress. Finding the personal touch that will provide the bookend is important and allow for that critical sense of finality and closure.

I've offered or performed this ritual with individuals who ended a relationship, endured an untenable work environment, experienced a harrowing divorce, and who suffered severe discrimination within the confines of the Jewish community. Of course, one could utilize it at other times as well after physical or psychological abuse, a debilitating accident, a traumatic experience with a sibling, etc. Can Jewish ritual offer a sense of healing and closure to the pain suffered? As rabbis it is part of our mission to provide prayers, rituals, and traditions wherever we can as a way to mend the emotional and spiritual wounds suffered. After all, one cannot expect depression or existential pain to heal on its own. Judaism and its rituals, traditional and creative, offer a means to the end—a sense of a peaceful whole self.

The ritual of release is an interactive experience taking place in front of a few witnesses, who will be a source of support and sign this ritual document, essentially a personal "*get*" from the hurtful event. The document and ritual can be modified according to individual needs and circumstances. While this ceremony can be conducted anywhere, ideally it should take place where there is a sense of peace, privacy, comfort, and spirituality (e.g., a chapel or sanctuary).

Ritual of Release

Even today my speech is bitter; my wound is heavier than my sigh.[14]

Rabbi:

Life takes unpredictable twists and turns. Some of these unanticipated events yield joy, learning, and satisfaction, while others yield hurt, embarrassment, and existential crisis. We can never fully know how we will react to any given situation, and our Jewish tradition is rich enough to offer insight and wisdom throughout our lives.

Congregant:

Past events dictated that my life changed. These changes, while beyond my control, have taught me that I must mourn the loss of my self in some way. At present, I must look within to redefine myself, and for the future move forward from these difficulties to embrace a full life. I know this is not an easy task, but one that needs to be addressed for my health and well-being.

Rabbi:

The journey of life differs from one person to another, and meaning and faith are unique and deeply personal. You stand here today to recapture your sense of purpose and make a separation from past events. "Consider nothing impossible because there is no one who does not have her/his time, and no thing that does not have its place."[15] This is your time to conquer fears and disappointments, to create a sacred moment moving you to wholeness and peace.

Congregant:

(Time to share personal words/prayers/reflections)

I seek refuge in You, *Adonai*;
may I never be disappointed.
As You are beneficent, save me and rescue me;
incline Your ear to me and deliver me.

Be a sheltering rock for me to which I may always come;
decree my deliverance,
for You are my rock and my fortress.
My God, rescue me from the hand of the wicked,
from the grasp of the unjust and the lawless.
God, do not be far from me,
My God, hasten to help me.[16]

Congregant:

בָּרוּךְ אַתָּה, אֲדֹנָי אֱלֹהֵינוּ, מֶלֶךְ הָעוֹלָם, הַגּוֹמֵל לְחַיָּבִים טוֹבוֹת, שֶׁגְּמָלַנִי כָּל טוֹב.

Baruch atah, Adonai Eloheinu, Melech haolam, hagomeil l'chaiyavim tovot, sheg'malani kol tov.

Blessed are You, *Adonai* our God, Ruler of the universe, who bestows goodness upon the responsible, who has bestowed every goodness upon me.

Witnesses:

אָמֵן. מִי שֶׁגְּמָלֵךְ טוֹב הוּא יִגְמָלֵךְ כָּל טוֹב. סֶלָה.

Amen. Me sheg'maleich tov hu yig'maleich kol tov. Selah.

Amen. May the One who has bestowed goodness upon you continue to bestow every goodness upon you forever.

יְבָרֶכְךָ יְיָ וְיִשְׁמְרֶךָ.
יָאֵר יְיָ פָּנָיו אֵלֶיךָ וִיחֻנֶּךָ.
יִשָּׂא יְיָ פָּנָיו אֵלֶיךָ וְיָשֵׂם לְךָ שָׁלוֹם.

Y'varech'cha Adonai v'yishm'recka.
Ya-eir Adonai panav eilecha vichneka.
Yisa Adonai panav eilecha v'yaseim l'cha shalom.

May God bless you and keep you.
May God's presence shine upon you and be gracious unto you.
May God's presence be with you and grant you peace.

Meaning is possible even in spite of suffering.[17]

_____

Self

_____   _____

Witness   Witness

Ultimately, I hope that this ritual will provide a comforting Jewish ceremony or service for emotional and sacred healing. Knowing we cannot change past events, we must empower ourselves to bring relevant aspects of our tradition to provide a mechanism to move beyond the past in order to embrace the present and future. Whether it is this ritual or another, let Jewish tradition seep into these cracks in life's journey.

In the book *Necessary Losses*, Judith Viorst wrote, "We must never forget that we may also find meaning in life even when confronted with a hopeless situation, when facing a fate that cannot be changed. For what then matters is to bear witness to the uniquely human potential at its best, which is to transform a personal tragedy into a triumph, to turn one's predicament into a human achievement. When we are no longer able to change a situation we are challenged to change ourselves,"[18] or find a course of action that will allow us to feel that sense of closure or triumph.

In one of Shel Silverstein's poems, "If the World was Crazy," he writes:

If the world was crazy, you know what I'd do?
I'd walk on the ocean and swim in my shoe,
I'd fly through the ground and I'd skip through the air,
I'd run down the bathtub and bathe on the stair…
And the greatest of men would be silly and lazy
So I would be king . . . if the world was crazy.[19]

Sometimes the world we live in is crazy, as Silverstein's composition so creatively points out. Life doesn't follow predictable rules like those of gravity or physics. Instead we are subject to the randomness of people, personalities, and circumstances. It is when we collide with these in challenging ways that Jewish tradition and ritual can become most helpful and meaningful. Ritual is not a cure-all, but it can be an act of empowerment, comfort, and peace. The rituals we incorporate into our lives must fulfill certain needs—like "meaning and community"[20]—even, as Arnold Eisen articulates, "in the absence of God's felt presence." However, we must compensate for that absence with the invocation of God's felt presence in song, text, and blessing.[21] As rabbis we can draw upon tradition to help others, as well as ourselves, find resolution to what ails us spiritually in order to create healthy, whole individuals and communities.

Notes

1. Isaac Mayer Wise, *Reminiscences* (Cincinnati: Leo Wise and Company, 1901), 155-172.
2. Alexander Moreira-Almeida, Francisco Lotufo Neto, and Harold G. Koenig, "Religiousness and Mental Health: A Review," *Brazilian Journal of Psychiatry* 28, no. 3 (2006): 243.
3. Harold G. Koenig, Michael E. McCullough, and David B. Larson, *Handbook of Religion and Health* (Oxford: Oxford University Press, 2001), 214–15.
4. Ibid., 228.
5. Moreira-Almeida, et al., *Religiousness and Mental Health: A Review*, 247.
6. Job 23:1.
7. T *B'rachot* 60b.
8. Irwin Kula and Vanessa L. Ochs, eds., *The Book of Jewish Sacred Practices: CLAL's Guide to Everyday and Holiday Rituals and Blessings* (Woodstock, VT: Jewish Lights Publishing, 2001), 1.
9. E.M. Broner, *Bringing Home the Light: A Jewish Woman's Handbook of Rituals* (San Francisco: Council Oaks Books, 1999), 2.
10. Judah Goldin, "Of Change and Adaptation in Judaism," in *Studies in Midrash and Related Literature*, ed. Barry L. Eichler and Jeffrey H. Tigay (Philadelphia: The Jewish Publication Society, 1988), 215.
11. Judith Viorst, *Necessary Losses* (New York: Simon and Schuster, 1986), 266.
12. Chaim Stern, ed., *On the Doorposts of Your House* (New York: CCAR Press, 1994), 148–50.
13. David Lieb, "On Private Prayer: A Covenantal Experience," *CCAR Journal* (Fall 1998):45.
14. Job 23:1.
15. *Pirkei Avot* 4:3
16. Ps. 71:1–4, 12.
17. Viktor E. Frankl, *Man's Search for Meaning* (Boston: Beacon Press, 2006), 113.
18. Viorst, *Necessary Losses*, 112.
19. Shel Silverstein, *Where the Sidewalk Ends* (New York: Harper Collins, 2004), 146.
20. Arnold Eisen, *Rethinking Modern Judaism: Ritual, Commandment and Community* (Chicago: University of Chicago Press, 1998), 256.
21. Ibid., 262–63.

The Intermediate Blessings of the *Amidah* as the Model for a Personal Twelve-Step Program

Jeffrey Ableser

Over the past twenty years, because of their widely perceived success, Twelve-Step programs have been adapted to a wide range of addictions and dependencies. The purpose of this article is to examine the intermediate twelve (or thirteen)[1] benedictions of the *Amidah* as the paradigm for a personal twelve-step program. Popularly known as the *Sh'moneh Esreih* (eighteen), the normative form of this prayer at weekday services involves eighteen (now nineteen) benedictions. (This rubric of prayer is reduced to seven benedictions during Shabbat or Holy Day services and to nine benedictions during the traditional Rosh HaShanah *Musaf* service, at which the shofar is sounded.) It makes sense to refer to the "intermediate weekday benedictions" because, in all forms of the *Amidah*, the first three and last three benedictions remain essentially the same.

The primary reason for pursuing this course of inquiry is that a twelve-step program imbedded in something as central to Judaism as the *Amidah*, which is also known as *HaT'filah* (the Prayer, par excellence), would hold an immediate authenticity for Jews. This issue of authenticity has been addressed by the two leading Jewish exponents of Twelve Steps, Rabbis Kerry Olitzky and Dr. Abraham J. Twerski.[2] While they are persuasive that the Twelve-Step approach is in line with Jewish values, Jews continue to be wary of these programs.

There is already solid spadework that suggests that the intermediate blessings serve as a coherent process towards *national* redemption, this despite the fact that many of the benedictions

JEFFREY ABLESER (C81) is the rabbi of Congregation Beth El in Windsor, Ontario, Canada.

seemed to be couched as personal prayers. This hypothesis was first promulgated by Professor Leon Liebreich, who declined to publish it except in abbreviated form due to its apparent unprovability.[3] Still, others, including such Conservative scholars as Reuven Hammer and Reuven Kimelman, have come to similar conclusions, apparently independently.[4]

In brief, the hypothesis is based in the Talmudic statement that Rabban Gamaliel fixed the order of the benedictions of the *Amidah*, even though, as evidenced by fragments found by Solomon Schechter in the Cairo Genizah, the actual text of each benediction remained unfixed for centuries. Liebreich's theory is that Rabban Gamaliel fixed the order of benedictions as an antidote to the messianic impulses of his time, a generation after the destruction of the Second Temple and the Fall of Judea in the first war against Rome.

The main themes of the intermediate blessings are:

4. For knowledge (or acknowledgment)
5. For repentance (or return to God)
6. For forgiveness
7. For deliverance
8. For healing
9. For "years" (agricultural fertility in the Land of Israel)
10. For the ingathering of the exiles
11. For justice (the restoration of just judges)
12. For punishment of heretics
13. For reward of the righteous
14. For the rebuilding of Jerusalem
15. For the coming of the Messiah (restoration of the Davidic dynasty)
16. For God to hear and accept prayer

Liebreich makes a compelling, if unprovable, case that these thirteen blessings teach us on a daily basis of the possibility of an incremental process towards national redemption. Several of the blessings speak to our quotidian aspirations as individuals. But can these intermediate blessings serve as a blueprint for recovery and personal redemption?

I believe these blessings can be relevant to us as individuals if we can allow ourselves to see them as an incremental approach to individual integrity and personal redemption. The most popular paradigm for an incremental approach to recovery in our time is the Twelve-Step approach made popular by Alcoholics Anonymous. The purpose of this article is to propose that, with a little metaphorical interpretation, particularly for those prayers couched in a "national" context, we can see the twelve or thirteen intermediate blessings of the *Amidah* as a series of *kavanot* that can serve as the basis for an authentically Jewish twelve-step approach to recovery from a personal affliction or addiction.

The Blessings and Their Interpretation

The twelve intermediary benedictions form four triads of blessings, each triad responding to a different sensibility. The first triad focuses on *t'shuvah*, which, as Soloveitchik[5] has noted, is linked to the aesthetic sensibility that one is in need of spiritual cleansing. (It is noteworthy that much of the argot surrounding the combating of addiction uses language about "cleaning up.") The second triad focuses on restoring health to one's body and relationships. The third triad appeals to the ethical sensibility and restoring balance to one's critical and self-critical faculties. The last triad uses imagery that can excite the religious imagination.[6]

Blessing 4, the first of the intermediate benedictions, is a prayer for wisdom or knowledge. Liebreich understands this blessing to be the critical first step in making changes. He submits that Rabban Gamaliel understood that the first step was for people to acknowledge the mistakes that had been made that led to their downfall and to the destruction of the Second Temple, much of Jerusalem, and the subjugation of the Judeans by the Romans in the year 70 C.E. On a personal level, the first step towards turning one's life around must also be acknowledgment that one has a problem. Logically, if one refuses to acknowledge a problem, one will not take steps towards ameliorating the situation. Not coincidentally, this is also the first step in any twelve-step program.

Blessings 5, 6, and 7 then present us with a three-stage process towards getting back to square one. Blessing 5 is a prayer for repentance. Having acknowledged our affliction/addiction, we must repent our complicity in the hold it has had over our lives and acknowledge that we can't break its grip on our lives by ourselves. This corresponds to step 2 of the classic Twelve-Step approach. Blessing 6 is the logical consequence of successful repentance, which is a prayer for forgiveness. Interestingly, the prayer asks God for forgiveness not for our inherent worthiness, but because of God's mercy. The next step is a blessing for deliverance, not because we deserve it but "for God's name's sake." It explicitly asks God to "Look upon our affliction." While this blessing is widely understood to be a prayer for national redemption, Kimelman, based on the interpretation of Abudarham, sees it as a cry for personal redemption. He also notes that it is a fitting blessing between benedictions for forgiveness and healing.

One might feel that this step is the end of the process. It is possible to read the remaining classic Twelve Steps as a delineated approach to the process addressed in blessings 5 through 7. But this is really only the end of the beginning. A hallmark of twelve-step programs is the acknowledgment that the slate is never wiped completely clean. At best one is a recovering alcoholic. What is to keep the addiction/affliction from taking root again in the soul of the individual? The remaining blessings can be viewed as an incremental approach to giving the individual's soul the strength to resist a relapse into active addiction/affliction.

The next three blessings, 8, 9, and 10, focus on the physical or external forces that, if not addressed, can lead to and perpetuate addiction/affliction. Blessing 8 is a blessing for health. Liebreich understood that, on national terms, the Jewish people had been decimated by the war against Rome and needed to be physically "healed" in order to engage in the revitalization of their nation. On a personal level, the prayer for health at this juncture also makes perfect sense. With respect to the relationship between the individual and God, the body is still fertile ground for the affliction. It needs to be detoxified from the addiction. It needs to recover from the psychic wounds that led to the affliction in the first place, that made the individual susceptible to the affliction. It is a prayer to create a firm physical foundation for psychic health.

Echoing the words of the prophet Jeremiah, the blessing for health begins: "Heal us, O Lord, and we shall be healed; save us and we shall be saved . . . grant a perfect healing to all our wounds." While the addict can and should turn to medical and other professionals to help him combat his disease, God is invoked as the source of healing.

Blessing 9 is a national blessing for either "the land" or years. Gamaliel understood that for the Jewish nation to be reborn, the Land of Israel needed to be healed after years of warfare, exploitation, and neglect. On a personal level, this blessing can be seen as a prayer to break the cycle (years) of dependency. We can read this as a prayer for *shanim* (years), but also for *shinuyim* (positive changes). Blessing 9 can be used as an affirmation of the positive steps the addict has taken towards recovery. Blessing 10 is a prayer whose main themes are freedom and the ingathering of exiles. It invokes the images of a banner and of the shofar. On a national level, it acknowledges that after the Land and People of Israel have been restored to health, those exiled by the Roman war could now return to their home. On a personal level, the images evoke two prerequisites for a successful recovery. The shofar evokes the story of the *Akeidah*, the Binding of Isaac. Blessing 10 is thus a request that we no longer suffer from the addictions, afflictions, and neuroses that *bind* us. The banner can be seen as a sign to all those whom we have estranged through our previous bad behavior to return to us and become a support in our recovery. Just as a banner is raised, the addict is in the process of raising himself above his addiction. In this context, blessing 10 echoes steps 8 and 9 of the Twelve-Step program.

The next triad of blessings has the common theme of restoring judges and justice. Following Liebreich's thesis, Roman rule of Judea was accompanied by harsh Roman judges who promoted heresy and betrayal, and who persecuted the righteous. On a national level, a critical step in national recovery was the reestablishment of a Jewish judiciary, the punishment of heretics and collaborators, and the honoring of the righteous, including righteous converts. Blessing 12 is an attack on the *malshinim* (the badmouthers) that can exist inside our heads as well as within earshot. In the national context, the *malshinim* were the enemy within, messianists with unrealistic expectations of perfection. According to R. Ishmael, they incited hatred between God and Israel (*Shabbat* 116a). On a personal level, a key foundation for successful recovery is the ability to develop a balanced perspective on one's problems, perhaps through interaction with others (blessing 10). How often is self-destructive behavior a response to an irrational internal critic? Blessings 11, 12, and 13 combine to form a prayer for the restoration of sound judgment, suppressing the internal critic and promoting that which in us is upright and ethical.

Having restored our physical and moral equilibrium, we now turn to the last triad of blessings. Blessing 14 calls for the restoration of Jerusalem. Blessing 15 calls for the restoration of the rightful Davidic dynasty. Finally, blessing 16 asks God to hear our prayer. On a personal level, these benedictions can be seen as the culmination of the process of recovery—the realization that we are holy beings made in God's image. The prayer for Jerusalem can be interpreted as a personal appeal that we may once again be a vessel of God's presence. As such, we are beings capable of nobility and majesty, not unlike King David. But if our self-perception becomes too majestic, we may create fertile ground for a relapse into affliction. Blessing 16 serves as a potent corrective to the previous blessing evoking majesty; we once again appeal to God to have mercy and pity us, and in genuine humility to accept our prayer.

The wisdom that can make for national redemption can also serve as a blueprint for personal redemption. After an initial prayer for the wisdom to acknowledge our affliction, we perceive four triads that bring us towards recovery. The triad for successful *t'shuvah* is followed by an appeal for physical circumstances that are a prerequisite for spiritual rebuilding. The next triad acknowledges the importance of a balanced perspective and sound judgment in keeping us from falling back into old patterns of self-destructive behavior. Once achieved, we can begin to look at ourselves as vessels of holiness.

Benefits and Concerns of This New Approach

What would be the positive consequences of creating a twelve-step program based on the *Amidah*? As stated above, one of the concerns that Olitzky and Twerski have had to address is Jewish resistance to Twelve-Step programs. Despite their persuasive arguments that Twelve-Step programs are consonant with Jewish life, many Jewish addicts remain unconvinced. Some of their resistance is circumstantial; most Twelve-Step programs are based in churches, and often conclude with the Lord's Prayer.

A Jewish twelve-step program rooted in the *Amidah* could not be so easily dismissed. I could envision Jewish twelve-step meetings that would be an organic outgrowth of a weekday service. Such a service would have a specific audience and focus, not unlike the Healing Services that exist in many of our congregations. Perhaps there would be special meditations attached to the *Amidah* when it was recited in the service. Since there is a long tradition of praying the *Amidah* silently before praying it aloud, there would be additional time for the participants to focus on these mediations.

A major question is whether these services would include the public confessions, which are a hallmark of the Twelve-Step process. Jewish confession, or *vidui*, plays a prominent place in Jewish worship, particularly during the High Holy Days. But that confession is couched in the first person plural, and is recited privately. Is this traditional form of Jewish *vidui* as effective as the public confessions that occur at Twelve-Step meetings? If *vidui* is kept silent, do such services have to focus on a specific addiction, or just reflect on the addiction recovery process itself? Would Jews accept the risk of public confession before fellow congregants? A broader question, which may go to the heart of Jewish resistance to Twelve-Step programs, is that while we Jews are all-too-well acquainted with guilt, we are relative novices when it comes to the shame that comes with public confession.

Ultimately, the proof of the pudding will be in the eating. Scientists still grapple with how the Twelve-Step process is so successful, but few deny its success in combating addiction for countless souls. I would encourage rabbis and others committed to combating Jewish addiction to explore the creation of "recovery services" or weekday *minyanim* that utilize the metaphorical approach to the *Amidah* outlined above. Perhaps these services will only stimulate the impulse to join a traditional Twelve-Step program. But I believe there is wisdom, particularly for Jews, in pursuing a Twelve-Step model based in the directives of Rabban Gamaliel, who understood that the *Amidah* could lead the Jewish spirit from degradation to recovery.

Notes

1. There are currently nineteen benedictions in the weekday *Amidah*. There are two dominant theories concerning which benediction was added to the original eighteen. One theory is that the fourteenth and fifteenth blessings were split apart to honor the Exilarch in Babylonia. The other theory is that the "blessing" against heretics is the added blessing.

2. Olitzky and Twerski have written several books on the Twelve Steps and addiction that have added immeasurably to Jewish support for combating addiction. Olitzky's works include *Twelve Jewish Steps to Recovery*, which ties the classical Twelve Steps to twelve Jewish values, and *100 Blessings Every Day*, which, pointedly,

includes a foreword by Rabbi Neil Gillman entitled "Are the Twelve Steps Jewish?" Both are published by Jewish Lights Publishing. Twerski has written many books on addiction and recovery, including *Addictive Thinking* (Center City, MN: Hazelden, 1990) and *I'd Like to Call for Help, But I Don't Know the Number* (New York: Henry Holt and Company, 1996). Rabbi Rami Shapiro has also contributed to the field with his *Recovery—The Sacred Art* (Woodstock, VT: Skylight Paths, 2009).

3. L. Liebreich, "The Intermediate Benedictions of the *Amidah*," *Jewish Quarterly Review* 42, no. 4 (April 1952): 423–26.

4. Reuven Hammer, *Entering Jewish Prayer*, (New York: Schocken Books, 1994) and Reuven Kimelman, "The Daily Amida and the Rhetoric of Redemption," *Jewish Quarterly Review* 79, no. 2–3 (1988–1989): 165ff.

5. Pinchas H. Peli, *On Repentance: The Thought and Oral Discourses of Rabbi Joseph Dov Soloveitchik* (Northvale, NJ: Jason Aronson, 1996).

6. Soren Kierkegaard wrote about three categories of the aesthetic, the ethical, and the religious in *Concluding Unscientific Postscript*. This will be explored in a future essay.

A Very Personal Reflection: Debbie Friedman's Setting of *Mi Shebeirach* as a Sonata

Evan Kent

One of the archetypal musical forms of the Western musical canon is the sonata. The sonata came into maturity during the classical period—that epoch that roughly extends from 1750–1830 and is defined by the likes of works of Mozart, Haydn, and Beethoven. The term "sonata" occurs as both a descriptive term of the larger forms of music (as when we refer, for example, to Beethoven's *Moonlight Sonata*) or as a way of referring to the first movement of many compositions of the classical period, including string quartets, concerti, and symphonies. It is this latter usage of the term "sonata" of which I am speaking here. The sonata form is generally comprised of three sections: exposition, development, and recapitulation. The exposition introduces a musical theme and often a second, contrasting melodic idea. In the development section, the composer artfully plays with the musical themes previously introduced. Typically, this includes harmonic modulations, melodic sequences, and rhythmic alterations. Finally, in the recapitulation, the composer commonly returns to the original melodic material and the initial key center. This first movement sonata form is essentially a musical sonic journey. As listeners, we enjoy the comfort of the exposition, revel in the excitement of the development, and are soothed as we return to the familiarity of melody and harmony as we experience the musical return: the recapitulation.

As a cantor, music is the medium through which I communicate the best. After a quarter of a century in congregational life, I understand the power sacred vocal music has in expressing the innermost yearnings of the heart and soul. I am blessed to

---

EVAN KENT (SSM NY 88) is the cantor at Temple Isaiah in Los Angeles and is on the faculty of the Los Angeles campus of HUC-JIR.

reside in a world of music as I often hear melody and rhythm in the quotidian sounds of the urban landscape and I am particularly aware of musical structures, shapes, and forms manifest in both the musical and the nonmusical. Like the painter who sees geometry and symmetry in the landscape, I perceive music and observe structure in the soundscape of my own life. This personal sonic backdrop includes the thousands of songs and prayers, chants, and *nigunim*, the panoply of sacred and secular music that are embodied in my soul and being. Familiar songs and chants are continually renewed each time they are sung and new meaning and awareness develops as part of this process of continual evolution.

After many years of chanting and singing Debbie Friedman's version of the *Mi Shebeirach* for healing, I see this prayer as a type of personal spiritual sonata. The words and music have allowed me to embark on a spiritual journey with *Mi Shebeirach* as the anchor. It is through this lens of the sonata form—the familiar musical structure of exposition-development-recapitulation—that I view this prayer's development as a part of my own repertory and I appreciate how it has informed my personal theology and philosophy. When I am singing the prayer at the bedside of a congregant, whispering it for an ailing loved one or friend, or singing it with my congregation at a Shabbat service, this sonata structure is apparent to me. This exposition-development-recapitulation exists when the *Mi Shebeirach* is sung, and it informs my understanding of the prayer not only in my life but in the lives of my congregants as an inherent and important part of our worship.

Exposition

Although I was aware that traditional settings for healing existed, my first encounter with a contemporary *Mi Shebeirach* for healing was that written by Debbie Friedman, z"l. It provided me with words and music for those situations in which I as a cantor needed to express hope and comfort to those who were ill as well as to caregivers. While I cannot exactly recall the first time I experienced Friedman's *Mi Shebeirach*, I do know it created a seismic shift in my own theology and my philosophical understanding of the power of liturgy.

I grew up in the sort of suburban Judaism of the 1960s and 1970s that has been well chronicled. We prayed from the *Union Prayer Book*, read responsively English text in italicized print, sang hymns in unison aided by a hidden choir accompanied by organ. Acts of social action loomed large in my life and that of the congregation and provided me with both a formidable grounding in understanding the Reform Jewish pursuit of *tikkun olam* and the concept of "prophetic Judaism." However, an honest and personal connection to prayer and to the sacred was lacking from my own faith. Over time the synagogue experienced some liturgical changes. The *Union Prayer Book* was replaced by *Gates of Prayer*, the choir was traded for a series of young, eager cantorial students from Hebrew Union College, and the unison hymns were supplemented by some of the newer melodies I had heard at summer camp and winter conclaves. Although liturgies and music might have changed, my personal ability to encounter holiness both in the sanctuary and beyond its walls was lacking.

It was because of my initial encounter with Friedman's *Mi Shebeirach* that I began to conceptualize a God who was present and intimate rather than a God perceived as aloof and distant. The *Mi Shebeirach* allowed me to comprehend how prayer might have a real and tangible place in my life. The liturgies in which I had previously participated were void of intercessory prayer and my early synagogue experiences had me question the validity, legitimacy, and effectiveness of such prayers. The strictures of the Reform Judaism I had known made me question if these sorts of prayers were not a little too magical or rooted in the supernatural. But these initial doubts were minimized when I sat with the ill and their families and caregivers and we sang *Mi Shebeirach* together, and voices once replete with fear and sadness transformed into voices of hope.

For me as a cantor, Friedman's *Mi Shebeirach* provided me with a voice that offered hope and comfort not only to the ill, but to caregivers and family. I had sung at the bedsides of the ill—often the words of a psalm or a setting of *Oseh Shalom*. But Friedman's *Mi Shebeirach* succeeded in providing comfort by providing accessibility to a prayer text and a mode of prayer that until this time had been the bastion of a more traditional Judaism. *Mi Shebeirach* was my personal exposition—an awakening to the power of prayer—especially intercessory prayers.

Development

The second section in the sonata form is the development. The theme modulates, it is excerpted, extracted, and often the composer will change keys—sometimes in rapid succession. But at the core of the development is the essence of the exposition. So it is true with the *Mi Shebeirach* for healing. Friedman's *Mi Shebeirach* had been presented at various conferences and biennials, but its development as a part of the congregation's prayer was still to be determined. Thoughtful debate in clergy and staff meetings ensued over the theology of praying for the ill. We discussed the historical nature of the prayer and where it would be placed in the Friday night service. We wondered if it was truly appropriate for members of the congregation to call out names or was it enough to just sing Friedman's melody. We earnestly discussed issues of confidentiality (e.g., What if someone called out someone's name who did not wish to be identified as ill?). Initially we collected names on a handwritten list before services began, but that proved difficult as often handwriting was illegible. Subsequently, we then asked congregants to telephone a secretary with names for a list that was printed for the clergy. That presented an additional challenge as names often were placed on the list but often never taken off. Finally, the manner of announcing names at services as Friedman herself had done in a prayer setting was utilized.

In my congregation, the singing of *Mi Shebeirach* and the mentioning of names transforms prayer from the often abstract and theoretical into a prayerful moment that is real and vivid. Whether the choreography of the moment of offering names was announced as "as my eyes meet yours" or "as my hand passes through the room" the congregation became alive and alert and eager to share the names of loved ones. From my perspective of standing in front of the congregation, I could see how earnest and deliberate this annunciation of names was. Congregants waited patiently to call out the names of the ill and obeyed a self-imposed code of behavior to assure that the name they were mentioning was heard by all. Some wept as they called out a name; others held the hand of a friend or family member. As we joined in the second verse of the *Mi Shebeirach*, arms were often placed around shoulders and remained there until the prayer's final "Amen."

Initially, I envisioned that Friedman's *Mi Shebeirach* would be just one of many prayers for healing that the congregation would sing. I tried to introduce other musical settings of healing texts, but the strength of Friedman's melody was too pervasive. After singing an alternate healing composition on a Friday evening, a congregant approached me at the *Oneg Shabbat* and told me how much they wanted me to lead them in the "real *Mi Shebeirach*" or the "traditional melody." Although I favor a wide and diverse palate for most liturgical settings, it was evident that Friedman's melody had become "*Mi Sinai*" in a short time.

The singing of *Mi Shebeirach* and its announcement of names presents the congregational community with an opportunity to simultaneously experience the prayers of the community as well as the prayers of the individual. The calling out of names provides a momentary break from our first-person plural liturgy and presents a detour toward the first-person singular. At that moment of announcing names, the community is concurrently comprised of the individual and the collective with a constant vacillation between these two. *Sh'ma koleinu* and *sh'ma koli* (hear our voice and hear my voice) reside side-by-side.

Mi Shebeirach presents a unique moment where the individual voice rises and rides on the wave of the community's support. The congregation, informed of all those who are ill, then embraces those names, takes those names and all the hardship, sadness, and the hope these names represent and holds onto them as the second verse of the setting is sung. This sense of the community embracing itself and all whom these names represent is one of the unique features of this liturgical moment. The profound experience of the singing of *Mi Shebeirach* has prompted me to examine how other parts of our communal worship can present moments of prayer that are as engaging and vibrant and lend themselves to as salient a liturgical moment as that of the *Mi Shebeirach*. For example, could a similar moment be presented as part of the prayer of thanksgiving *Modim Anachnu Lach*? If a "*Modim* moment" were presented as the *Mi Shebeirach* is—with congregants sharing with each other all that for which they are thankful—would we rejoice in communal gratitude? Or perhaps a creative composer might write a new setting of *Birkat HaGomeil* that would enable a congregation to share another member's escape from danger? Would any of these other attempts be as powerful as that of the *Mi Shebeirach* or would they just be seen as derivative and imitative? Could the recitation of Mourner's *Kaddish* be recast to provide an even greater impact for both the mourner and the congregation? The words and music of *Mi Shebeirach* provided me with a doorway into achieving greater understanding of how prayer might be most expressive and effective within the congregational setting.

Recapitulation

In the classical sonata form, the recapitulation brings the listener back to the original thematic material. After the development takes us on a melodic and harmonic journey, we arrive back at that which is familiar. Debbie Friedman was famous for her instruction on how the *Mi Shebeirach* would be sung. Debbie would sing the first stanza. Her plaintive rendition would cause each of us to draw closer and to embrace each other more firmly. At this moment of healing, Debbie essentially held all of our ill and cared for them as a nurse, loving parent, physician, and healer. The second verse was sung in unison as we coalesced into a community of caregivers.

In many congregations, including my own, the first verse is sung, then names are presented by the congregation, and then the second verse is sung. The first verse of the prayer is the exposition and the interval between the verses functions as the development. The music playing in the background as names are called out marks the development—not in the classical sense, but it is a development nonetheless. In the interval between verses the initially presented melodic material becomes a recipient of an overlay of names in need of healing and adds texture and richness to the melody. When the congregation has called out all the names in need of healing of body, mind, or spirit and the second verse is sung, the worship space is transformed. Although the music is the same and the words are similar, we as a congregation have changed. As a community we have become aware of "those in need of healing" in our midst, and when we sing the second verse the names hover above us as if supported by scaffolding constructed of care and love.

I witnessed Debbie Friedman sharing her *Mi Shebeirach* with various congregations on numerous occasions and the power in her presentation was extraordinary. Even though Friedman's instruction for the *Mi Shebeirach* was always similar, the prayer never felt static or mundane or preplanned. The sanctuaries, convention halls, chapels, or auditoriums in which she offered the prayer were never the same, and those in need of healing and consolation were different each time the prayer was sung. Friedman's *Mi Shebeirach* had an almost electric vibrancy each time she sang it, and this vitality is apparent in my own congregation (and congregations throughout the world) when the prayer is sung.

Coda

Debbie Freidman wrote her setting of *Mi Shebeirach* in 1987, and it was adopted by my congregation as a prayer for healing within a few years of its composition. I have sung it hundreds of times and it has never become tiresome or weary because each week it changes. The interlude between the verses is filled with names that are forever evolving. Some weeks there are more names than others. Some names are called out for only a week or two; other names are recited for months, even years. Like the finest of classical sonatas we have yet to grow tired of this rendition of *Mi Shebeirach*. The power of prayer, the strength of faith, and the potency of community is manifest in those words that have become so familiar to many of us:

Bless those in need of healing with *r'fuah sh'leimah.*
And let us say: Amen.

Standing in Life before God: Report and Reflection on One Congregation's First Steps for Creating a Congregation-Based Program on Health and Wellness

Richard F. Address

One of the unexpected outgrowths of the Sacred Aging program of the Union for Reform Judaism's Department of Jewish Family Concerns[1] was the interest that was evidenced in issues related to health and wellness. As we looked at this fact, it became clear that this heightened interest was being driven by the rising number of baby boomers. Faced with the challenges of extended life spans, caring for their own aging parents over a longer period of time, and the desire to delay the reality of aging as long as possible, boomers have emerged as an active cohort in seeking physical, emotional, and spiritual avenues that seek to promote health and wellness. Longevity has also meant that more people are living with chronic medical conditions that in a previous generation may have meant death. However, the miracle of medical technology has now made it possible for many to live long and fulfilling lives. Their interest in maintaining a healthy lifestyle is more than just theoretical; it may be life saving. On the other end, longevity has also seen the gradual rise in instances of dementia and Alzheimer's, which bring into sharp focus the frail and random nature of health. With these blessings and curses has come a greater awareness of the mystery of health and the importance of our need to take care of this most basic of gifts.

Department staff observed a slow rise in the number of synagogue programs that began to look at various aspects of health and wellness

---

RICHARD F. ADDRESS (C72) serves as senior rabbi of Congregation M'kor Shalom in Cherry Hill, New Jersey. He previously served as founder and director of the URJ Department of Jewish Family Concerns and how Jewish texts could inform this new interest. Congregations have begun to develop support groups and programs for families dealing with dementia and Alzheimer's as well as diseases such as cancer. Numerous communities have created major programs, either on a yearly or random basis, that look at issues that speak to Judaism and issues of mental health.[2] A renewed emphasis on what we put into our bodies informs how congregations add healthy food choices to *Oneg Shabbat*, youth group events, and snacks served at meetings. It is no longer unusual to find apples and fruit next to the cakes and candy, or juices and water as an option to sodas. As baby boomers expand their own searches for spirituality, congregations have responded by adding classes on yoga and meditation, even incorporating some of these techniques into worship. Gradually these ideas are permeating the psyches of congregational life. There have even been congregations that have taken health and wellness on as a yearlong project or as a theme for a scholar-in-residence weekend. All of this is slowly impacting the world of Jewish communal programming—one project at a time. An interesting challenge that has grown from this is whether these disparate programs can be harnessed to create a holistic, congregation-wide approach to health and wellness—an approach that would encompass not a segment of a community, but be cross generational in nature.

Congregation M'kor Shalom is representative of many of our congregations. It is located in a suburb of Philadelphia and has a membership that spans the generations. The congregation is approaching its fortieth year of life and has an active and involved membership. I came to the pulpit in the summer of 2011 and presented a challenge to the lay leadership to see if we could evolve a congregation-wide program on Judaism, health, and wellness that would involve the entire congregation—from preschool through older adults. What I wanted to try was to see if we could create an integrated cross-generational approach to the issues of health that would involve a variety of people and resources and that would possibly provide new opportunities for leadership development, programmatic integration, and creativity. This effort could fall under a common united theme of health and wellness and emerge from Jewish texts and tradition. The congregation had an existing Caring Community committee and I approached them initially with an overall outline of the project as much of what I envisioned would fall under their purview.

The Caring Community membership along with the congregation's executive leadership and my clergy team agreed that we would launch this idea after Yom Kippur with a Sunday morning think tank open to the first thirty-six people to respond to an open invitation, distributed through the congregation's electronic and print communications. We were hoping that people who had an interest in this subject, and may not be ordinarily involved, would come forward for the discussion.

We filled our quota with two weeks to spare, and the group represented the desired cross sections: youth group through older adults, board members and new members, healthcare professionals and consumers. The stage was set.

The Think Tank

The Sunday after Yom Kippur we held the think tank from 9:00 A.M. to noon. To model some of the food issues, we served fresh fruit, yogurt, and energy bars along with coffee, tea, and water. A week prior to the session we sent out a kit of material that included a sample of texts that spoke to the issue of health and wellness, a collection of sample best practices culled from the work of Jewish Family Concerns, sample articles and a series of ideas for the congregation sent in by several people who were unable to come to the think tank due to family conflicts.

We began the morning with a *Shehecheyanu* and proceeded to outline the goal of the day: to share ideas on what a program on health and wellness would look like for the congregation. We explained that the ground rule was that we were not to worry about money or logistics; we were there to dream. We followed with about twenty minutes of text study. We asked the group (seated around tables, eight to a table) to look at one of three texts that spoke to the theology of health. The discussion set the stage for an overview of existing programs that have been tried in various congregations around North America. We outlined how they emerged and what resources were available to assist in their being developed for the congregation. These two preliminary conversations allowed us to see what the theological foundation was for our overall project, as well as to observe that this discussion was not taking place in a vacuum—that indeed, other congregations had developed bits and pieces of programming on health and wellness issues. Our next task was then to spend a significant amount of time in table discussion with the goal of asking each other what a congregation-wide program would look like.

What was surprising and inspiring in the early sessions was the conversation that ensued about our body's relationship to God. The three texts that we studied were the Physician's Prayer, attributed to Maimonides; the morning blessing that thanks God that our veins and arteries work so that we can stand in life before God; and a midrash (*Vayikra Rabbah* 34:3) that featured a dialogue between Hillel and students on the mitzvah of caring for our bodies. The ideas that our bodies come as a gift from God and that health is a command based on our relationship with God provided a fascinating and challenging few moments of dialogue. It was fascinating to observe how the attendees related to the idea that they may not have "control" over their own bodies, and challenging because a variety of questions were raised about the tension between what someone would want and what Judaism may say. This tension found its way into questions that touched on end-of-life issues and that was pursued even further when we overviewed congregational programs developed to teach the Jewish approach to decision making at the end of life.[3] These conversations pointed out the need for allowing congregants to freely discuss how they see God and the role of tradition in these issues. Our contemporary Western medical model, indeed our secular society, is fine with compartmentalizing the role of God in medical issues. Yet, when we open the conversation to the Jewish holistic mind-body-soul model, it is as if a floodgate opens for many of our people. The role of spirituality in the conversations around health and wellness is coming under increasing scrutiny and is reflective of our people's desire for something more than a scientific approach to these issues. One senses in these conversations the need for meaning and purpose, a need to see the emphasis on health not as an end in itself, but as part of a larger psycho-spiritual quest. It is to this point that synagogues can be of significant importance for, through our texts and traditions, we can again show that we are part of something beyond the self.

For about an hour the members of the think tank discussed their ideas on how to bring this project to life. The conversations around the table were animated. Each table was given the responsibility to record the major suggestions in order for them to be reported out to the group as a whole. We made it clear that this enterprise would be ongoing and evolving and that we would begin implementing some of the ideas this program year. There were five tables in the room and thus five recorders reporting their ideas. The ideas spanned the range of possible programs and included suggestions from pre-school through all ages. Ideas suggested everything from classes to large-scale congregation-wide educational forums. There were calls to broaden the base and include other congregations and Jewish organizations (JCC, Jewish Family Service), as well as to increase the congregation's Caring Community portfolio and presence.

It was possible to break down the dozens of suggestions into several broad categories. The first were calls for major congregation-wide education programs. These are scheduled to include a session on how Jewish texts and tradition looks at the issue of caregiving and another on how texts and tradition can inform people on making sacred decisions at the end of life in light of medical technology. These subjects reflect the broad practical need for such educational opportunities given the congregation's demographic.

A second rubric looked at community-wide suggestions such as creating, as some congregations have, a regularly scheduled health fair that would include teaching segments on health issues, information on local resources in health-related fields, and direct service sessions such as blood pressure screenings and flu shots.

A third area that attracted a lot of attention can be labeled niche programs. For example, there were several suggestions on creating a more comprehensive curriculum on health for the religious school. Likewise, several tables commented on the need to address the emotional and spiritual health of teens in light of the increased pressure on young people. We also noted calls for the development of programs and support for *b'nei mitzvah* families who were dealing with stresses of blended family, interfaith, and single-parent issues. Finally, and not unexpectedly, we were asked to consider increasing awareness of the issue of Judaism and addiction. This idea also led to a suggestion that we consider developing a staff position for a congregational healthcare worker who would visit members as well as work in teaching issues related to Judaism and health to the entire congregation. This suggestion emerged from some of the Sacred Aging conversations and from previous attempts on the part of a very few congregations to create such a position. This position was an interpretation of the Catholic Church's Parish Nurse program. It has not translated so well into our world. The conversation at our think tank around this subject has led to our developing a relationship with our local Jewish Family and Children's Service, which has seen them assign a full time concierge to work with us in the development of the Health and Wellness Initiative.

A fourth area involved some kind of enhanced direct service to congregants: classes in such areas as yoga and meditation, support programming for individuals, and a patient advocate project. This latter idea would see the development of a person or persons within the congregation who would work with clergy to assist congregants in dealing with insurance issues, Medicare and Medicaid issues, assisting in consulting on placement of parents or family members and the like. The idea behind this is to have, as a first line of support, the ability for clergy to refer a person or family to a fellow congregant who had some expertise in these areas. The creation of our Jewish Family Service concierge, as noted above, has helped move this idea forward. Individuals from the congregation who are interested in developing programs can call on our concierge to assist in developing additional support and service to members. The first line of contact will remain within the congregation. We hope this partnership will also model a more cooperative, communal approach to serving the needs of members.

Priority-Setting Session

Two weeks after the think tank, nine people, who had volunteered to return to discuss priorities, came back to review the suggestions that emerged from the think tank and to begin a process of prioritizing the suggestions as to what was possible in the near term and what could be looked at later. At that meeting, we agreed that we would schedule congregation-wide educational forums titled The Art of Care-Giving and Making Sacred Decisions at the End of Life. We also decided to offer support and supplemental programming in each of these areas if the need arose. One participant then agreed to research the development of a cancer survivors' network for the congregation. The issues of illness support continued to be a major topic, and we discussed mechanisms to create a more relationship-based approach to deal with this issue using the existing Caring Community as a prime means of interaction. We decided to move forward and enhance the existing "friendly visitor" program that was in place and to explore additional support in areas of transportation to congregation events.

A second area that meeting participants prioritized was offering programming to respond to the stresses of being a young person. The group decided to immediately implement discussions and classes for confirmation and post-confirmation that dealt with issues such as bullying, peer pressures, body image, self-inflicted violence, addictions, and other self-destructive behaviors. The group suggested that we work with the director of religious education to overview how these subjects could be introduced in middle school grades and how we could develop a healthy-living curriculum that would embrace the entire school.

The discussion of priorities gave rise to a third concern. Those at the session were very interested in following up suggestions from the think tank on creating educational and direct support programs around the issue of cancer. The number of individuals in the congregation, from teens to older adults, who are living with or have been touched by cancer is noteworthy. This discussion has generated the beginnings of the creation of a support network of individuals who will be available to people who are dealing with the disease, and we will move forward with a major educational program within the year on the spiritual issues related to cancer. It was surprising that the overwhelming theme of the priority-setting meeting dealt not with issues of physical health, but with issues related to mental health. The attendees seemed to feel that spiritual health was very much related to a sense of mental health and well-being—more so than physical health. Even the discussion at the end of our session that dealt with creating the patient advocate project was focused around the idea of lessening stressors for care-givers, thus "making their life easier and relieving the stress of having to make decisions in a crisis."

Before the meeting ended the group strongly suggested that a serious "needs assessment" be undertaken to better understand the needs of the congregation that relate to the general areas of health and wellness. Everyone in attendance sensed that we needed to do everything we could to strengthen the interpersonal relationships within the congregation and to work in concert with committees and existing resources in the community ("to not reinvent the wheel"). The desire to create a cross-generational, integrated programmatic approach to issues of health and wellness will take several years to unfold. At the heart of the project is not just the creation of a program, but the desire to reach into the hearts and souls of our members to strengthen our relationships and to provide a safe nonjudgmental environment of spiritual health that, over time, engages an entire community. The application of Jewish texts and tradition to the life issues relevant to members has already begun to create a greater appreciation for the insights that our texts and tradition can provide. For example, various committee discussions raised questions as to how a particular idea would reflect our Health and Wellness project. The programs already done in confirmation and post-confirmation class have sparked ideas for next steps. Changes in foods that are served at meetings have been put into place. A weekly yoga class for synagogue staff was created. This is a project that is in its infancy but has the potential to reach into every household and bring a message and awareness of how Judaism can inform our views on health, healing, and wellness. It shall be an interesting ride.

Notes

1. The Sacred Aging program of the Union for Reform Judaism was a major part of the URJ's Department of Jewish Family Concerns. The program was created in order to produce programs and resources for congregations that would provide responses to the revolution in longevity that is now impacting our congregations and community. Special emphasis evolved on the growth and impact of the baby boom generation on contemporary synagogue life. For further examination of this issue, see Richard F. Address, *Seekers of Meaning: Baby Boomers, Judaism and the Pursuit of Healthy Aging* (New York: URJ Press, 2011).

2. Examples of such programs on mental health issues are those developed by Temple Israel in Minneapolis, Minnesota; Beth Emeth in Evanston, Illinois; Temple Sinai in Atlanta, Georgia; and Temple Chai in Scottsdale, Arizona. See also Richard F. Address, ed., *Caring for the Soul: R'fuat HaNefesh: A Mental Health Resource and Study Guide* (New York: URJ Press, 2003) and Edythe Held Mencher, *Resilience of the Soul: Developing Emotional and Spiritual Resilience in Adolescents and Their Families* (New York: URJ Press, 2007).

3. Richard F. Address, ed., *A Time to Prepare: A Practical Guide for Individuals and Families in Determining a Jewish Approach to Making Personal Arrangements, Establishing the Limits of Medical Care, and Embracing Rituals at the End of Life* (New York: URJ Press, 2002) and *Preparation and Consolation: An End of Life Resource Manual for Congregations* (New York: Congregation Rodeph Shalom, 2010).

Sacred Communities:
The Potential for Synagogues to be Communities of Caring and Meaning in the Older Population

Marion Lev-Cohen

The oldest of the baby boomers, the generation born between 1946 and 1964, turned sixty-five in 2011. Their sheer numbers bespeak their outsized influence. Throughout their lifetime, baby boomers have shaped American culture, politics, consumer patterns, and so much else—and they continue to do so, even as they age into what once were the retirement years. Baby boomers comprise the largest segment of North American Jews affiliated with Reform synagogues. "They are healthier, wealthier, more mobile and more highly educated than any preceding generation."[1]

With greater longevity, we have an increasingly large population of elderly in general, and of Jewish elderly in particular. As this large, accomplished, influential population grows older, their needs for services of all types related to aging will increase. For understandable reasons, the organized Jewish community, in its many manifestations, has begun to pay increasing attention to the needs and concerns of this growing population, one with extraordinary skills, resources, experience, and wisdom, as well as a concomitant list of physical, medical, and spiritual issues related to their aging and increased longevity.

Jewish baby boomers, and the older aging population, present both a challenge and opportunity to American non-Orthodox synagogues, the vast majority of which have as yet failed to prioritize empty nesters and those currently, or soon-to-become, age

MARION LEV-COHEN, ACSW (NY10) serves as an educational and pastoral rabbi at Central Synagogue. With Rabbi Rachel Cowan, she is working on developing resources for a Jewish spiritual approach to aging.

sixty-five and over. Over the years, Reform and Conservative congregations have devoted extraordinary efforts to educating children for bar/bat mitzvah, arguably making parents of school-age children their primary focus. As anxieties over dwindling membership rosters have mounted, some congregational leaders have of late shifted their energies to other population groups and related membership strategies, such as seeking to retain teenagers' families and to recruit young adult members. In short, the prime attention of rabbis and congregational lay leaders currently seems to center upon a younger demographic. However a large percentage of members are in their middle and senior years, as the Jewish population is aging. If for no other reason, the changing demography of congregations demands a shift toward focusing on those in their fifties and beyond. Such a shift would also be coherent with the Jewish values of the obligation to respect, care for, and meet the needs of our elderly. But doing so would require rethinking how the synagogue can support the psychological, social, and spiritual needs of this population, one with significant human and financial resources.

I am both a member of this age cohort and a rabbi who has spent some years working with those in their sixties and beyond. Drawing upon that interest, and the experience gained primarily at New York's Central Synagogue where I serve, I want to offer some reflections about the special needs and opportunities presented by two somewhat distinctive older adult populations. One is the middle-aged empty nesters (the current baby boomers); the other is the post–sixty-five population. As I hope to demonstrate, by weaving together the pastoral, the educational, and the social dimensions of our work as rabbis, we can build and strengthen the bonds of community among those in their later, still-vital, years.

Empty Nesters and Their Distinctive Features

In the wake of their adult children leaving home, many empty nesters take this opportunity to take stock of their lives. Social circles that have often been previously defined by children's school friends are now in flux and open to reconsideration as are, in some cases, their longstanding marriages. For some, it is a time to move to new communities, rupturing ties with long-cherished friends and deeply familiar communities. For many stay-at-home parents, it is a time to reenter the job market. For those who have been working outside the home, this can be a time to contemplate or undertake significant changes in lifelong careers, to consider meaningful volunteer activities, or even retire.

Many empty nesters have elderly parents for whom they serve as the primary caregivers. Some become caregivers for their partners. Regardless of the nature of the illness, being a primary caregiver engenders stress, changing the nature of the dynamics between the cared for and the caregiver, as well as affecting the greater family dynamics. Caregiving creates time demands on already busy people and generates financial concerns for families, especially those strapped with paying college tuitions. Recent studies have shown that caregivers get sick more often. They clearly need tangible and emotional support.[2]

Midlife is also a time when people experience increasing and sharpening concerns about health and longevity, sickness and mortality—be it of themselves, their spouses, or their lifelong friends. They are situated at a liminal point in their lives, on the threshold of what sociologist Sara Lawrence Lightfoot calls a "Third Chapter"[3] of life, one that raises discomfort but also presents opportunities to create new beginnings in the domains of sociability and work.

In his famous work on the developmental tasks of each decade of life, psychologist Erik Erikson described each stage as an attempt to master crucial milestones of identity.[4] Although we have come to appreciate that the stages are not quite as sequential as he depicted them, they still help us to examine the crucial elements of ego development. He described the task of midlife as being generativity, the primary task of which is to pass along one's wisdom to the next generation. Failure to do so can lead to stagnation, generativity's polar opposite.

The Post–Sixty-Five Population

In contrast with the empty nesters, people in their late sixties and older encounter even more occurrences of illness and loss of functioning. For many, deterioration in health, in themselves and those close to them, raises anxieties, not only about health, but also about relationships and legacy. With increasing amount of available time and a sharpening awareness of life's limitations, growing older evokes a sense of urgency about *doing* something useful and productive and *being* someone useful and productive.

Erik Erikson sees the main psychosocial task for people in this later stage of life as achieving ego integrity. This task is achieved primarily through a *cheshbon nefesh* process of assessing one's life and ideally arriving at the conclusion that one has indeed made a contribution to society. Failure to do so can result in despair.[5]

Central Synagogue as a Locus of Community

The congregation in which I am privileged to work and from which I draw much of my thinking about vital aging is New York's Central Synagogue. A thriving Reform congregation on Manhattan's Upper East Side, Central Synagogue has two thousand member units and a two-year waiting list of three hundred families that enjoy some of the services of member families. Unlike many congregations, most families choose to remain members even after celebrating their youngest children's *b'nei mitzvah*. Central Synagogue is a popular choice for affiliation of empty nesters who move back to Manhattan from the surrounding suburbs after their children leave for college. As a result, the congregation is blessed with a large complement of empty nesters and post–sixty-five congregants.

The overarching purpose of my work at Central Synagogue is to make the congregation the locus of community for this vital aging population. Toward that end, we offer a Caregivers' Group for those caring for elderly parents and spouses who are ill, as well as a spousal bereavement group.

Beyond these explicitly pastoral groups, I teach classes using texts that ask some of the existential questions of this stage of life. One class entitled Values and Virtues has included a focus upon character virtues (*midot*); we have studied Ecclesiastes, the Book of Ruth, the Book of Esther, and Psalms through the lens of the most salient issues for people at this life stage. We also offer an affinity group for people over the age of sixty-five to meet socially. Each of their meetings includes a Jewish educational or cultural component. Plans are currently underway to start an affinity group for empty nesters.

Although one could easily categorize my work with this population as falling into the domains of education, ritual, pastoral, and social opportunities, in truth there is no clear distinction between any of these categories. Each component is part of a virtuous circle that informs and enriches each other. All are embedded in the wisdom of our texts and tradition. And all serve the purpose of helping congregants to feel connected to a sacred and caring community.

Meaning Is the Question; God and Duty, the Answer

My first adult study class with this population, Making Meaning at Mid-Life, taught me to distinguish the two major population segments: empty nesters and post sixty-five. The class was composed primarily of women who were empty nesters, with a smattering of women in their mid- to late sixties.

In one session, a widowed congregant poignantly recounted a fulfilling life as a school psychologist, a satisfying marriage, rich friendships, and raising two children to be functioning independent and happy young adults. She said that at this stage of her life, her primary identity was none of these things—not mother, not psychologist, and not wife. She held out her hands and said plaintively, "Who am I?" This question of self-identification has resonated throughout the groups and individual pastoral counseling I have conducted. In all these settings, congregants ask, in effect, "What is my purpose, my function, my contribution here on earth?"

This question—asked in different ways at all life stages—can be destabilizing and frightening; or it can be challenging and invigorating. At its essence is the search for meaning and purpose.[6] As rabbis, we need to recognize that this question of ultimate meaning readily lends itself to specifically Jewish answers—those rooted in our texts, traditions, and narratives as a religion and a people.

As Rabbi Dayle Friedman suggests, older adults benefit when they are imbued with a sense of purpose and obligation by making explicit their duty of covenantal obligation.[7] This obligation stems ultimately from the covenant, or mutual contract, that the Israelites made with God at Mount Sinai. In the Torah portion, *Nitzavim*, the text goes to great length to make the point that all Israelites are obligated by this contact including, "Your little ones, your wives, the proselyte who is in the midst of your camps, from the hewer of your wood to the drawer of your water" (Deut. 29:9–11, 13–14).

According to the Or Chayim, as quoted in the *Stone Edition of the Chumash*, God specified these groupings to underscore the point that each and every person is obligated to take on those responsibilities of covenant, each according to his or her capacity.[8] These seemingly ethereal notions of covenantal duty and obligation actually provide an important framework of purpose and obligation for older members of our congregation.

To take an illustrative case, a congregant, deeply concerned about her husband's depressed mental state, asked me to visit her ailing husband at their home. A once active and vigorous businessman, Alvin was now confined as a result of a debilitating illness to a wheelchair, rarely able to leave his home. When I visited, he decried his physical impairment when so many of his contemporaries still led full and interesting lives. He ruminated as to what purpose he served on the earth. All he did, in his view, was eat and sleep.

I agreed with him that it was unfair that his illness caused him to be confined to a wheelchair in his mid-seventies. But I disagreed with him that he served no useful function. I argued that indeed he served a very important purpose to fulfill, in fact a covenantal obligation as a Jew, to discharge. I reminded him that as a member of the Jewish people, as a beloved husband and father, and as the bearer and shaper of his family's legacy, he still had an important task before him. His challenge was to model for his children and others how to conduct himself with such a disability. Like our forefather Jacob, who had given each of his children a personalized message, he had a legacy to transmit. I asked him to think of what values and messages he wanted his young adult children to learn. What would his legacy be to his children?

Alvin immediately shifted to speaking about his children, describing where they were currently in their lives, and of his aspirations for each of them. He agreed that he would speak to them to share his love for them and hope for their future. Alvin actually sat taller in his wheelchair. At least for that moment, he was imbued with a sense of duty, purpose, and mission. As Alvin's story demonstrates, helping someone reframe his or her situation can make the difference between feeling purposelessness and despair or feeling buoyed by an abiding sense of purpose and mission.

Like so many people in this age category, Alvin cannot be physically cured from his chronic illness. But for those who cope with long-term or terminal illness, pastoral intervention can help achieve at least in the moment, a state of emotional acceptance, healing, and wholeness.[9]

Particularly appropriate here are a few lines from Abraham Joshua Heschel that beautifully describe how purpose and meaning emanate from a sense of indebtedness: "The need to be needed corresponds to a fact: something is asked of man, every man. Advancing in years must not be taken to mean a process of suspending the requirements and commitments under which a person lives."[10]

Issuing Personal Invitations

We are beginning to see a shift in the Jewish communal world to a more personal, individualized approach to engaging people in Jewish life. Although labor intensive, the power of the personal invitation is becoming patently evident as clergy seek to build community one cup of coffee at a time.

Critical to my work in forming community is the judicious use of personal invitation. This means spending time one-on-one with individual congregants, hearing the stories of their lives, learning about their individual concerns, and discovering what gives their lives a sense of purpose. I have found that each time I invest as little as a half hour with a congregant, in a one-on-one conversation, they invariably begin to show up in classes, groups, and social gatherings at the synagogue.

Personal invitation is rooted in the biblical concept of honoring the uniqueness of each individual. Each time we extend a personal invitation to congregants to be involved in some aspect of congregational life, we acknowledge them as valued and valuable, holy and sacred individuals, created *b'tzelem Elohim* (in God's image). In *Parashat K'doshim* we read, "God spoke to Moses saying: Speak to the gathered Israelite community and say to them: 'You shall be holy, for I, your God *YHVH*, am holy'" (Lev. 19:1–2). These powerful words immediately raise several intertwining questions: Why be holy? What does holy mean? And, perhaps most importantly, how are we to be holy?

Underlying the answer to all these questions is the key feature of holiness: Holiness is an attribute of God. We are commanded to act like God (*imitatio dei*), for each of us has the capacity to be like God.

In my work with congregants, I view holiness as the capacity to see each human being as a unique manifestation of God. To quote Martin Buber:

> Every person born into this world represents something new, something that never existed before, and something original and unique. It is the duty of every person in Israel to know and consider that she is unique in the world in her particular character, and that there has never been someone like her in the world, for if there had been someone like her there would have been no need for her to be created. Every single person is a new thing in the world and is called upon to fulfill her particularity in the world.[11]

One example of this phenomenon at work is almost comical in nature. Two years ago, a gentleman appeared in one of my last classes of the semester. As he was late, he did not sign the roster. Since he was unknown to me, I called another congregant to ask his name to call and invite him to our next class. She inadvertently gave me the wrong name. Instead of the congregant I sought, I phoned a high-powered attorney who told me that he would probably be unable to make my classes as he had a very busy work schedule, but said the class sounded interesting. Not only did he come, he has rarely missed a class since!

Building Personal Connections

One of the most insidious elements of aging is the loss of people who have been significant in one's life, such as partners and close friends. Retirement and moving also disrupt the networks of friendship and colleagues, the key people who give richness to our lives and sustain us through the difficult times. Loneliness and lack of social networks are major challenges for the aging population. As a result, I find that one of my most important functions is weaving bonds of connection. I often act as a connector, a *shadchanit* of sorts, making sure that newcomers become integrated into the community by connecting people of similar interests and backgrounds. A woman who had been widowed four years earlier decided to retire from a fulfilling career as an attorney. The executive director of our synagogue suggested she speak to me. She had been married to a Jewish communal professional but had never had much opportunity to study Judaism. She wondered how she could learn about meaningful volunteer opportunities. I invited her to one of my classes and on her first evening introduced her to a retired attorney who volunteered his time pro bono one day a week.

On another occasion, I met individually with Carol, a recently widowed congregant, and invited her to come to the spousal bereavement group. I called Julie, a member of the group, to ask if she would be there. In fact she had tickets to go to a lecture that night. I told her that she could be tremendously helpful with this more recently bereaved woman. Not only did Julie change her plans and come, the two have become friends and now have dinner weekly. Additionally, Julie convinced Carol to come to Friday night services, explaining that they had been very spiritually uplifting for her. Carol, who had previously not come to services, now attends regularly. The two have started attending more of the adult education classes. They serve as a prime example of how each strand of community reinforces the next step and how synagogue can become the locus of community.

Personally Appreciating the Overlooked

Our texts tell us to respect the elderly. But "ageism" is a societal issue, not just a Jewish problem.[12] As Sylvia Boorstein teaches us with great humor and pathos in her book *Happiness Is an Inside Job*, an ongoing issue for this age cohort is feeling overlooked.[13] Their accomplishments are often unknown to a younger generation; they are ignored in social settings and bypassed for mentorship or as sources of knowledge. Recently I invited friends to Shabbat dinner. I seated my friend's elderly mother who is legally blind in the middle of the table next to people who I thought would engage her. Sadly, I watched the conversation flow around her as she sat silently. No one paid attention to her. Toward the end of the evening, she responded to a question that someone had asked the group with tremendous insight and acuity. My guests seemed surprised. I realized that not being able to see physically is not as isolating as not being seen metaphorically.

In broader terms, it is therefore especially important for congregations to find ways to honor their congregants in the post–sixty-five cohort such as by asking them to share their histories and the contributions that they have made to their families, congregation, and society. Older congregants can serve as valuable resources to the congregation in their field of expertise and can act as mentors to younger people interested in pursuing careers in the same field.

Ritual and Text as Context

Judaism is a religion rich in holiday and life-cycle ritual. As people live longer, we need to develop new rituals to mark the transitions that take place in later stages of life. Rabbis Richard Address and Dayle Friedman urge congregations to develop rituals to mark such life passages as retirement, becoming grandparents, moving to an assisted living facility, or taking on a new work or volunteer role.[14]

A participant in the Central Synagogue Caregiver's Group whose mother had Alzheimer's spoke to me about how difficult and painful it was for her and her children to watch her mother "slip away." I suggested that the next time the family visited her that they each bring a special item that symbolized their unique bond with her. The family sat in a circle with their beloved mother/ grandmother and shared their favorite stories and memories. They were able to express their love, as well as their sadness, as they said goodbye to that chapter of their lives with her.

One of the tasks of aging is letting go and passing on leadership roles to the next generation. In *Pirkei Avot* we read of Rabbi Judah's milestones of adult life and compared them to Erik Erikson's developmental stages. The class I teach used these texts as the context to discuss their own lives. With increasing comfort and confidence, they shared with each other their own struggles around letting go—be it giving up the high-powered career track or letting a daughter take over making the Passover seder. Moses' standing on Mount Nebo took on personal resonance as they discussed their own letting go of previous roles.

The text classes serve to link congregants' narratives to the Jewish canon and to each other. The discussions are laced with questions that create opportunities for participants to share stories about themselves. For example, in the Values and Virtues class, we explored *tochacha* (the duty to reprove) as participants engaged in compelling conversations on the difficulties of giving adult children reproof.

As we have seen for people at the empty nest stage and beyond, congregations can serve as a forum to come together to share concerns and aspirations, to give and receive care and sustenance. In essence, congregations can build sacred community for the empty nesters, vital aging, and all others. All this can be undertaken enriched by the wisdom of ancient and contemporary texts and enduring Jewish values.

Meaningful Volunteering

Synagogues have the opportunity to harness the energy and expertise of this population to create a cadre of volunteers. A major moral imperative for the larger Jewish community is to provide for the needs of the elderly. At the moment, trained professionals, such as home health aides and social work coordinators, are mainly in charge of many of the support services. But trained professionals are not the only ones who can deliver such services.

Psychotherapists in my synagogue have volunteered their time to help congregants who are ill and their families to cope. Another congregant has offered to set up a network of people to visit homebound elderly congregants to share our live-streamed *Kabbalat Shabbat* services with them. The opportunities for congregants to volunteer to help other congregants (including elderly congregants tutoring religious school students) are almost limitless. In order for this endeavor to develop to its fullest potential, and operate at a level of excellence, synagogue resources will need to be devoted to establishing volunteer training and coordination.

In the meantime, such efforts are springing up organically. At Central Synagogue, members of the various pastoral groups, affinity groups, and classes have strengthened their ties to each other. They socialize with each other, sit together during services, visit each other during hospitalizations and illnesses, and generally serve as support networks for each other.

Conclusion

Many congregations are beginning to recognize that they have both an obligation and an opportunity to make themselves into engaging and fulfilling places for middle-aged and older adults. Synagogues are uniquely situated to work successfully with this population owing in part to the three historic functions: *beit k'neset*, *beit midrash*, and *beit t'filah*. None of these functions stands alone. All help build thick bonds of connection and community. Synagogues have the potential to offer what empty nesters and older adults seek: to be valued and respected members of sacred communities and to participate in strong social networks of caring, purpose, and meaning.

Our sacred texts provide a rich resource for engaging older adults in exploring the distinctive challenges and opportunities they face. Our congregations are (or at least aspire to be) strong and sacred communities, readily lending themselves to building connections among older adults, and between them and the congregation at large. Older adults in congregations are often highly educated, and vital, and have much to offer to the rest of the congregation. They are available for volunteering, ready to share their personal histories with younger members, and predisposed to provide philanthropic support, large and small, to congregational endeavors. In short, attending to the needs of older Jewish adults is not only congregations' responsibility, it is also congregations' opportunity to capitalize on the skills and resources older adults have to offer. Conversely, the growing physical, social, and emotional needs of an aging population serve as an opportunity for younger and healthier congregants to do good.

Clergy who serve this population need awareness, readiness, and a sense of the sacred. Awareness of the life-stage issues make it possible for us to serve the needs of individual congregants as well as to capitalize on opportunities to create supportive communities. Having a sense of the sacred is what sets synagogues apart at this stage of life. The larger questions of purpose and meaning can best be addressed with the wisdom of our tradition and a spiritually committed rabbi able to stand with their congregants at times of existential and physical crisis.

Notes

1. David Elcott, "Baby Boomers, Public Service and Minority Communities: A Case Study of the Jewish Community in the United States," *Public Policy and Aging Report*, 16.4,2000. P. 147, Berman Jewish Policy at NYU Wagner and Research Center for Leadership in Action, Wagner School of Public Service, NYU, p. 4.
2. Gail Sheehy, *Passages in Caregiving; Turning Chaos into Confidence* (New York: Harper, 2010), 50.
3. Sara Lawrence Lightfoot, *The Third Chapter: Passion, Risk and Adventure in the 25 Years After 50* (New York: Farrar, Straus and Giroux, 2009), 4.

4. Erik F. Erikson, *Identity and the Life Cycle* (New York: W.W. Norton & Company, 1980), 103.

5. Ibid., 104.

6. Richard Address, "The Next Frontier: Baby Boomers and their Challenge to the Communal Status Quo," *Contact: The Journal of the Jewish Life Network/Steinhardt Foundation* 13, no. 1 (Fall 2010): 9.

7. Dayle Friedman, *Jewish Visions for Aging: A Professional Guide for Fostering Wholeness* (Vermont: Jewish Lights Publishing, 2008), 17.

8. Nosson Scherman and Meir Zlotowitz, eds., *Stone Edition of the Chumash* (New York: Mesorah Publications, 1998), 1093.

9. William Cutter, "Healing and Curing," in *Healing and the Jewish Imagination,* ed. William Cutter (Woodstock, VT: Jewish Lights Publishing, 2007), 3.

10. Abraham Joshua Heschel, *The Insecurity of Freedom: Essays on Human Existence* (New York: Jewish Publication Society, 1966), 78.

11. Martin Buber, *The Way of Ma: Ten Rungs* (New York: Citadel Press Books, 2006), 13.

12. Rachel Cowan, "Wise Aging," *Contact: The Journal of the Jewish Life Network/Steinhardt Foundation* 13, no. 1 (Fall 2010): 8.

13. Sylvia Boorstein, *Happiness Is an Inside Job* (New York: Ballantine Books, 2007).

14. Dayle A. Friedman, "Gearing Up for the Age Wave: A Guide for Synagogues," in *Highlights of Aging and the 21st Century Synagogue: A Think Tank on Creating Positive Future* (co-sponsored by Hiddur: The Center for Jewish Aging, Rabbi Dayle A. Friedman; URJ Sacred Aging Project, Rabbi Richard Address).

Experiencing Judaism through Thematic Temple Programming

Richard Steinberg

There are many models of congregations. There is the *pastoral model*, in which the rabbi is at the center of all the synagogue does and congregations experience their Judaism through the rabbi.[1] When I arrived at my congregation in 2001 it was a pastoral congregation, which according to Mann's definition means that the congregation is centered on the clergy or pastor. But as the congregation began to grow rapidly it became clear such a model was neither sustainable for the congregation to function in a healthy manner nor was remaining a pastoral congregation preferable for my particular make up as a rabbi. My congregation needed to move from the *pastoral model* to the *programmatic model*, in which people experience their Judaism through the environment, Shabbat and holiday rituals, and programs offered. The rabbi is the guide of those programs, but not the sole being through which people enjoy their Judaism.

As an assistant rabbi from 1995 to 2001, with very good guidance and direction, I was able to hone my skills as a programmer. I realized I did not want to be the conduit through which people experienced their Judaism (the pastoral model). I liked being the vehicle (who planned and executed programs) that helped Jews and Jewish families get from one point to another. I relish being the teacher and the tour guide of Judaism, but I am very cognizant that my job is to support the congregants' journey, and whatever program or lesson I might be able to offer would hopefully only enhance their voyages in Judaism (the programmatic model).

But even with this perspective, when I became the senior rabbi, my programming was haphazard in that there was no

RICHARD STEINBERG (C95) is the senior rabbi at Congregation Shir Ha-Ma'alot in Irvine, California. He recently received his master's degree in Marital Family Therapy.

overarching theme connecting the program I would plan. Often times the programs we decided to offer were based on the interests of the staff and by their particular views of Judaism. People seemed to enjoy many of the programs offered but there was no structure to any particular year of programs. There was nothing that elevated any of the programs in order to help the congregants raise their consciousness about Jewish living and that made sure what we were offering had a significant impact in their lives. Each program touched them a little, but given the eclectic nature of a year's worth of programming, much did not stick for the long term.

Theme for the Year

Many summers ago I was on sabbatical and had the honor of traveling to Kenya to build a hospital in the depths of the Kenyan countryside. Each day for a month, there was a single purpose to that which we were doing—nothing was ancillary. Nothing was extraneous. There was singularity of purpose to build that hospital. That experience will stay with me for the rest of my life.

When I came back from the trip, even though our temple programming had been planned and calendared for the upcoming year already, we started from scratch and we started with purpose. Every program we planned was centered on a single theme so that every time a person entered the synagogue they would understand what our message was for the year and hopefully such encounters would add up and make an impact to last a lifetime. Our first year was entitled A New Shabbat Experience. For A New Shabbat Experience we offered programs ranging from Hot Challah Club to Thought for Shabbat to Torah Readers Club to prayer classes to Chardonnay Shabbat to Dress in White Shabbat to so many other programs, each trying to capture a different aspect of Shabbat. This year our theme is family and is entitled Mishpacha Family Moments. We are offering a family retreat, parent/teen workshop, family Torah study, lecture series, and so much more. In any given year, there are as many as thirty different theme-based programs, each speaking to different constituencies and yet broad enough to include anyone. Singularity of purpose and a clear theme is the best way for the synagogue to have the largest impact in a person's life.

The *Alef*, *Bet*, and *Gimel* of Theme Programming

Every February/March, prior to the staff calendar meeting in April, we gather a lay focus group (this group can be hand selected by lay leadership and staff, the board of trustees can serve this role, or the focus group can be an open meeting for the congregation). In said group, we brainstorm for the year ahead. Truth be told, the staff has already had a conversation prior to the focus group. And, yes, the staff has a strong idea about the direction they want the group to go (perhaps this is unpopular to say, but it is the truth).

That being said, we only want to provide programs desired, needed, and possible, plus those that will be well attended, and hence the group has much sway over what is determined for the next year's theme.

Shortly after the focus group, the staff meets once again to determine how to proceed. A committee is formed and the specifics detailed, fleshed out, and initiated.

In April, the staff blocks out a whole day, with twelve huge sheets of paper on the walls—each a different month—and the programming begins. We start calendaring with the essentials:

1. Shabbat and holiday services and times
2. Religious school days
3. Vacation days of staff
4. Thematic programs

There are dozens of other things that are put on the calendar from when the choir sings at services to staff meetings, etc.— anything that happens within the synagogue for the next year (July 1–June 30) is calendared on that day (we bring in lunch for the staff on this calendaring day and it goes from 9 A.M. to 5 P.M. usually).

From April until June, the planning of each program takes place. For example, if we desire a particular speaker to come, we invite him or her and negotiate the deal for one of the specific dates already selected, if possible. The calendar is not set in stone in April, but by June it is.

The most important piece of the programming process is the tangible end result: an expansive full-color and detailed catalog is produced. Every program offered in the temple for the upcoming year is printed in this catalog with color pictures, dates, times, and specifics for congregants to put in their personal calendars for the year to come. The catalog is not only a wonderful publicity and public relations piece, it is also the central guiding document of the year—highlighting the theme of the entire year. We spend more money producing that book than we do on all other publicity combined. It is worth every cent. This catalog of seventy pages or more is sent to every congregant and prospective member.[2] Other considerations to use for theme-based programming:

1. I always deliver a High Holy Day sermon on the theme of the year.
2. During the summer, we have a famous speaker kick off the programmatic year.

The L'chaim Project: Balance of Mind, Body, and Soul

In January of 2010, a congregant, whose husband had died tragically a year before, came to visit me. She said, "I love our temple, but it is too joyous." I asked her what she meant. She went on to explain she loved how family oriented we were and how we make a point to celebrate life at every turn. She then reminded me that life is more than just celebrating—there is an ebb and flow to all that we do. She suggested we look at the span of life in our temple programming and speak to the needs that the vicissitudes of life bring upon us. I was so taken with her thoughts that I brought her concerns and ideas to the staff. Soon thereafter we brought together a lay group of the helping professions to assist in fleshing out what she was saying. I asked her to be the chair of the focus group. It also so happened that in this particular year, for months the staff and lay leadership were discussing the vacuum of support groups in our Jewish community, as the Jewish Family Service was in transition and not providing the array of programs they had in the past. After much brainstorming at the staff and executive committee level and then with the focus group, it became clear that providing a program based around healing, growth, and spiritual and emotional support was sorely needed in our temple community. Due to this confluence of circumstances from my lay person's expressed need, to the lack of outside Jewish community support, and to great interest in our temple, we pushed forward.

Following the focus group meeting, the staff started to devise a skeleton plan on what a program like this might look like or entail. At the same time, we transformed the focus group into our standing committee to help form, create, and publicize the program to the rest of the temple community.

At that time, the lay chair and I presented all that had taken place prior to the first committee meeting. The skeleton outline was then presented to the committee. This nameless healing program proposed a program divided into three sections:

1. Support groups
2. Lecture series
3. Interactive workshops

The lay committee liked the structure very much. The idea behind the structure is the programs would be lay led by members with professional expertise. At this point in the meeting, we separated into three groups and gave each group one of the three sections and asked them to brainstorm relevant, meaningful, and doable programs under their given rubric. After reviewing all the ideas, we then asked what might be an appropriate name for this program to connect all of the different pieces.

The word "balance" came up several times as an overarching theme, as it was clear people desired to find ways to have more balance in their lives. After much back and forth, and with attention to how Judaism would guide, help, and be an essential part of whatever we offered, we came to the name The L'chaim Project: Balance of Mind, Body, and Soul. Now, as a staff, we had dozens and dozens of possible programs from which to choose and then find leaders. Some of the programs the staff would lead, and most of the programs congregants would lead.

Many of the lay leaders on the committee were experts in their given fields and they would end up being our greatest resource. In his book *Spiritual Community: The Power to Restore Hope, Commitment and Joy*, Rabbi David Teutsch writes:

> What draws us into community? It could be an enlightening speaker or a wonderful teacher; a soulful choir or the opportunity to learn new rituals in a supportive environment; a gentle counselor or an effective liturgical leader. It could be the caring

commitment of a circle of people who provide support during difficult personal crisis. Or dozens of other things . . . These activities can move people from the periphery toward the center . . . In a thriving congregation, there are multiple radiant centers. Because the radiant centers do not involve all the same people, they create several centers of congregational life rather than just one single one . . . Radiant centers tap into people's best talents by calling on them to undertake risks and experiments . . . As radiant centers develop, more people on the periphery bask in their warmth. The more radiant centers there are in a congregation, the more people will be affected and the more they can be sustained as part of the community. Radiant centers bring institutional vibrancy, programmatic change, and religious renewal.[3]

Our radiant centers included the three rubrics of support groups, lectures, and workshops. Along with the lay chair, the staff chose who they thought would be the best leaders, lecturers, and facilitators for each of the enterprises. There were some hurt feelings when a person was not chosen to lead, but with creativity, we tried to make sure every person felt valued. If a person was not leading a group, they were asked to write an article for the newsletter. Hurt feelings seemed hard to avoid in an endeavor such as this, but for the overall programmatic success, it was a necessity.

As for those who attended the programs, the support groups and workshops were for members of the congregation only. The lectures were open to the public. Membership ought to have its privileges, and participating in our program, especially something like a support group, must be one of those privileges.

Here is a snapshot of the L'chaim Project: Balance of Mind, Body, and Soul.

Support Groups

Support groups included:

- Bereavement Support Group—led by a clinical psychologist
- Parenting Support Group—led by a clinical social worker
- Chronic Illness Support Group—led by a marital family therapist
- Women's Support Group—led by retired clinical psychologist

- Men's Spirituality Group—led by me (I did not think men would come to something entitled "support group")
- Teen Support Group—led by a marital family therapist

All the facilitators were congregants. Many of the groups worked well and continue to this day. It is often hard to determine "how well" a group does because the outcomes for each participant are different. I followed up with each facilitator many times and with several members of each group to assess how they felt. There was some tweaking along the way. For example, one facilitator was letting a particular person in the group have too much time to talk about herself to the exclusion of others having the chance to participate, and the tweaking kept that participant from monopolizing the group. From my anecdotal discussions, however, congregants felt connected to each other and that brought great meaning to their lives. They felt bonded in a significant way to their synagogue for having provided such a venue for them to feel supported. Their Judaism was enriched as many of the group leaders provided texts and Jewish concepts for healing and support. But just being in a Jewish environment to talk about the issues of their lives was a Jewish experience in and of itself.

There were those groups that did not work, however. The Teen Support Group met twice, but attendance was low and the teens reported that they were not interested nor were they able to find time in their schedules to come.

Depending on the group, its leader, and the availability of the temple, each group determined their own schedule and frequency.

Lecture Series

When I began to thematically program, I thought it was best to begin the year with a nationally recognized speaker. This kicks off the year in a powerful way, initiates a theme, and, mostly, gets people in the door to frame the coming year. This piece of the program is one of the few that requires a funder. We look for the most well-known figure who can teach, entertain, and draw an audience to open our theme, and this usually costs money. It is quite compelling for a funder to know that it is not just a onetime lecture, but an opening to a whole year of programming. I have had funders cover the expenses for the whole year once they understood the context of what we were trying to accomplish.

Our overall lectures were based on two criteria: (1) People's genuine interest in the topics as brainstormed at the committee and (2) Were there experts in our community able to teach/lecture on the subjects? We soon discovered that each lecturer was glad to volunteer his or her time and share his or her expertise with the congregations.

Lectures included:

- How to Create Shalom in the Home—by Rabbi Shmuley Boteach (He also taught Torah study the next day.)
- Laughter and Health—by a retired pediatrician and professional clown
- Heart Health—by a professor of nursing
- Memory—by a neurologist and professor of medicine
- Jewish Genetics—by a genetic counselor
- Lecture and Service of Healing—by Debbie Friedman

Workshops

Workshops included an eclectic group of programs. As with the lecture series and support groups, choosing the workshops was dependent on the needs raised by the lay committee and staff ideas as well as local resources available. For the workshops, we had more than a dozen ideas and through discussion about the (1) relative importance, (2) the probable attendance, and (3) what would have the largest impact, we whittled down to a manageable set of workshops. They included:

- Freedom Song: For Teens and Parents; One Jewish Family's Struggle with Addiction; One Nation's Path to Recovery— This program was held during our high school night for over 130 kids in attendance with their parents. It was performed by residents and former residents of the Jewish rehabilitation facility known as Beit Teshuva. It is important to utilize as many community resources as possible. The facility was more than glad to do it. In our brainstorming sessions, the idea of teens taking stock of their lives in a responsible way came up many times. This workshop was planned to address this need.
- Meditation Workshop—led by an experienced teacher of meditation. Our hope in offering this workshop was to reach

people not just in words, but through other mediums. This was very popular as it spoke silently to the souls of those in attendance.

- Soul Food Workshop—led by a local rabbi/chef using biblical texts as he taught them to cook. Food is such an essential part of health, we thought the combination of food and Judaism was a perfect match for this theme.
- Yoga Flow Workshop—led by a yoga teacher for weekly yoga classes. In much the same spirit as the Meditation Workshop, this program intended to use the body as the medium for teaching about health and balance (literal and figurative).
- Couples' Retreat—an all-day intensive led by me (a rabbi and marital family therapist intern) and a sex/relationship therapist. We had more than twenty-four people in attendance from morning till night. To have balance in one's life, it requires balance in one's relationships. This workshop looked at the ways we can realign ourselves in relation to our spouse and vice versa in order to attain a sense of equilibrium in our daily lives. Again, the richness of our Jewish tradition was not only informative, but the guiding principle in this workshop.

Analysis and Assessment

In the L'chaim Project: Balance of Mind, Body, and Soul, through support groups, lectures, and interactive workshops, there were myriad ways for the congregant to wrestle with and address the issues of health and healing, of balance and centeredness in one's life. The synagogue was the place and Judaism the backdrop for addressing these issues.

Having a single theme for a yearlong program allowed for a direct approach of addressing the needs of people's lives. For example, someone spiritually adrift could participate in several programs through the L'chaim Project and all would lead to the same end of using Judaism to help center him or her in life. From meditation to lectures on health issues to being in a support group, a point of balance could be found. I believe that if, for example, during 2010–2011 we had offered a random Talmud class and another class on chanting Torah, a participant might have experienced learning, but not experienced the possibility for greater insight, growth, and community building offered by participating in a theme-based programmatic year.

The board of trustees spent a whole meeting evaluating and discussing the virtues and constructive criticisms of the program. The overall comments were exceedingly positive. Some suggested, however, we did not do enough for teens. Others commented that we ought to join forces with other congregations. There were three people I know of who joined the congregation simply to participate in the support groups and now are involved in many other aspects of temple life. It is difficult to a do an objective evaluation of such subjective matters, but it is clear to me after having done this thematic work for years that thematic programming is the way to go. Singularity of purpose is palpable for people for they will understand what it is the temple is trying to offer. The Talmud teaches, "The Holy One created nothing without a purpose" (BT *Shabbat* 77b). Let us not create a temple program without a purpose. People will gravitate to that which is clear to them. Theme programming is purposeful, meaningful, and one of the best vehicles for transporting Judaism to and through people's lives.

Notes

1. See Alice Mann, *Raising the Roof: The Pastoral-to-Program Size Transition* (Herndon, VA: Alban, 2001).
2. See www.shmtemple.org to view the catalog.
3. David Teutsch, *Spiritual Community; The Power to Restore Hope, Commitment and Joy* (Woodstock, VT: Jewish Lights, 2005), 39–41.

The Rabbi Does Handstands: An Exploration of the Emerging Field of Jewish Yoga in North American Synagogues and Beyond

Marcus J. Freed

Religious Diversity and the Relationship Between Judaism and Health

A person should aim to maintain physical health and vigor, in order that their soul is upright, in a condition to know God.
—Maimonides, *Mishneh Torah*, *Sefer Mada / Hilchot Dei-ot* 3:3

We are witnessing a time of change in Judaism. There have always been Jews who are disenfranchised by traditional spiritual practices and in many cases this has led to the creation of new movements. In the past there was a level of communal division, whether it was the different streams of Orthodox and Reform Judaism, or the religious-secular divides seen in the eighteenth-century Enlightenment, when the Haskalah saw the burgeoning of a secular Jewish culture. This time it is different. We are seeing an emerging field of Jewishly focused meditation and yoga, bringing together practitioners from across the Jewish spectrum and often integrating their work into mainstream synagogue life.

In the course of this article, I'll explore the emerging field of Jewishly informed yoga, consider some of the main practices that are currently being developed, and suggest how we can incorporate

MARCUS J. FREED is the creator of Bibliyoga (www.bibliyoga.com) and the Kosher Sutras and president of the Jewish Yoga Network (www.jewishyoganetwork. org). Based in Los Angeles and originally from England, he received teacher certifications from Tripsichore Yoga and Purna Yoga, and studied at the Universities of Birmingham and London, as well as Yeshivat HaMivtar in Israel.

these ideas into more mainstream spiritual practices on a personal and communal level.

Twenty years ago there was a wide gap between Orthodox and non-Orthodox Jewish approaches to healthy living. While I was at yeshivah, exercising was considered *bitul z'man* (a waste of time) that could otherwise be spent learning Torah. As we become more aware of the need to keep our bodies fit, we better appreciate Maimonides' profound teachings that bodily health is connected to spiritual health. Today, the gap is closing. All streams of Judaism are shifting towards a greater consciousness that keeping our bodies healthy is not *bitul z'man*, but rather an essential part of having a healthy body and soul.

We are moving into a new era of increased consciousness about the connections between Judaism, health, and healing. I was recently teaching a series of Bibliyoga workshops during a scholar-in-residence visit to the Jewish Community Center in Detroit and was delighted to see the ultimate integration of healthy body and soul displayed on the walls of the gymnasium at the JCC. The designers had inscribed quotations from the Jewish tradition about health and healing on the wall of the gym.

The coming years may see this shift become even more clear, where these teachings come to the forefront and we will realize that a holistic approach is the truest approach to our spiritual lives. This is the vision of Rabbi Mani who wrote about the custom of holding all four species of plants in one hand as part of the Sukkot ritual:

> R. Mani opened his discourse with the text, *All my bones shall say: "God, who is like You?"* (Psalm 35:10). This verse was said in allusion to nothing else than the lulav (date-palm). The rib of the lulav resembles the spine of a man; the myrtle resembles the eye, the willow resembles the mouth, and the etrog (citron) resembles the heart. King David said: "There are none among the limbs greater than these, for they outweigh in importance the whole body. This explains [the verse] *'All my bones shall say'* [who is like You?]" (*Vayikra Rabbah* 30:14).

Every part of our being, body and soul, connect us to God.

"A Kind of Yoga"

A quiet turning point was reached when Rabbi Aryeh Kaplan[1] published his translation of *Sefer Yetzirah* (The Book of Enlightenment), a pivotal work of Kabbalah. Kaplan made a profound and significant statement:

> Meditative Kabbalah deals with the use of divine names, letter permutations, and similar methods to reach higher states of consciousness, and, as such, **comprises a kind of yoga.**[2]

Before we even consider the importance of this comment, let's just review what yoga is, and what it isn't.

The word "yoga" comes from the Sanskrit word *yuj*, which means "to yoke" or "to unify." It refers to the connection between the body and soul or the unification of body and soul, or mind and the spirit. It can even refer to the unification of the individual and God. The aims of yoga are to unify our body and mind, to bring us to a higher consciousness, and this is the objective of all kinds of meditation. Yoga, as we've come to understand it, is so much more than the aerobic-style physical exercises that we see in gyms. Although the asana/vinyasa[3] (yoga postures and poses/styles) are an important part of the mix, they are ultimately a tool for attaining inner balance and spiritual peace. Side benefits include physical and psychological health, which is why it has gained such popularity throughout the world.

The renowned yogic scholar Georg Feuerstein explained that "all forms, branches of Yoga, have the same goal. [These are] liberation, enlightenment, freedom, the transcendence of the human condition, or the fulfilment of our highest potential."[4] Yoga has been coupled with various religious philosophies and a strong Hindu influence can be seen in the names of the postures and the use of Vedic texts (e.g., the Bhagavad Gita). Nonetheless, one of the most influential yogic texts is Patanjali's *Yoga Sutras* (c. 200 B.C.E.), which deliberately moved the practice away from traditional Hindu philosophy and towards a more universal and deistic spiritual outlook. For many Jewish practitioners, this shift effectively makes it "kosher." For others, one primary challenge remains: the popularity of Hindu-god statues in yoga studios and the use of Hindu chants.

At the 2011 World's Yoga Day in Lisbon, Portugal, I explained this Jewish dilemma to a global gathering of yogis, swamis, and gurus. Bhava Jain, the general secretary for the World Council of Religions at the United Nations, publicly responded by stressing the closeness between Hinduism and Judaism. There is a popular misconception, he explained, that Hindus are polytheistic, when actually their belief is that there is one God with many different visual manifestations.

Now let's consider one of the more controversial terms that has emerged.

Jewish Yoga?

When Aryeh Kaplan suggested that the Book of Creation was a "kind of yoga," he was most likely referring to the way that meditative stillness leads us to unite with God. The term "Jewish Yoga" is one that I am reluctant to use because yoga is an independent discipline that is, by its very nature, nondogmatic. However, if the pursuit of yoga is the pursuit of God, as Patanjali and this author believe, then it is a process of experiencing oneness with the Divine. If you are breathing then you are able to do yoga.

The term "Jewish Yoga" is an unhelpful one because it implies that yoga is a Jewish practice, when it is purely a form of meditation. As we will explore here, there are many ways of presenting yoga in a Jewish context. We can attempt to Judaize yoga, rather than suggesting that the yoga itself is Jewish, when, in actual fact, it is a neutral practice. Yoga is about bringing inner healing and stillness to everyone *regardless* of their religious or ethnic background; nonetheless, there are many ways to connect it with Jewish spiritual wisdom.

The great yogi B.K.S. Iyengar is reported to have articulated this important distinction in a conversation with Ida Unger, a yoga teacher based in Los Angeles. He explained to Ida that she should not call her work "Jewish yoga"[5] because the focus needed to stress the yoga name, not detract from it. Yoga is not to be put into a box that makes it smaller than it is, as a practice only for Jews. The guru also explained that the problem with rebranding yoga into a "Jewish" box implied that a new form was being created, which was not true—after all, it is still the same recognizable yoga that includes asana and vinyasa.

The Jewish Yoga Network

The name may not be perfect—whether it should be the Jewish Yogi's Network or a Network for Jewish Yoga Practitioners—but the name explains what it is. In the 1980s, an English yoga teacher, Estelle Eugene, began Yoga Mosaic, a group under the auspices of North London's Yakar community, led by Rabbi Mickey Rosen. Since that time, she has led over twenty biannual seminars with yogis and yoginis from across the United Kingdom. Now, we have assembled a network of Jews who are teaching and practicing yoga and meditation. The first Jewish Yoga Network seminar was held in the yoga studio at the Los Angeles Jewish Federation building during August 2011, and subsequent programs are planned. The network is in contact with other Jewish Community Centers and other communities that regularly practice and teach yoga.

What began with Aryeh Kaplan's popular book *Jewish Meditation* can now be found in classes offering Jewish-themed yoga and meditation in almost every major city in the United States, while Europe and Israel are gaining speed. Practitioners in Australia and South Africa are also offering workshops, and this points towards a greater trend.

Although the standardized *t'filah* (prayer) is essential for continuity of tradition and providing a communal vocabulary for worship, members of mainstream Jewish communities are expressing frustration with traditional services, and people are repeatedly asking the question: "If I feel so calm/relaxed/centered/balanced/spiritual after my yoga/meditation class, why can't I achieve that within my Judaism?"

Some have published books; others train teachers of yoga to incorporate Jewish teachings into their work; while others record music that is suited to a yogic flow, uses Hebrew chants and Jewish music, and is devoid of references to Hindu gods

Diane Bloomfield's *Torah Yoga* (2004) laid the groundwork for a Torah-based approach to yoga, as she took key themes such as *yetziat Mitzrayim* (the process of being liberated from Egypt) and translated them into physical metaphors that could be experienced through yoga, with postures that open the body and free it from restrictions and tightness. Steven Rapp's *Alef-Bet Yoga* (2002) takes a more physical asana-based approach that is echoed in Ida Unger's *Sacred Shapes* poster based on the Hebrew alphabet, and the Canadian teacher Audi Gozlan's *Kabbalah Yoga*, exploring kabbalistic teachings through the letters. Judy Greenfield and Tamar Frankiel created *Minding the Temple of the Soul: Balancing Body, Mind, and Spirit Through Traditional Jewish Prayer, Movement, and Meditation*

(1997). Their book is not purely limited to yoga, and they take a broader view of the Jewish meditation field and suggest a series of physical applications. Jay Michaelson's *God in Your Body* (2006) presents an excellent overview of sources and spiritual practices, while Steven Gold's *Yoga and Judaism* (2007) considers the shape of this emerging field.

Although there is still no systematized practice that frames yoga and spiritual healing within a Judaic context, there are many teachers who are developing their own methods and approaches. The strongest support currently comes from Rabbi Myriam Klotz and Diane Bloomfield (of *Torah Yoga*), who have trained three student cohorts in their teacher training program at the Elat Chayyim retreat in Connecticut. This training helps Jewish yoga teachers create programs of their own and gives them support with resources and a teaching methodology. Both the teachers and students come from a variety of Jewish affiliations, and in this sense it is a nondenominational practice. There is also the New York–based Institute for Jewish Spirituality, which works with rabbis, cantors, and educators, teaching spirituality within a Jewish framework.

Recent years have seen a growing number of spiritual music recordings, with music appropriate for synagogue settings, without traditional Sanskrit chants that invoke the name of Hindu gods. Rabbi Andrew Hahn, promoted as the "Kirtan Rebbe," often performs a live-action call-and-response Kirtan concert based around Hebrew chants and Jewish music. Yofiyah and a cadre of Los Angeleno musician-yogis are making their own recordings with a yogic flow.

Many synagogues have introduced some form of yoga and/or meditation classes into their programming mix, although they are of varying quality, due to teachers' differing levels of yogic and Judaic knowledge. These valiant starts are growing in force. I believe that we are still at the start of a curve that will only increase during the next twenty to thirty years.

Kosher Sutras: Bridging the Gap

The question that really bothered me was how we could bridge the gap between Jewish practice and health and well-being. Jews like to eat, talk about food, celebrate with food, and there is an oft-repeated joke that the calories we eat on (the Sabbath) don't count.

This has led to a dislocation between the body and the soul, when most major Jewish sources affirm the opposite.

The Talmud instituted a prayer to be said immediately after leaving the bathroom:

> Praised are You, Lord our God King of the universe, who with wisdom fashioned the human body, creating openings, arteries, glands and organs, marvelous in structure, intricate in design. Should but one of them, by being blocked or opened, fail to function, it would be impossible to exist. Praised are You, Lord, Healer of all flesh who sustains our bodies in wondrous ways.[6]

Maimonides, the thirteenth century rabbi and doctor, specified the need to match physical exercise with a spiritual intention:

> The person who regulates their life in accordance with the laws of hygiene, with the sole motive of maintaining a sound and vigorous physique and having children to do their work and labor for their benefit, isn't following the right course. A person should aim to maintain physical health and vigor, in order that their soul is upright, in a condition to know God. It is impossible for someone to understand science, to learn and think about them when they are hungry and sick, or when any of their limbs are aching. (Maimonides, *Mishneh Torah, Sefer Mada / Hilchot Dei-ot* 3:3)[7]

He also focused on the process of eating and how we fill our stomachs in the first place:

> Any person who sits around and does not exert themselves, or anyone who does not properly relieve themselves, or whose belly is [distended and] hard—even if they eat the right foods and look after themselves medically, they will suffer pain their whole lives long, and they will be feeble. Overeating is tantamount to poison; it is the root cause of all illness . . . "He who guards his mouth and his tongue guards himself from trouble" [Prov. 21:23]—that is to say, a person who guards their mouth from eating the wrong things or from gluttony, and who guards their tongue from speaking, except for what is necessary. (Maimonides, *Mishneh Torah, Sefer Mada / Hilchot Dei-ot* 4:15)

Our challenge is to help contemporary Jews become mindful of the mind-body connection that our tradition has long-recognized.

The sage Hillel summed up an entire philosophy of mindful living in *Pirkei Avot* (1:14) when he famously said, "If not now, when?" Many Jews, including kabbalists such as Abraham Abulafia, have shared teachings about mindfulness. Rabbi Kalman Kalonymous Shapira—the *"Piaseczna Rebbe"*—wrote a meditation manuscript while in the Warsaw Ghetto, before he perished in the Holocaust.[8]

My work has focused on finding connections between Jewish wisdom and the body, and creating resources for every *parashah* (Torah reading) and festival, as well as for many aspects of Jewish living. The Kosher Sutras take a simple verse and explore yogic and meditational applications. For example, for the festival of Sukkot, which ends with Simchat Torah and a public reading of the final chapters of Deuteronomy, the Kosher Sutra, a physical yoga posture—in this case it is a simple, seated mudra (yogic hand pose)—is applied to spiritual health and physical well-being:

Happy Endings: The Yoga of Sukkot (Parashat *V'zot Hab'rachah*)

KOSHER SUTRA: "He showed his love to the peoples" (Deut. 33:3)
SOUL SOLUTION: Feel loved and complete at every moment, regardless of what's going on on the "outside."
BIBLIYOGA POSE: *Anjali-mudra* (the lotus of the heart). Seated in prayer pose with both hands pushed together, thumbs on heart chakra.

There is a poignancy to this week and it is a time for anticipating new beginnings. Nature runs its course and we are coming to the end of various cycles. The leaves are beginning to fall, the annual Torah reading is ending, another Kosher Sutra cycle is complete, and animals would be beginning to think about hibernating if we hadn't singed the ozone layer and messed up the seasons through prematurely triggering global warming.

"He [God] showed his love to the peoples," explains Moses in his farewell speech (Deut. 33:3). The Rabbinic commentators go for an ethnocentric translation of this, explaining that it is talking about the twelve tribes (Onkelos and Rashi), but the Hebrew word *amim* suggests a wider scope. *Am* usually refers to the Israelites, but the plural word refers to the other peoples on the earth (e.g., everyone, regardless of race or nationality). God loves you, baby. Hallelujah.

The final yogic teaching of the year is simple: all is one. And incredibly complicated: all is one. We can quote endless Sanskrit sources, or Hebrew sources for that matter, but the mind games will distract us from the work of our hearts—to understand that we are living in a space of divine love, and that we are all part of one huge spiritual organism. When we can live in this space of deep knowing, we remove our fears, pains, and sense of lack. This is an idea that our hearts understand, but our heads often complicate.

The yogic meditation of *anjali-mudra* takes us into this place. It is performed by pushing both palms together into prayer position and lightly pressing your thumbs on the sternum, or heart center.

This week is the festival of Sukkot where Jews gather in the temporary structure of the sukkah and invite guests in throughout the whole week. We sit in this physical-spiritual space and remind ourselves of the oneness of God and the Universe. We hold four species of plants together (the *lulav*/*etrog*/willow/myrtle) and remind ourselves that we are all one people. But can we feel it in our hearts?

Here is a simple meditation. Close your eyes and meditate on the word "love." Allow yourself to feel it in every cell of your body. If your heart is beating anxiously, breathe and allow yourself to come back to the meditation focus. If your mind wanders in another direction, bring your mind back to it.

A couple of days ago my friend Peter Himmelman beautifully summed up Reb Aryeh Kaplan's approach to meditation: "Think of a thing. When you stop thinking of it, think of that thing again. Do it for fifteen minutes."

Back in the days of the Temple in Jerusalem, Sukkot was a time of joint prayer for all peoples of the world, of all religions and nations. We all joined together as one.[9]

The style of writing is deliberately light and amiable for online readership, inspired by Patanjali's *Yoga Sutras,* which are typically written as short aphorisms that can be committed to memory. Their form is similar to mishnaic texts, which I seek to replicate in these contemporary teachings.

This Kosher Sutra is an example of the materials that are currently being disseminated to synagogues, JCCs, and individuals. Several synagogues and communities currently use them as part of their regular worship and/or in ongoing yoga workshops.

Judaism and Well-Being

One of the truly beautiful aspects of the Jewish tradition is that it has such a wealth of wisdom and information, it is possible to find teachings and sources that stay relevant and contemporary in any historical period. This is one understanding of the notion of *Torat Chayim* (a living Torah), and it certainly applies to Jewish teachings about health and well-being. Although recent generations may not have stressed Maimonides' ideas on healthful eating and fitness, or the kabbalists ideas on meditation and stillness, this generation is increasingly discovering the true power and depth of our tradition.

There is one area in which we can still improve: silence and stillness. Although King David wrote "Be still and know God" (Ps. 37:7), Jewish tradition is not best known for its aptitude for silence. There is a brief respite from talking during prayer while we recite the silent *Sh'moneh Esreih* (the nineteen blessings of the *Amidah*. However it is sandwiched between the recitations of many prayers.

Various new siddurim are frequently published, although it is exceedingly rare that a "New and Revised Prayer Book" involves *fewer* words than its predecessor. As a result there are increasing numbers of Jews who are drawn towards Buddhist meditation and other silent practices, because the sound of silence is all too rare in synagogue reflection. As more "Bujus" surface (the Buddhist-Jewish followers), books like *The Jew in the Lotus*[10] become ever more widely distributed, and more Jewish yogis emerge, it is inevitable that Jewish forms of silent meditation will continue to become more prevalent. Perhaps we will develop new forms of "Jewish silence," not that there is such a thing as "Jewish silence," but you get the idea.

We are moving towards a new era that is increasingly conscious of the connections between Judaism, health, and healing. The forthcoming years may see a shift where these teachings come to the forefront and we will realize that a holistic approach is the most effective approach to our spiritual lives. This takes us back to the vision of King David who presented a vision for an integrated body and soul: "Let all my bones proclaim: God, who is like You?" (Ps. 35:10).

Notes

1. 1934–1983. Kaplan's translation of *Sefer Yetzirah* was published posthumously.
2. From Kaplan's introduction to *Sefer Yetzirah* (The Book of Enlightenment).

3. Most Westerners are familiar with variations of hatha yoga that started to gain popularity in the United States from the 1960s onwards, and this form is primarily centered around asana (physical postures), vinyasa (flowing movements that are choreographed with specific breathing, such as Sun Salutations), and pranayama (yogic breathing-meditation). There are, however, many more forms of yoga that exist: Jnana Yoga is the Yoga of Wisdom, centred around applying deeper knowledge; karma yoga is the yoga of action, which has been described as "aiming at liberation through self-transcending service, often considered especially suitable for those who lack the necessary qualities for concentration and meditation"; and bhakti yoga is the yoga of devotion, described as "aiming at liberation through self-surrender in the face of the Divine." Interestingly, all three of these translate directly into Jewish terminology: *chochmah* (wisdom), mitzvot (positive actions), and *chesed/korban* (loving-kindness/sacrifice.

4. Georg Feuerstein, *The Deeper Dimension of Yoga* (Boston: Shambhala Publications, 2003), 372.

5. Reported in a private conversation from yoga teacher Ida Unger, who lives in Los Angeles, www.yogagardenstudios.com.

6. Translation from anonymous source.

7. Translation from various sources.

8. Eventually published under the title *Conscious Community*.

9. From: http://bibliyoga.com/sutra.php.

10. *The Jew in the Lotus* by Roger Kamenetzky retells Rabbi Zalman Schachter-Shlomi's encounter with the Dalai Lama.

Verbatim with God

Robert Tabak

Learning Goals/Reason for Presenting

This dialogue relates to two learning goals: to assess how I will do at chaplaincy on a daily basis; and second (although this was not one I wrote down at the beginning of the CPE program) in the theological/spiritual realm to evaluate the sincerity of what I do as a chaplain.

Known Facts

This takes place at a quiet moment in the pastoral care office late in the day. I am somewhat tired, and perhaps a bit discouraged as to how effective my visits have been that day. The conversation was initiated by the Partner's visit, not the chaplain.

Observations

The Holy One appears as a slightly glowing formless warm shimmering light. God apparently uses a form of voice projection, with a slight hint of a Yiddish accent. The Partner has many names, among them Holy One of Blessing, the Source of Life, Ruler of the Universe, Companion, Wondrous One, Healer, *Shechinah*. No one else is present.

C1: Hello, shalom—is this who I think it is?

G1: Of course, you can recognize me!

C2: This is amazing! What are you doing here? Why are you appearing as a light?

G2: You were expecting maybe a burning bush? And George Burns was busy.

C3: But why are you appearing to me, now?

RABBI ROBERT TABAK, Ph.D., BCC (RRC77) is a staff chaplain at the Hospital of the University of Pennsylvania and an adjunct faculty member at St. Joseph's University (Philadelphia) and Cabrini College (Radnor, Pennsylvania). He is also editor of the Reconstructionist Rabbinical Association newsletter, the *RRA Connection*.

G3: Sometimes I want to check up on something. I under-
     stand you've been working in the hospital this summer
     as a chaplain.

C4: Yes, I have. Wait—don't you know all this?

G4: Listen, aren't you the one who has trouble with an omni-
     scient, omnipotent God?

C5: Yes, but . . .

G5: So let's say that is true. With a few billion galaxies to look
     in on, sometimes I need an update.

C6: I'm honored that you think I can tell you something.

G6: Don't get too uppity. Let's say you are something like a
     reporter or human weather station for the moment. You'll
     share some observations that will give me a better picture.
     But don't get too inflated. You aren't the only weather sta-
     tion on earth.

C7: Sorry. So what can I tell you?

G7: These human feeling things are always blurry long dis-
     tance. I understand you talk about them a lot with people.

C8: Well, I try.

G8: Look, I had plenty of humbleness with Moses, and there
     were still times when he was a pain in the neck. Just skip
     that part, please.

C9: This is a bit overwhelming for me. You sound irritated. You
     did want to talk about feelings.

G9: Give a gold star to your CPE supervisor. But I didn't stop
     by to talk about MY feelings. I want to ask about you and
     the patients you visit.

C10: What feelings in particular?

G10: Well, first, what do people say about God?

C11: I guess that is one topic people are more likely to talk about
     with chaplains than other hospital staff. I often hear
     people say, "God gives me strength" or "All we can do is
     pray" or "God must have a plan for me."

G11: And what are people feeling when they say these things?

C12: I'll try to generalize, but I think it varies. Overall, people
     are feeling alone or abandoned, or the limits of what doc-
     tors or nurses or family members can do.

G12: And how do you feel when you hear these phrases?

C13: On the one hand, I feel glad that people have some sense of
     the spiritual at a moment of crisis. On the other, I don't al-
     ways have a sense of how that faith works, what it means,
     or how it fits into a life. For example, I read of a chaplain
     once who was working on a book called *There Are No Athe-
     ists in the Neonatal Intensive Care Waiting Room.*

G13: So, are you disappointed in yourself because you can't understand someone's entire spiritual journey in ten minutes in a hospital room?

C14: I suppose so. But really, what I don't know is whether I am touching a deep spot, or sharing a cliché that fits the moment.

G14: Listen—don't get off on the atheists and foxholes business. I'll give you the short answer: you can't always tell.

C15: So how can I be effective? Some people say "God bless you" when they hear a sneeze but don't really think about You.

G15: So if they're calling on me but not really thinking of me, it matters?

C16: Wait, there were all these debates in the Talmud and later Rabbinic literature about how important was *kavanah* (intention) when performing certain mitzvot (commandments) or reciting certain prayers.

G16: OK, Mr. Scholar, I won't embarrass you by asking when was the last time you actually studied those sections. And what do you remember as the summary of this great debate?

C17: (Hesitatingly) Well, while *kavanah* was required for reciting the *Sh'ma* (Central declaration of Unity of God—Deuteronomy 6), for a lot of other actions it was nice to have but not absolutely necessary.

G17: That will do for now—you can guess what your homework is. So you expect people who are in a hospital bed or waiting room, in a crisis, maybe with tubes coming out of them and strangers coming in and out and poking them, worried about life or death or healing or sickness, to only talk to me when they have *kavanah*?

C18: I didn't say that, exactly. Do you mean it doesn't matter whether people really believe it when they pray?

G18: Don't forget who came here to ask the questions. Can you really tell what they feel? Anyway, do you usually pray for people who ask you not to?

C19: No—if they just want to talk, or have a supportive human presence, or be left alone, that's OK with me, too.

G19: And is any of that prayer, too?

C20: Well, in my theology, God—You—are experienced through godly actions of other people as well as in other ways. So if I looked at it right, then my presence might be a shadow of your presence in the world, a kind of prayer, whatever words I say.

G20: Listen, as I recall you were stronger in history and Rabbinic texts than theology. You're doing better than I expected, considering to whom you are speaking. But don't discount the words. Try going into a few rooms and reading the phone book or your CPE orientation manual.

C21: So do prayers for healing really help?

G21: You tell me—what do you think?

C22: The prayers can help. They help the patient to feel care, hope, and healing. But I now also believe there is a sense in which prayer can reach beyond the hospital bed and help in healing in a way that cannot be measured.

G22: Don't be too sure about the last point. Several human weather stations tell me about people trying to measure the effects of prayer. But this theology business for you is a bit fuzzy. So this interpersonal interpsychic immanent God can also heal people?

C23: Yes, I believe so—but I'm not certain how, or even if my belief is consistent.

G23: Well, I could have chosen another address to get consistency. When you pray for a sick person, what are you praying for?

C24: I am praying for courage, and *r'fuat hanefesh* and *r'fuat haguf* (spiritual healing and physical healing). I am praying so that they are not alone at a moment of pain.

G24: And what do you feel when you are visiting or reciting one of these prayers?

C25: I wish I could say I always have complete attention and *kavanah* (intention) but sometimes it can be a little routine.

G25: Again with the *kavanah* business. Do you mean it is "routine" for you or "routine" for the patient?

C26: For me—I may say a prayer or supportive word many times a day, but the patient will probably have only one chaplain's visit.

G27: And is this just a job, or something more?

C28: Sometimes, I feel that I am a messenger for You and your community of caring.

G28: Bingo. I did come to talk about feelings. Don't get so hung up on the valleys that you forget the plains and the mountains.

C29: Can I tell other people about this visit?

G29: That's up to you. Look, I have to go soon. I have an appointment on Vega.

C30: Are you going to leave me with one teaching to remember or share?

G30: This is Hahnemann University hospital, not Mount Sinai. But how about a quick trade? You'll tell me one favorite text of yours, and I'll tell you one of mine.

C31: (Pausing) OK, in *Pirkei Avot* [Ethics of the Fathers] Rabbi Tarfon says "You may not complete the task, but neither are you free to desist from trying" [*Pirkei Avot* 2:21].

G31: That's fine. Don't forget his words in the preceding passage: "The day is short, the work is much, the workers are lazy, the reward is great, and the Master of the house is insistent" [*Pirkei Avot* 2:20]. (Pause) Now I'll share my favorite text for today: *Min hametzar karati Yah, anani va'merchav Yah* (From my distress/the narrow place I cried out to Yah/God, Yah/God answered me, bringing great release [Ps. 118:5]).

C32: Wait, there's a lot more I want to ask you. We talked mostly about God and feelings. What about Torah and Israel? What about peace for Jerusalem? When will the Messiah come? What about life after death?

G32: You're full of questions. Next time I want to do an interview, I'll be sure to stop by. Anyway, I've given you guys the building blocks and the tools. Keep studying, keep working, and keep creating stories. (shimmering light starts fading, and voice starts growing fainter)

C33: Hold on—why is there so much pain and suffering?

G33: Oy, now you think I have all the answers? Check out Job or Harold Kushner or Elie Weisel. I have to be going.

C34: Shalom *aleichem* (peace unto you).

G34: *Aleichem* shalom (unto you, peace).

Evaluation

While this is a somewhat surprising dialogue (to take place at all), there are several things to note. God mostly asks questions, so my responses are key. In C9, I try responding to God's feelings. The Holy One is not interested in this discussion. A major issue that I explore is when I am being "real" or whether I am delivering clichés (C14–C15). I express a number of doubts about my role. I am also pushed to say that I believe prayer can help (C22) and that I sometimes am a messenger (C28) of a higher source.

Theological Implications

Many implications (doubt/sincerity/effectiveness of chaplaincy or prayer) are noted just above. God is willing to respond in terms of my theology, without specifically answering whether it is true, but pushing me as to its limits and implications: G5, G22, and especially G33 ("now you think I have all the answers?"). I also note that God had a few things to leave me to think about. G28: "Don't get so hung up on the valleys that you forget the plains and the mountains." (Not every moment or encounter will be great or even modestly successful. Don't focus only on the ones that seem unsuccessful or superficial.) In response to one of my favorite sayings, about not completing the task, God reminds me of the context. I was struck by the "workers are lazy." There are times when I am tired, or don't do as much as I could. That is the other side of the coin of trying to accomplish "everything."

God's favorite text could be a prayer for a hospital patient (or frustrated chaplain) calling from the narrow straits. God resisted my attempts to answer the ultimate questions by telling me to go study more (G17, G33) and telling us to "keep studying, keep working, keep creating more stories" (G32).

This article was originally published in *The Journal of Pastoral Care* 53, no. 4 (Winter 1999): 481–84. Reprint permission has been granted by JPCP, Inc.

Maayanot (Primary Sources)

The Origins of the Reform Concept of Prayer: An Eighteenth Century Essay by Isaac Euchel

Translation and Introduction by
Michael A. Meyer

Traditionally, Jewish prayer is understood as a substitute for the sacrificial service in the ancient Temple. It is a continuation of עֲבוֹדַת קוֹדֶשׁ but with an offering of words rather than animals. Even in Reform Judaism we continue to use the word "service" to describe prayer, thereby implying that by our acts of prayer we do something for God, just as a slave or servant performs services for his or her master. For many still today, prayer is considered a mitzvah similar in its intent to serving God with sacrifices as was done in ancient times and, according to Orthodox belief, as will be done again in the future.

However, Reform Jews have also long questioned whether the purpose of prayer is really to serve God. Does God need our prayers to substitute for the pleasant aroma of bullocks roasting on the altar? Should prayer at all be seen as a continuation of the ancient sacrificial service? Or is it for Reform Jews something quite different not only in using words rather than fire pans, but also in its intent?

Back in the year 1812 the radical reformer David Friedländer had suggested that the proper term for Jewish worship should not be *Gottesdienst* (service to God) but *Gottesverehrung* (showing

---

MICHAEL A. MEYER is Adolph S. Ochs Professor of Jewish History Emeritus at the Cincinnati campus of HUC-JIR and the author of *Response to Modernity: A History of the Reform Movement in Judaism*.

reverence to God).[1] Such reverence directed to God, unlike service to God, he believed could be understood as having moral consequences for the individual engaged in prayer. In prayer he or she accepts the yoke of heaven and thereby also certain consequences for the individual's life.

However, the notion that prayer is not for God but rather for the one who prays has an earlier point of origin. The first occurrence I have been able to locate comes from the year 1786, well before there was a definable Reform Movement. Isaac Euchel (1758–1804) was a disciple of Moses Mendelssohn and one of the editors of *Ha-Me'asef*, the Hebrew periodical of the German Haskalah. The leading scholar of the Haskalah today, Professor Shmuel Feiner, considers him to have been its chief organizing force. Even as Moses Mendelssohn translated portions of the Bible from Hebrew into German for a Jewish population that was making the transition from Judeo-German to High German, so did both David Friedländer and Isaac Euchel in the identical year publish a High German translation of the traditional prayer book. Friedländer's translation used Hebrew characters; Euchel preferred to use Gothic type.

Euchel's introduction to his translation, a portion of which appears in my translation from the German below, seems to me especially significant for the way we in the Reform Movement regard prayer.[2] Few Reform Jews come to the synagogue in order to render service to God. They go there for what has increasingly been termed the "worship experience." In Euchel's words, they go there for the important purpose of their "own improvement and perfection." Put differently, they attend in the hope that prayer will in some way change their lives for the better. Using the language of our time, they hope that being in the synagogue and praying to God will be personally "transformative."

Euchel's views anticipate the Reform Movement also with regard to his rejection of prayer that is purely mechanical. Prayer, he suggests, gains importance only if it has consequences for the individual, if as its result not only is the individual praying spiritually elevated, but also has a deepened devotion to the social justice propagated by the biblical Prophets.

However, prayer is also not an exercise in which God plays no role and that could, as well, be conducted outside the synagogue. In Euchel's view, God is the source of the "illumination" that makes the transformation possible. It is in the presence of God that our moral sensitivities are revived and raised to a higher level. This idea was already expressed in the last mishnah of *Masechet Yoma*, which the Jewish philosopher Hermann Cohen set as the motto for his 1919 posthumously published *Religion of Reason out of the Sources of Judaism*:

אמר רבי עקיבא : אשריכם ישראל, לפני מי אתם מטהרים, מי מטהר
אתכם ? אבינו שבשמים.

("Said Rabbi Akiba: Happy [in the sense of blessed] are you Jews. Before whom do you purify yourselves? Who purifies you? Our Father who is in Heaven.") Prayer as self-purification before God, a process that leaves its effect not upon God but upon the person praying, is, I suggest, still the essence of prayer in Reform Judaism.

Gebete der hochdeutschen und polnischen Juden aus dem Hebräischen übersetzt und mit Anmerkungen begleitet, von Isaac Abraham Euchel [**Prayers of the High German and Polish Jews, translated from the Hebrew and accompanied by notes, by Isaac Abraham Euchel**] (Königsberg: D. E. Kanter, Königl. Hofbuchdrucker, 1786), iv–x.

People have gotten so used to using the words "prayer" [*Gebet*] and service of God [*Gottesdienst*] synonymously that they associate one concept with them both. And since it is thought to be a general obligation to serve God, they think that they serve God through prayer. Hence they see prayer—which is only a means—as an end. The term "service of God," which we owe to the priests—who called the sacrificial transactions and the Temple service by that name—would be most inapt if it were understood according to its original meaning.

God does not desire our service; rather He allows us to engage in ritual acts as means in order to reach the important end of our own improvement and perfection. Moses says (Deut. 10:12–13): "And now, O Israel, what does the Eternal require of you, but to revere the Eternal your God, to walk in all His ways, to love Him, and to serve Him with all your heart and with all your soul; that is: to keep the commandments of the Eternal and His statutes that I give you this day—and this for your own good."[3] And the Psalmist sings (Ps. 40:7): "You have no delight in sacrifice and meal offering. You have opened my ears [to hearken to the Lord's voice]; burnt offering and sin offering You do not require." The sacrifices at the time of the Temple were only means to guide the human being to the complete subjugation of his senses and to submission to God.

Aside from that, they were spurned by the Eternal One and not accepted for grace. All external acts and customs that were connected with them were indeed called "service," but by no means could they justifiably be referred to as service of God.[4]

It is from this perspective that we have to regard prayer. Prayer is our spirit's[5] occupation with God. It cannot flow from the heart and be acceptable to the Eternal One until we come before Him with a clean conscience, a heart free of impure thoughts with regard to our fellow human beings, free of doubts regarding divine providence, justice, grace, and goodness, and fully submissive to His will. If we pray in such a spiritual state, then our prayer is agreeable to Him and, as once the sacrifices, a *reiach nichoach*. God heeds and helps us; we leave with unstained soul and clear conscience, our heart is consoled and our suffering relieved.

But woe to him who thinks otherwise with regard to prayer, who believes that he fulfills his obligations through merely moving his lips or through loudly shouting out empty words—like those Indians who constantly spin a wheel outfitted with lots of clappers.[6] Woe also to him who accompanies his prayer with a variety of bodily gesticulations and self-mortifications, believing through such unnatural actions to be pleasing to God! Of him the Prophet says (Isa. 58:5–9): "If a person afflicts his body, bends down his head like a reed, puts on sackcloth and spreads ashes on himself—that is supposed to be fasting and a day desirable to the Lord? The fast that I desire is to loosen the bonds of evil; to remove the tyrannical bands; to let the oppressed go free and to cast off every yoke. Break your bread with the hungry; lead the abandoned needy to your house; if you see a naked person, clothe him; and do not evade your fellow human beings. Then your light will shine like the dawn, your righteousness will march before you, and the majesty of the Eternal will accompany you. Then call out, the Eternal will answer. Beseech, He answers: Here I am."

If a person finds himself surrounded by the adversities of life, his heart oppressed by a burden of grief, his mind, out of desperation, occupied with evil thoughts, hideous imaginings, and wicked designs—then let him take refuge in a heartfelt prayer. By asking God for illumination of his gloomy spirit, by recalling His fatherly goodness and grace, and by considering well that the

All-Benevolent desires only the well-being of His creatures and does everything for their welfare, he will soon turn inward, inspect his deeds with an attentive eye, and realize that he is himself the cause of his distress. He will recognize how through divine wisdom and benevolence everything can work out for the best. He will feel better during the greatest suffering than a person who lives in the fullest enjoyment of sensual pleasures and with an abundance of seeming goods.

Such is the case with the hymns that contain partly praise of the Deity and partly thanks for His goodness and beneficent deeds. God requires our praise just as little as our thanks. Yet He is pleased to accept both if they have our own perfection as their purpose. It is as the Psalmist in his song has God say (Ps. 50:23): "Whoever offers a sacrifice of thanksgiving honors Me." By praising Him, by declaring in solemn words the works of His omnipotence, by observing with a watchful eye the wisdom and goodness that shines forth from every point of the vast cosmos, God desires the human being to cast his glance back upon himself and to consider how insignificant his being in the endless order of creation, how little he is entitled to lay claim to all those great things that his heart desires. And yet he finds his place in Creation so exalted and his majesty bordering on that of the angels. As the Psalmist sings (Ps. 8:4–7): "When I behold the work of Your fingers, the heavens, the moon, the stars, that You have set in place—what is the human being that You are still mindful of him, the son of the earth, that You look after him? Nonetheless, You have set him but little below the angels. You give him dominion over all [Your] works and lay everything at his feet."

These lofty ideas put the human being on the path to his eternal happiness [Glückseligkeit]. A heavenly fire flames up within him, his heart comes to abhor all earthly lusts and beats only for the good, the noble, and the perfected. He looks about him, sees how everything is animated by the benevolent hand of God and is arrayed before him, preserved for his enjoyment. All things invite him to celebrate [God's] benevolence and omnipotence. He feels moved to allow the stream of his emotions to flow from the spring of thankfulness. Finally, he learns from his experience to be thankful to benefactors and beneficent to the thankful. His heart grows tender and loving to his fellow human beings, and with every new step he approaches his perfection [Vollkommenheit]. This is the great end that we should achieve through our devotions; this is the thanks that God requires. David, the sacred poet, speaks of it and closes his song with the words (Ps. 50:23): "To the person that gives heed to his acts I will show divine salvation."

Notes

1. See David Friedländer, *Ueber die durch die neue Organisation der Judenschaften in den Preussischen Staaten notwendig gewordene Umbildung . . . Ein Wort zu seiner Zeit* (Berlin, 1812).

2. Interestingly, the introduction appears again in the 1817 edition published in Berlin and Leipzig (without indication of publisher), but it was omitted in the editions published in Vienna in 1815 and 1824 by Anton Schmidt. The Vienna editions were apparently intended for Orthodox congregations, who could not accept Euchel's view of Jewish prayer. The 1785 edition was produced by the official publisher of the royal court.

3. In rendering Euchel's biblical citations, I have tried to follow his sometimes rather loose translation of the text as closely as possible.

4. In the sense of a modern *Gottesdienst*.

5. The German term is *Gemüth*, not *Geist*; the former encompasses emotion as well as intellect.

6. As used in Tibetan Buddhism.

Poetry

I Met a Man Today

Daniel S. Alexander

I met a man today
who retains his youthful vigor
even at sixty-two.
He engages avidly in the world around him,
in issues of politics and philosophy.
He never misses the daily paper
and sometimes peruses two or three.
He reads literature and watches films.
He exercises his body
and takes strenuous hikes and rides a bicycle.
He enjoys the sunsets,
and the mountains,
and conversation with friends.
He loves his family
and is grateful for each day,
expressing his gratitude in constant prayer.

I met another man today
who, though not yet among the elderly,
feels himself aging in every bone and every organ.
He longs for the vigor of his youth,
the sharpness of vision now aided by prescription lenses,
the acuity of hearing now replaced by missed punch lines,
the trim physique a mere memory.
He misses the passion that only yesterday
motivated his eager engagement,
the drive to expand his capacities,
to make an impact,
the desire for human contact, intimacy.

DANIEL S. ALEXANDER (NY79, D.Min. Wesley Theological Seminary) is rabbi of Congregation Beth Israel in Charlottesville, Virginia, and an occasional lecturer in the Department of Religious Studies at the University of Virginia.

He wonders if he has much to say or much to give,
when giving requires a greater sense of self.
Gratitude's been supplanted by emptiness.

I met these two men today as I stared into the mirror
and watched with curiosity
as they conversed.
Yetzer Tov.
Yetzer Ra.

Between Earthquake and Hurricane

Daniel S. Alexander

Between the rumblings of the earth and the crashing of the
    heavens;
Among shaking of knees and buildings and howling winds;
Among fearful shudders, fallen trees, and broken power lines,
We pause,
A time to elevate awareness,
And make connections
Between rumbling earth
And the One who fills it with Her Glory;
Between crashing heavens and the One who rules the heavens;
Between our fear and the One who holds us in our fear,
As a parent who comforts his child
With "Sha, sha, it's all right."

After Psalm 16

Daniel S. Alexander

God, remind me that I need protection . . . when I forget.
And when pain or fear rise within me,
be there to embrace me,
to calm my shaken nerves,
to support my wobbly bones.

Remind me, You who drop hints in all the obvious places,
that Your hand enfolds my fate
as Your grace allows my portion.

Keep me in mind of the unending blessings showered upon me,
that I may take joy in them,
that I may express appreciation for them.

I thank You, God, for the guidance of wise mentors,
empathetic listeners, caring models of the way,
and for the knowing heart, the urgent bladder,
insistent peristalsis.

Do not abandon me to dread of night
Do not release my hand
in the hour of my anguish.

Hold me even in my dying
for at the end, I know,
there is none but You,
no comfort but Yours,
no trust but in You.

In You do I find fullness and truth.

A Meditation:
Healing the Broken-ness

Paulette Rochelle-Levy

Giving my sigh to God . . . .
Releasing the breath,
Releasing the holding
Of the ribs around the breath.
Like loosening a net around my heart,
Softening—gently—kindly
Giving my sigh to God.

And, now, being with myself in the stillness.
Deepening into the quiet movement of breath,
Allowing my breath to draw awareness
Deeper into my body,
Becoming aware of places of holding,
Of the places where pain has congealed.

Perhaps there has been shock
Where the breath is caught and doesn't quite let go.

Perhaps the wound is old or renewed
And there is a frozen place in my heart.

Wherever the energy is trapped,
For now, I just notice.

Listening to the sensation of energy,
Where energy moves freely and
Where there are obstacles.

PAULETTE ROCHELLE-LEVY, MFT is a multifaceted psychotherapist, educator, and Jewish spiritual leader. Paulette is the author/artist of *Dancing with the Divine: Prayers & Meditations for Movement & Stillness, And You Shall Be a Blessing*, and the CD *Medicine Words*. A Reform rabbi's daughter (Paul Richman, HUC32), she has been deeply involved in Jewish Renewal for many years.

For now—nothing to do—
Only to breathe
Observe,   listen,   feel.

The pulse of the stillness
So many times going to this wall of pain and retreating.
Now, I gently approach,
As much as I, now, am willing and able,
At this time,
To move through.
One step at a time
One breath at a time.

Breathing into the broken-ness,
Being with myself,
Being with all
That cries out for repair.

Allowing the breath
The in and out of breath
To bring me into wholeness
To be touched with holiness.

Not Knowing

Abby Caplin

Are you still breathing?
I can't tell if you've flown off
with the butterfly
that came to you in a dream
while you floated
on ocean foam.
As tender as a lover,
it held you in
the folds of its wings.

What is your hope? I asked.
When it's time, I want to go fast, you said.

Are you still breathing?
I detest this deficit of mine.
I should be able
to feel the departure
from your body,
in my body.

Maybe it's time to
call your friends, I suggested.
No. I'm a very private person,
you reminded me,
cocooned in blankets.

Our last time together
you didn't speak,
but your eyes flew open

ABBY CAPLIN, MD, MA practices Mind-Body Medicine and Counseling in San Francisco, California, combining her medical and counseling training to help people with chronic illness lead meaningful and empowered lives. Abby is also a writer and poet whose work has been published in *Sh'ma*, *Poetica Magazine*, *Tikkun* magazine, and the anthologies *The Healing Art of Writing* and *Pulse: Voices from the Heart of Medicine*.

once, as if surprised by
metamorphosis.

Are you still breathing?
Or has your breath stilled,
as I picture you now
borne up on sunlit wings,
beating the path
to another world?

MRI

Linda Hepner

"Please take a seat," she said.
"Fill out these forms." Obedient,
I did. "In full please." Smiling, white blouse. "Name:
Mother's name too, and your abode."
"Where are you from?" I asked. "Russia," she said,
Magnetic north.
"The ice, Siberia." What shall I write?
The house I dwell in or my home, near but receding?
"Who is your next of kin?" (in case you die).
"What implants do you have?" Just one, I say,
A wedding ring I can't pull off.
"OK," she says, "Then leave it,
All the rest just give to him."

The young man, white shirt, white shoes, calls me through
The heavy door which clangs behind me.
Tu nombre? I ask him. No reply.
The Valet from *No Exit*, I assume,
And follow him down the marble passage to the locker room.
"Leave all your clothes here, your purse, your book,
Your jewelry, papers, underwear, and shoes. Put on this gown
    and come to me."
A white robe, tied with ribbons, loose, my skin cold, crawling.
I pad along the passage, enter.
A chamber, high and shadowy, walls pallid.

And there it stands, the grand machine,
Petrified in metal paint, splendid, hollow.

Over the sarcophagus, an emblem, scrolled: GE.
Imagine. SPQR. Out slides the board, narrow and silent.
On it I climb and lay me down.

LINDA HEPNER lives with her family in Los Angeles and comes from England, where she began writing poetry at the age of six. Her poem "Potiphar's Wife" appears in part in *The Torah: A Women's Commentary* (URJ Press, 2008); and the complete version, with many of her other poems, can be seen online at Poemhunter.com.

Priestly: "You'll hear a noise, do not be scared,"
And he plugs up my ears with wax.
Smoothly, in it slides, bearing me deep enclosed, entombed.
Above me a vault, small glow
Like a last gleam behind my eyeballs when I sleep.

But this is French theatre: Knock knock knock
The giant broom handle warns the waiting crowd
The play will now begin! A Corneille kill? or Racine
With his slow, excruciating Bérénice farewell
To Titus, lover, emperor, and *pour jamais! Jamais*
Jamais will she ever live again
Seeing his eyes, touching his mouth, waking each day
Like night, a night ahead, a wilderness
Of resonating Rome, Jerusalem,
And now she hears how resonance has culled her life,
An exile in her palace, country, years of death.

Thump thump thump thump!
Such heavy nails!
And then a buzzing, deafening my thoughts and so
The furies come and pierce my hearing,
Nightbat screeches screaming in my brain,
Crickets not owls, captor torturers!
Oh Beelzebub, pilotless drone
Buzzing my castle, desist
And I shall lie quite still, holding my breath
Submissive captive, come what will.

Forty minutes. Time enough
To circle the world, to find the herb
That transforms life and memory
And then return
To sudden freedom:
Slide out. Light! "Now you are done. Now you can go."
I rise like dry bones from my slab
Slowly and I see the priest,
Smiling, a helping hand.
He passes me my watch.

What is your name? I ask,
Gratefully turning at the door.

"Angel," he says.

Words of Wisdom
from Four Poets

I.

A guaranteed ending—mortality.
No cure. But a healing.

* * *

"Know your fears" it calls,
"then they are no longer enemies."
. . . maybe even blessings. . . .

* * *

I received a call from my mother-in-law
     someone who loves me
     someone trying to reconnect me to the world I once knew
(someone who assumed they knew *the* plug to resume this flow
of life . . .)

I was asked how I was.
My sincere succinct reply,
     "Fair"
(the turmoil below too ugly
too messy, too explosive
to release).

"Still struggling with the death of your father?" her assump-
tive, crystalline retort.
     My heart stunned, and contemplating pause,
     quickly reconsidered and continues to beat.

Wow, what a bold, brash, heartless
question (so it felt).

"*Still* struggling . . ."
Like at some point I won't.
Like we are all waiting
for this to go away
     and be done.

* * *

only those
watching their loved ones reach the precipice dare ask,
"How does it happen? How do they die?"

* * *

I think that if I don't speak my hatred
or anger then you don't know it. If I don't
speak it, then somehow it doesn't exist.

* * *

When you die,
I will have a hole in my heart that by
finding the bridge over the celestial waters
to eternity, will I have found my path to healing.
This is my prayer to you. May you always know I
will come looking for you. I will always want
you. I will always crave your arms around me.
I will always dream of your breath above me.
The tinkling sound of your spoon stirring your
coffee will forever be the music of your peace
and comfort. You will be well and whole once
again (soon enough). You will, forever, be my
glorious father.

DAWN GROSS, MD, Ph.D. is a published author and poet who practices Hospice and Palliative Medicine at UCSF and with VITAS Hospice in the San Francisco Bay Area, where she lives with her husband and three children.

II.

God,
Do you have time for me in this moment?
For my little desires and confusions?
For the aching of my heart and the pain of my body?

Where are You?
Who are You?
I want to touch You.
I want You to touch me.

* * *

Open my heart to the stillness of being
Let me become an empty vessel
Receiving the nourishment of grace.

* * *

God, this is a new breath, a new day, a new moment,
You open me up to the possibility of holy renewal
Let wholeness be now.

PAULETTE ROCHELLE-LEVY, MFT is an artist/author of books of prayer and meditation. Her website is creativepathwithpaulette.com.

III.

I am not afraid of dying
But I am afraid of declining.

So I will change from hiking briskly in the mountains
To walking slowly in the valley,
Looking at birds, flowers, and trees.

ALLEN S. MALLER (C64) retired in 2006 after thirty-nine years as rabbi of Temple Akiba. His website is rabbimaller.com

IV.

If I grow frail, gait unsteady,
will you wrap your arms around me,
gently guide my step?

If dark seals my sight, and I lean
my head toward you,
will you stroke my hair?

PATTI TANA is the Walt Whitman Birthplace 2009 Poet of the Year and the author of eight collections of poems, most recently *Any Given Day* (2011). Her website is http://www.pattitana.com.

Book Reviews

Midrash and Medicine: Healing Body and Soul in the Jewish Interpretive Tradition
edited by Rabbi William Cutter, Ph.D.
(Woodstock, VT: Jewish Lights Publishing, 2011), 315 pp.

Midrash and Medicine: Healing Body and Soul in the Jewish Interpretive Tradition is an exceptional contribution to the healing movement. If Torah is revealed throughout the ages, Rabbi Cutter and his co-authors bring new awareness to Jewish and non-Jewish chaplains, clinicians, and academicians who will benefit from the wisdom and innovation of its pages.

The book's ten chapters and nineteen contributors explore the gains and risks of utilizing metaphor in the meaning-making process; biblical personages who inspire us to expand our hearts, effect change, and accept life's changes; biblical poetry, contemporary interpretation, and music for the elderly; a plea for doctors to invite God-talk into their patient encounters; a personal narrative of the tragic loss of a spouse; narrative bioethics; and a personal and textual analysis of suffering.

A captivating aspect of the book is that it includes *machlokot* (disputes or different angles on a conversation), as some of the contributors respond to the writings of others within the pages. For instance, in the chapter entitled "Contexts of Suffering, Contexts of Hope," Ruhama Weiss suggests that stories in *Masechet B'rachot* of the Babylonian Talmud may indicate a Rabbinic movement that she entitles the "Underground against Suffering." Weiss's personally and textually based chapter ponders whether human interaction and pastoral encounter, which the Rabbis in the midrash exchange, can liberate individuals from the depths of pain and suffering.

Aryeh Cohen, in his response to Weiss, questions the historicity of her argument and her use of fictional interpretation to make the Talmud appear and feel more factual to her own circumstance. Cohen challenges Weiss to consider the theological questions of the Talmudic text as being concrete, rather than personified narrative. Cohen proposes that the concrete question of the Rabbis was: "Is physical suffering good or bad, helpful or hurtful spiritually?" (p. 130). Herein exists the tension between the pastoral narrative interpretation and theology of Weiss, and the more systematic textual analysis of Cohen.

A second example of contemporary discourse and debate arises when psychologist Philip Cushman, in his chapter, "The Danger of Cure, the Value of Healing," warns the Jewish healing movement to beware of the "surprisingly ahistorical discipline" (p. 211) of the therapeutic worldview. His caution is centered in his perspective that psychotherapeutic innovators tend to claim success with relatively little or no clinical testing or verification, which puts the autonomy and self-empowerment of the client at risk. Cushman's social concern is evident when he writes: "Preoccupation with the intrapsychic tends to obscure the effects of the material causes of suffering and blames the victim" (p. 218). Cushman illuminates the similarities between midrashic processes and relational psychoanalysis, which he proposes "engages us in a continuing group experience of interpretive study that helps develop a way of being" (p. 220).

Professor of Midrash Lewis Barth responds to Cushman by writing that Cushman's negative opinion of psychoanalysis is likely shaped by his own classical psychoanalytic tradition and overemphasis on cognitive behavioral therapy, which is prompted by corporate and fiscal agendas (p. 235). Barth acknowledges this as a legitimate concern. However he also encourages Cushman to consider that the "positive qualities Cushman sees in midrashic processes—'interpersonal engagement, critical interpretive processes, and playfulness,' as well as strongly anti-authoritarian attitudes—have informed much of the writings of contemporary psychoanalysis for more than a quarter century" (p. 235).

It is fitting that Rabbi Cutter's clever construction of his book includes the psychologist, Cushman, advising the Jewish healing movement to utilize a midrashic rather than psychoanalytical approach in its development of programs, and that the midrashist, Barth, would in turn persuade Cushman to see that midrashic text (citing *P'sikta D'Rav Kahana*) challenges legal institutions, societal structures, and corruption in the same manner that Cushman is challenging his own psychotherapeutic field. This is an intersection worth noting.

Effective pastoral education and meaningful spiritual care encounters are reliant on authentic and heart-felt communication.

The book engages us in a variety of theological, philosophical, and most of all, pastoral conversations that spark compassion, personal reflection, intellectual friction, and communal responsibility. Rabbi Cutter and his colleagues provide thoughtful and essential dialogue about what it means to be pioneers in this next phase of Torah revelation. *Midrash and Medicine: Healing Body and Soul in the Jewish Interpretive Tradition* is a powerful next step in discovering the Jewish imagination and its impact on health and healing within the Jewish world and beyond.

RABBI ROCHELLE ROBINS (NY98) is a certified ACPE Supervisor and pastoral educator. She lives in San Diego.

No Offense, Self-Defense, and On the Fence: Rabbis in Search of American Jewish Identity
A Review Essay

Richard Hirsh

Reviewing

What the Rabbis Said: The Public Discourse of Nineteenth-Century American Rabbis by Naomi W. Cohen
(New York and London: New York University Press, 2008), 261 pp.

Speaking of Jews: Rabbis, Intellectuals, and the Creation of an American Public Identity by Lila Corwin Berman
(Berkeley: University of California Press, 2009), 266 pp.

Jewish Preaching in Times of War 1800–2001 by Marc Saperstein
(Oxford: Littman Library of Jewish Civilization, 2008), 619 pp.

In the modern and now postmodern eras, the category of "identity" has been among the most volatile and contested. Rabbis in the United States, from the first arrival of European-trained ravs and reformers, have been struggling spokespersons in search of a way to articulate an American Jewish identity that would, as one of our authors under discussion puts it, "formulate Jewishness as an ideology to mediate between Jews' desire for acceptance into the United States and their commitment to Jewish survival" (Berman, p. 7).

The Enlightenment bequeathed numerous blessings on the Jewish people along with unprecedented challenges to Jewish tradition, texts, communal structure, theological content, and religious practice. In America, each of those challenges was amplified by the open and secular nature of the society, the newness of what America represented, and by the absence of what Mordecai Kaplan in 1934 in *Judaism as a Civilization* called "environmental factors of [identity] conservation" such as the ancestors of European and Russian Jewish immigrants could assume and often had to endure under duress.

In the nineteenth and early twentieth century it fell primarily to rabbis to take up the task of "defining a collective identity... [and] . . . crafting an ideology about the relationship between Jews and non-Jews and the role that Jews could play in a non-Jewish society" (Berman, p. 2). As Lila Corwin Berman notes, the emergence and subsequent ascendency of what she names "Jewish social science" in the period between World War I and World War II correlated with the appearance of other spokespersons who were equally if not more adept at trying to understand, interpret, and define American Jewish identity through the academy, rather than from the pulpit.

The ownership of Jewish identity became and remains a debate among rabbis, academics, demographers, Federation and JCC professionals, lay leaders and, as the twenty-first century began, the Jewish "sovereign selves" (Cohen and Eisen, *The Jew Within: Self, Family, and Community in America,* 2000), who are in many cases happily going about shaping their individual Jewish self-identity without any guidance from (or concern about the approval of) the communal elite. The 1983 CCAR resolution on patrilineality begins with language that surely would be challenged today: "The CCAR *declares* that the child of. . . ." As many rabbis can testify, interfaith families today do not come to ask us *if* their children are Jewish, they come to tell us they *are* Jewish. No one is waiting for rabbis "to declare."

As twenty-first century rabbis, we inherit the accomplishments even if we dispute the content of our predecessors who labored valiantly under a complex of conditions unprecedented in Jewish history. At the risk of belaboring a metaphor, trying to define Jewish identity in the past two centuries has been like trying to change a tire on a car that is not only moving, but accelerating, and headed in a direction that remains unmapped. If the ubiquity of GPS (Global Positioning System) technology teaches us one thing, it is to be prepared to "recalculate."

Each of these volumes under review proceeds from the insights of rabbis as recorded in sermons. Berwin and Cohen digest and present (enriched with ample quotation) words preached from the pulpit, focusing analysis on the interplay of evolving rabbinic roles and the challenges of explaining Judaism in America both to Jews and non-Jews. Saperstein, in contrast, offers the sermons themselves as documents upon which he then comments, placing the sermon itself as the center of attention.

Cohen and Saperstein both acknowledge the tangible problem of recovering manuscripts of the earliest American rabbis. Cohen notes that much of what survives comes predominantly from Reform rabbis, whose higher social status, use of the vernacular, and service to more established, wealthy congregations pushed them fastest into creating a Jewish version of what Protestant Americans and their clergy had defined as the centrality of (the) preaching in "worship" or "services." The *wort* or *d'var Torah* of the European-style rav remained subordinate to the davening and when offered was more often in Yiddish, so few such texts survive.

The twofold preaching task of nineteenth century American rabbis was both "no offense" and "self-defense." As Cohen puts it, "their primary aim was to ensure acceptance of Jews within the larger society...they could not afford to criticize or appear too different from non-Jews" (p. 5). But in the closing decades of that same century, wide-scale immigration and other social, economic, and political factors aroused what would become a rabid animus against "foreigners," especially those who clung to collective identity that seemed to diminish their "Americanism." Cohen cites numerous discussions from CCAR conventions in the 1890s where debate raged over whether and to what degree rabbinic preaching should or could address social and public policy issues, especially as Jews (and in some academic circles, Judaism—Solomon Schechter's scathing observation was that "the Higher [biblical] Criticism [was simply] the higher Anti-Semitism") came under increasing attack.

The battle between "religionists" and "nationalists" for the meaning of Jewish identity inevitably found its way into the sermons of rabbis. Both Berman and Cohen document and comment on the tensions that the nascent nationalism that emerged as Zionism created in the quest to clarify American Jewish identity, creating debate and dissent over the degree to which Judaism was a faith, culture, or ethnicity. Cohen touches on the end-of-the-century rise and subsequent demise of "Judaism as race" and Berman picks up with the emergence of a consensus on a sociological ethnicity that allowed for "groupness" while presumably not giving sanction to charges of dual-loyalty.

The preeminent spokesman of "living in two civilizations," Mordecai Kaplan, often held out the model of the American Catholic community as an example of how Jews could maintain their collective identity while also living fully as Americans. American Catholics, for example, endorsed parochial schools, wanted their children to marry Catholics, maintained visible rituals that conveyed identity, and clearly were committed to maintaining group identity within the larger American culture. Kaplan admired the ways in which American Catholics resisted assimilation while claiming their equal right to identify fully as Americans. This was not a position echoed in the sermons of most Reform rabbis, for whom the Protestant model of faith over ritual, individualism over collectivity, and integration over separatism was more in line with their version of American religious behavior and identification.

In the area of "no offense," it is instructive to note Berman's discussion of the debate that swirled around the 1947 publication of *Basic Judaism* by Rabbi Milton Steinberg, particularly with regard to his frank and unapologetic assessment of why Jews rejected Jesus. Steinberg's terse and elegant language did little to mask the implicit critique of the very foundations of Christianity. In the prior half-century, such a frontal confrontation would have been avoided by almost any rabbi, let alone one preaching from a most prestigious pulpit in the biggest city in the United States. But as the post–World War II American Jewish community struggled simultaneously to emerge from second to third generation in suburban America while under the cloud of the annihilation of European Jewry, rabbis began to engage the very civic (and inevitably, interfaith) issues that their nineteenth century ancestors either avoided or evaded.

Berman states that "the period from the end of World War I through the civil rights era saw the flourishing of Jewish attempts to create a public and synthetic American Jewish identity" (p. 7). Not surprisingly, this period also correlates with the emergence of the rabbinic sermon as a primary tool for shaping individual and collective Jewish identity within an American context while simultaneously engaging the great social struggles and civic issues of that period.

The ability of rabbis in this period to step out and to speak out was not simply a matter of being what Deborah Dash Moore called in the title of her 1981 study of American Jews in the period between the two world wars "at home in America." It was also a consequence of the loosening of what could be called the "content-control patrol" function of synagogue lay leaders, who often took for granted their right to review and approve rabbinic sermons both in terms of topic and viewpoint. The legendary battle on the bimah in the early 1850s between Rabbi Isaac Mayer Wise and his congregational president during Rosh HaShanah services is an exemplary if embarrassing anecdotal example of such "oversight." (See a description of the fight by Rabbi Lance Sussman at http://www.pbs.org/godinamerica/interviews/lance-sussman.html.) Anti-rabbinism has been an aspect of American Jewish life from its beginning, and was not limited, as Cohen artfully notes in a series of specifics, to those who rejected religious life.

Saperstein's collection is an invaluable asset for primary sources, and can be read selectively in parallel to the periods on which Cohen and Berman focus. Saperstein has previously gathered sermons in other contexts (*Jewish Preaching 1200–1800: An Anthology,* 1992), but this volume focuses specifically on rabbinic sermons during those very moments when "Americanism" would be preeminent in the American-Jewish equation: the times when our country was at war. The diverse voices that we hear with regard to, for example, the Civil War and Vietnam, are complemented by the common core of concern evidenced in the sermons from the periods of World Wars I and II. This collection concludes with three rabbinic reflections on the 9/11 terrorist attacks, stopping short of citing sermons that may have been preached following the beginning of the wars in Iraq and Afghanistan.

Saperstein's volume is especially valuable in that it exposes an inherent but often overlooked obstacle in the quest to define

"American identity," "Jewish identity," and especially "American Jewish identity." As the historical approach to the study of Judaism has demonstrated, there is no "Judaism" but there are many variations that sail under the name. Similarly, there is no one "American" identity but rather a spectrum of approaches along which are gathered all who claim that citizenship. And surely there is no one American Jewish identity, certainly not when we take into account the postmodern variables with which we deal.

This leads us to the current moment, where rabbinic roles continue to change and evolve, where the spectrum of engagement with Jewish tradition continues to expand to encompass innovations earlier generations could not have imagined. As the baby boomers yield to Gen X, Gen Y, and beyond, the presumptive value of collective identity can no longer be assumed, the prerogatives of personal identity construction are presumed, and what Berman names as "the bad politics of endogamy" have emerged with a vengeance. In this context, it is hard to imagine how the role of the sermon, and the coordinate issue of rabbinic authority and influence, could ever have been what it appears once to have been on the evidence of these volumes.

Rabbis are participating in the contemporary discussion of Jewish identity under often radically different sets of assumptions than those of our predecessors. Intellectual and academic parsings of the politics and dynamics of identity make it hard to take anything for granted. At the same time, our commitment to the continuity of Jewish tradition and the Jewish people does not necessarily always start from the head as much as from the heart. We are, as Berman insightfully states, "searching for a new language of volition: a language that describes Jewishness as a choice, not a social fact, not a religious mandate, and not a biological rule. Yet blood, God, and community are tough to replace or discount, as anyone thinking about Jewishness in the beginning of the twenty-first century would likely admit" (p. 10).

"Preaching" as represented here has yielded to "teaching" and the certitude of pronouncement has been displaced by the openness to questioning that seeks to engage rather than to inform, and to listen as well as to speak. We are challenged as rabbis to claim our place in the conversation that creates the new language Berman suggests, even as we acknowledge that while ours may be a primary voice, it is not likely to be the determinative one. When it comes to American Jewish identity, rabbis and laypeople may be settling in for an extended period of being "on the fence."

The earliest generations of American rabbis saw a major part of their task to be the "Americanizing" of immigrant Jews. The next generation took up the task of adapting Judaism into the "Jewishness" Berman notes as the "sociological identity" that sustained us from the 1920s until the closing decades of the twentieth century. More recent generations have moved towards recovering and elevating the spiritual practices, texts, and teachings that "modern rabbis" marginalized, such as Kabbalah and Chasidut. Having landed fully and comfortably in America, fourth-, fifth-, and now sixth-generation Jews provide rabbis with an inverted opportunity: the "re-Jewish-ing" of American Jews who are in search of spiritual meaning, authentic interaction with their tradition and texts, and in a variety of individual ways, still in search of a collective identity that can encompass choice as well as covenant.

RABBI RICHARD HIRSH (RRC81) is the executive director of the Reconstructionist Rabbinical Association and teaches at the Reconstructionist Rabbinical College.

The CCAR Journal: The Reform Jewish Quarterly
Published quarterly by the Central Conference of American Rabbis.

Volume LIX, No. 3. Issue Number: Two hundred thirty-three.
Summer 2012.

STATEMENT OF PURPOSE

The CCAR Journal: The Reform Jewish Quarterly seeks to explore ideas and issues of Judaism and Jewish life, primarily—but not exclusively—from a Reform Jewish perspective. To fulfill this objective, the Journal is designed to:

1. provide a forum to reflect the thinking of informed and concerned individuals—especially Reform rabbis—on issues of consequence to the Jewish people and the Reform Movement;

2. increase awareness of developments taking place in fields of Jewish scholarship and the practical rabbinate, and to make additional contributions to these areas of study;

3. encourage creative and innovative approaches to Jewish thought and practice, based upon a thorough understanding of the traditional sources.

The views expressed in the Journal do not necessarily reflect the position of the Editorial Board or the Central Conference of American Rabbis.

The CCAR Journal: The Reform Jewish Quarterly (ISSN 1058-8760) is published quarterly by the Central Conference of American Rabbis, 355 Lexington Avenue, 18th Floor, New York, NY, 10017. Application to mail at periodical postage rates is pending at New York, NY and at additional mailing offices.

Subscriptions should be sent to CCAR Executive Offices, 355 Lexington Avenue, 18th Floor, New York, NY, 10017. Subscription rate as set by the Conference is $75 for a one-year subscription, $125 for a two-year subscription. Overseas subscribers should add $36 per year for postage. POSTMASTER: Please send address changes to The CCAR Journal: The Reform Jewish Quarterly, c/o Central Conference of American Rabbis, 355 Lexington Avenue, 18th Floor, New York, NY, 10017.

Typesetting and publishing services provided by Publishing Synthesis, Ltd., 39 Crosby Street, New York, NY, 10013.

The CCAR Journal: The Reform Jewish Quarterly is indexed in the *Index to Jewish Periodicals*. Articles appearing in it are listed in the *Index of Articles on Jewish Studies* (of *Kirjath Sepher*).

ISBN: 978-0-88123-182-3

GUIDELINES FOR SUBMITTING MATERIAL

1. The *CCAR Journal* welcomes submissions that fulfill its Statement of Purpose whatever the author's background or identification. Inquiries regarding publishing in the CCAR Journal and submissions for possible publication (including poetry) should be sent to the editor, Rabbi Susan Laemmle, in electronic form via *Laemmle@usc.edu*. Should problems arise, call 323-939-4084.

2. Other than commissioned articles, submissions to the *CCAR Journal* are sent out to a member of the editorial board for anonymous peer review. Thus submitted articles and poems should be sent to the editor with the author's name omitted. Please use MS Word format for the attachment. The message itself should contain the author's name, phone number, and e-mail address, as well as the submission's title and a 1–2 sentence bio.

3. Books for review and inquiries regarding submitting a review should be sent directly to the book review editor, Rabbi Laurence Edwards, at *LLE49@comcast.net*.

4. Inquiries concerning, or submissions for, *Maayanot* (Primary Sources) should be directed to the *Maayanot* editor, Rabbi Daniel Polish, at *dpolish@optonline.net*.

5. Based on Reform Judaism's commitment to egalitarianism, we request that articles be written in gender-inclusive language.

6. The *Journal* publishes reference notes at the end of articles, but submissions are easier to review when notes come at the bottom of each page. If possible, keep this in mind when submitting an article. Notes should conform to the following style:

a. Norman Lamm, *The Shema: Spirituality and Law in Judaism* (Philadelphia: Jewish Publication Society, 1998), 101–6. **[book]**

b. Lawrence A. Hoffman, "The Liturgical Message," in *Gates of Understanding*, ed. Lawrence A.Hoffman (New York: CCAR Press, 1977), 147–48, 162–63. **[chapter in a book]**

c. Richard Levy, "The God Puzzle," *Reform Judaism* 28 (Spring 2000): 18–22. **[article in a periodical]**

d. Lamm, *Shema*, 102. **[short form for subsequent reference]**

e. Levy, "God Puzzle," 20. **[short form for subsequent reference]**

f. Ibid., 21. **[short form for subsequent reference]**

7. If Hebrew script is used, please include an English translation. If transliteration is used, follow the guidelines abbreviated below and included more fully in the **Master Style Sheet**, available on the CCAR website at *www.ccarnet.org*:

"ch" for *chet* and *chaf* "ei" for *tzeirei*

"f" for *fei* "a" for *patach* and *kamatz*

"k" for *kaf* and *kuf* "o" for *cholam* and *kamatz katan*

"tz" for *tzadi* "u" for *shuruk* and *kibbutz*

"i" for *chirik* "ai" for *patach* with *yod*

"e" for *segol*

Final "h" for final *hei*; none for final *ayin* (with exceptions based on common usage): *atah*, *Sh'ma*, <u>but</u> *Moshe*.

Apostrophe for *sh'va nah*: *b'nei*, *b'rit*, *Sh'ma*; no apostrophe for *sh'va nach*.

Hyphen for two vowels together where necessary for correct pronunciation: *ne-eman*, *samei-ach*, <u>but</u> *maariv*, *Shavuot*.

No hyphen for prefixes unless necessary for correct pronunciation: *babayit*, *HaShem*, *Yom HaAtzma-ut*.

Do not double consonants (with exceptions based on dictionary spelling or common usage): *t'filah*, *chayim*, <u>but</u> *tikkun*, *Sukkot*.